THE VERWOERD

WHO TOYI-TOYIED

Melanie Verwoerd

A memoir of politics and love

TAFELBERG

Tafelberg
An imprint of NB Publishers
Part of Media24 Books Pty Ltd
40 Heerengracht, Cape Town, 8000
www.tafelberg.com
First published by Liberties Press Dublin, Ireland
Copyright © Melanie Verwoerd, 2013

Set in Plantin
Edited by Roxanne Reid
Proofread by Louise Steyn
Cover design Michiel Botha
Cover photograph Morné van Zyl
Book design Nazli Jacobs
Photographs copyright the author, except where otherwise indicated
Printed and bound by Paarl Media Print,
15 Jan van Riebeeck Drive, Paarl, South Africa.
First edition, first printing 2013

ISBN: 978-0-624-05738-3
e-ISBN: 978-0-624-05739-0
mobi ISBN: 978-0-624-06452-7

For Wilmé, Wian and Gerry

Contents

Thank you . . .

I have been extraordinarily privileged to share my life with very special people. All these people formed me and influenced my life, which is the reason that this book exists. So my heartfelt thanks to . . .

Nelson Mandela and Archbishop Desmond Tutu, my African fathers and two of the most amazing men to ever live. You will always remain my moral compass.

The strong women I share my life and genetics with: my wonderful mum Lenie, my sisters Melissa and Nadine and my beloved grandmother Lenie Brandt. You are my anchors in life.

Philip for becoming a father and grandfather when it wasn't always easy.

Wilhelm for spending the first 21 years of my adult life with me. We did some amazing things together politically, but more importantly we made two extraordinary, special human beings. *Dankie vir alles.*

Sharon for giving Wilhelm happiness again and for accepting my children into your life.

Emily Nomajoni Makoena, my friend and my children's other mother. You taught me so much about politics, service to others and how to keep going when times get tough. *Enkosi kakhulu, Mama!*

Brid, Elaine and Abraham, three of the most special friends one could ever ask for. Thank you for always being there with love and support. Thank you that I could trust you with my hurts and pains, and for keeping everything I ever told you private.

Rita and Harry Crosbie for feeding Gerry and me and allowing us to camp on your couch when times were hard.

David Blake Knox and Fiona Looney for being such good friends to Gerry and for being there for me in the weeks after he died.

Paul McGuinness and Kathy Gilfillan, for an amazing time in France and for helping me on the day of the funeral. Gerry always loved spending time with you.

Lottie, Rex, Bonnie, Elliot and Babs. Thank you for the lovely times we spent together. I hope this will fill in some of the gaps and help with some of the pain that others caused after your dad's death. I love you all very much.

Gerry's brothers, Mick and Mano. We only got to know each other in very dark times. Your support helped a lot.

Gerry's accountant, MT, for helping me confirm what I always knew and for looking after Gerry and his children beyond the call of duty. He knew he could rely on you and admired and respected you deeply – as I do.

Niamh Sheehan, my amazing assistant. I am extremely thankful that you came into my and my children's life. There is so much I could not have done without you.

Paul and Susan Feldstein of the Feldstein Agency. Your professionalism, attention and personal care still astonish me. You are an author's dream.

Everyone at NB Publishers. From the beginning I felt at home. It has been a real joy to work with you.

Paul Tweed, Kathy Matthews and John Kerr from Johnsons Solicitors, for your patient guidance and support.

All the people I have been privileged to work with in the ANC, the South African Parliament, the Foreign Service and UNICEF and who are the fellow travellers on my journey.

The many people of Ireland who carried me through the last three years with letters, e-mails and phone calls. The kind gestures from so many strangers (such as the elderly gentleman who sent me a €20 voucher with instructions to buy Horlicks so I could sleep better) frequently 'rescued' me when life was very difficult. I was touched by your kind words and hugs.

My two children, Wilmé and Wian. This book would not have happened were it not for your love and care, which motivated me to write it. You are two exceptional young people and I am extremely proud of you both. I would not have survived the last few years if not for your support during times when you were also suffering. You were often the only light that kept the darkness from overwhelming me. *Daar is geen liefde groter as myne vir julle nie.*

And lastly for my love, Gerry Ryan. Thank you for choosing me to share your last years with. They were the best years of my life. Whatever happens in the future, 'I will love you till the end of time.'

Foreword

Melanie was never going to be just your ordinary run-of-the-mill kind of person. How could she be, marrying as she did into the Verwoerd family in South Africa? For all South Africans, black and white, her husband's grandfather, Dr Hendrik Verwoerd, was the architect of the policy of apartheid. Nearly all whites revered him, since they benefited so conspicuously from apartheid, and almost all blacks detested him, as the victims trodden under-foot by its viciousness.

She and her husband Wilhelm committed what was for the majority of white South Africans the ultimate treachery: they joined Nelson Mandela's African National Congress a few years before South Africa's first democratic elections in 1994. Wilhelm's grandfather must have been spinning in his grave.

After those elections, the ANC could justifiably boast that it was reflecting the new South Africa, which sought to be non-racial and non-sexist – more than any other party. Did it not, after all, have a Verwoerd on its parliamentary benches?

She went as South African ambassador to Ireland, accompanied of course by her family. She soon made her mark, so that when her term as ambassador ended, she was appointed as head of UNICEF Ireland – unusually, as she was not Irish. Sadly, she and Wilhelm divorced. She fell in love with Gerry Ryan, a hugely popular radio and TV personality. They were deeply in love but could not marry. One day, Melanie and her son discovered him dead. The inquest into his death led to all sorts of scurrilous stories in the media. Some were quite vicious.

This touching love story has been written in part to counter those awful media misrepresentations. Perhaps we should be grateful for these stories, though, since without them we might never have had the chance of reading such a lyrical and beautiful love story, which tugs at the heartstrings. She loved deeply and suffered much, but what a doughty and elegant human being. Thank you, Melanie, for your deep loving, and your courage to take them on. I admire and love you.

Archbishop Desmond Tutu

'Our lives begin to end the day we become silent about things that matter.'   *Martin Luther King Jnr.*

'What you cannot do is accept injustice . . . You must make the injustice visible and be prepared to die like a soldier to do so.'   *Gandhi*

Introduction

I met Nelson Mandela for the first time in 1990. I was 23 years old. We only spoke for a few minutes, but those minutes would change my life forever. At the end of our conversation, he said: 'You need to remember that . . . you have a voice. People will listen to you. You have to think carefully what to do with that power.'

So started a journey during which the challenge put to me by Mandela would become my constant companion. How to use my voice in service of others would inform almost all of the big decisions I would be confronted with, and the choices I made would lead me down a path that fills me with amazement even today, more than two decades later.

After all, what were the chances that a young Afrikaner woman, from staunch Afrikaner farming stock, who married the grandson of 'the architect of apartheid', would meet Nelson Mandela and be asked to represent his party in the first democratic parliament? Or that a few years later she would be asked to become an ambassador, and the head of UNICEF in a foreign country?

I suspect it is because they share my surprise at the unlikelihood of all this that many friends, colleagues and loved ones have over the years asked me to write my story. Despite their encouragement, I resisted the idea for a long time. I am a deeply private person, and the idea of exposing my life, my soul, and especially my precious and loving memories of the last few years, to scrutiny, filled me – and continues to fill me – with horror and fear. But over the last two years, I found myself writing late at night, not able to rest until I had allowed my thoughts and memories to take form on paper. And so the book seemed determined to write itself, whether I wanted it to exist or not.

During those long, dark nights, I gradually became aware that the writing was born from a deep desire to try to remember who I am. It felt as if the shock and pain that followed the devastating events of April 2010 and beyond had scrambled my DNA, leaving me at a loss when I tried to remember who I was and what I was meant to do in life. It seemed that the only way to fix things and to find my voice again was to write, and to remember the past.

But there was another even more compelling reason. Almost exactly twenty years after Mandela's challenge to me, I was asked to use my voice again. This time it was by the man I loved. He asked me to promise him that I would talk about him and his life after his death. Thinking that we still had many decades together ahead of us, it was an easy promise to make. Two weeks later, he was dead.

As the months went by, I knew I would never heal or rest until I had honoured the promise I had made to Gerry. After his death, I gave one interview. I had hoped it would never be necessary for me to talk publicly about him again, since everyone seemed to remember the man that he was. But as the months went by, and especially after the coroner's inquest, things changed. Gerry's legacy and memory were rewritten to the point where I could not recognise anything of the man I knew so intimately. This was exactly what he had feared so much, and why he had asked me to promise I would make sure to speak about him and his life, 'warts and all'.

Before this book was published in Ireland and the United Kingdom in October 2012, many people warned me that I should keep quiet, that my speaking out would have many negative consequences for me and even for my children. I was told that I would never find work again, that many people would hate me, and that I was putting my life and my children's lives in danger. When I decided to speak out against apartheid and joined the ANC in 1990, I received almost identical warnings. It would have been much easier to have kept quiet then, but my conscience would not allow me to. It is the same relentless stirring of my conscience that has driven me to write this book now.

When the book appeared in Ireland, it became the centre of a media storm. I expected beforehand that some people would be critical of the content, as would be the case with any publication. What shocked me, however, was that my right to have written the book, to tell my story, was questioned. Some commentators suggested I did not have the right to publish the book, and there was an attempt through the courts to stop the book from appearing. After the legal challenge was resolved, a few celebrities used their access to the media to encourage the Irish public not to read the book. These people readily acknowledged that they had not read the book, nor would they, and so had very little if any first-hand knowledge of the content. Yet, they still went on what can only be described as an orchestrated campaign to stop people buying the book. As someone who had grown up during the last years of apartheid, I was shocked that the basic right to 'freedom of speech', a fundamental cornerstone of any democracy and civilised society, could be called into question.

Thankfully many (also in the media) did not agree and defended my right to tell my story. And so despite – or perhaps because of – the attempts to silence me, thousands of people in Ireland bought the book and it became a number one bestseller, which surprised me. What was even more heart-warming was the number of letters and e-mails I received from those who had read it. Without exception they were kind and thanked me for speaking out. As was the case after Gerry's death, it was this caring and kind attitude of so many Irish people that helped me to weather the storm in the difficult weeks after the book's publication.

One of my biggest dilemmas in writing this book was how to deal with the stories of the seven children who shared Gerry's, and my, life. From the outset, it was important to me to protect their privacy as much as possible. I am thankful to my children for allowing me to tell a few of the personal stories of our life together. Since they were born, I have always protected my children from the media and public exposure. In fact, part of my motivation in taking up the diplomatic posting, and also to stay in Ireland, was to ensure as much anonymity as possible for them, and to take them away from the inevitable public interest in the Verwoerd legacy in South Africa. Of course, it became a lot more difficult to protect their privacy in recent times, but it is something I will continue to do as long as they want me to. It is for this reason that I am not publishing any current photographs of my children in this book.

Even though I know Gerry would have wanted me to write some of the stories that illustrate the extraordinarily close relationship he had with his children, and the central role they played not only in his life, but also in our life together, I decided not to. I love Gerry's children deeply, and feel very protective towards them. So in order to protect their privacy, I refer to them only in general, and in instances where it would have been bizarre not to. I am conscious that the telling of the story of their dad's last few years might be difficult for them. I can only hope that, in time, they will find comfort in the fact that in writing this book, I seek only to correct some of the terrible things that were said about him after his death.

I debated at length whether to write about everything that happened after Gerry's death. This period was so painful that I did not particularly want to revisit it. But over the months that followed I received a stream of letters and e-mails from women who were second partners and who found themselves in similar (or far worse) circumstances to mine after their partners died. Their letters spoke of the enormous grief and pain they experienced when they were left unacknowledged as the legitimate partner after the passing of their loved ones. Almost all of them begged me to speak out about this. So again it seemed to me that I was being asked to use my voice. I therefore decided to write about what I experienced after Gerry's death, in the hope that when faced with similar circumstances in the future, those involved would handle the situation with sensitivity, not only towards the second partner, but also towards the children involved.

I recently celebrated my 45th birthday. Given the average life expectancy, it is fair to say that I am at least halfway through this life. As I look back on the first half of my life, it strikes me that I did not plan much of it. It seems my journey has been determined by my response to the challenges and opportunities that crossed my path. Most of the decisions and choices I made led me on amazing journeys. A few resulted in a lot of pain and left me to deal with very trying consequences. But I agree with Mandela when he said: 'Do not judge me by my successes, judge me by how many times I fell down and got back up again.'

In the end, if there is one thing I learned from Mandela and from my own life experiences over the last four and a half decades, it is – in the words sung by Lee Ann Womack – that we should not fear the mountains in the distance or take the paths of least resistance. And when we are given the choice to sit it out or dance, we should always choose to dance.

PART ONE

South Africa

'I am an African! I owe my being to the hills and the valleys, the mountains and the glades, the rivers, the deserts, the trees, the flowers, the seas and the ever-changing seasons that define the face of our native land.'

Thabo Mbeki (at the adoption of the new constitution in the Constitutional Assembly, 8 May 1996)

S ince my earliest memories, my head and my heart seem to have been in a tension-filled dialogue. My intellect, filled with the writings of Shakespeare, the history of colonial powers, and art, music and religion from worlds far away, is most comfortable in the thinking patterns of Europe. Of course, my white skin, and the language I speak, make that even more evident. But something deep inside me has always rebelled against this European identity. Since I was very young, I have known that there is something else, something much deeper. Something that was formed by the red soil of Africa, the thunderstorms, the air, the harshness of the landscape, and the vast diversity of the continent's people. With time, I have come to understand and accept that I stand with my feet in two worlds: in the Europe of my head and in the Africa of my heart.

Physically, I came into this world at 5:40pm on 18 April 1967 in Die Moedersbond Hospital in Pretoria. It was a turbulent time in South Africa. Almost exactly three years after Mandela's famous speech from the dock, and his subsequent sentencing to life imprisonment on Robben Island, the National Party government was determined to keep the political insurgency under control by banning, among others, the ANC and PAC.

Seven months earlier, the prime minister, Hendrik Verwoerd, with whom I would become inextricably linked twenty years later, had been assassinated in parliament. After the Sharpeville massacre in 1960, the military wing of the ANC had increased its activities. In response, the apartheid government passed both the Defence Amendment Bill and the Terrorism Bill in June 1967. This made military service compulsory for white men, and also legalised the detention without trial of anyone who 'might endanger the maintenance of law and order'. Cut off by the rigorous division between people set up by apartheid, the white population was not really affected by the latter, and celebrated proudly when Dr Christiaan Barnard performed the first heart transplant later that year in Cape Town.

Like Dr Barnard, I know that my ancestors came from Holland centuries ago. However, as with many Afrikaners, the details are a bit hazy. Through an extraordinary piece of research done by Professor Geoffrey Dean from Ireland, I know that I am, on my father's side, a descendant of Gerrit Jansz and Ariaantje Jacobs. Gerrit Jansz came to the Cape in 1685 as one of the first free burghers sent by the Dutch East India Company to set up a half-way station at the southern point of Africa for the ships going to the Far East. Gerrit was given a piece of land, but had no wife. In 1688, the Lords Seventeen in the Netherlands, who directed the business of the Dutch East India Company, sent out eight female orphans on a ship called *China* as wives for the free burghers. One of them was Ariaantje Jacobs – or Ariaantje Adriaanse, as she was also known – an orphan from Rotterdam. The plan of the Lords Seventeen seemed to work, since the majority of the women were married within a month. Ariaantje married Gerrit Jansz and together they had eight children. But this is where my knowledge of the story ends.

During 1840, my ancestors must have joined the Great Trek. Bravely – some would argue, stubbornly – they faced enormous obstacles, including disease, war and almost impassable mountain ranges, in the firm belief and hope that their destiny lay somewhere else, free from British domination. This independent, courageous and adventurous spirit seems to be part of the genetic memory of most Afrikaners; it is certainly part of my genes.

But it was my maternal grandmother who ultimately had the biggest influence in my life. Our relationship was simple: I completely adored her and she completely adored me. A small but strong and determined woman, she had an extremely sharp mind and a great sense of humour. I loved nothing more than spending time with her on my grandparents' farm. During the day, I followed her when she collected the eggs and watched carefully as she made butter, dried peaches, baked bread and rusks, and cooked the most delicious food known to man on the wood-burning Aga stove. I would sit happily with her in the kitchen as she sang along to the religious music on the radio while ironing or cooking. In the afternoon, we would lie outside under the tree on a blanket, hoping to catch a cool breeze, and imagine that we saw human faces in the big white clouds drifting in the seemingly endless African sky.

But it was at night that I felt completely safe and comforted. As soon as I arrived, my grandfather would be exiled to the guest bedroom and I would snuggle up at night against my granny's back. In the winter, she would tell me endless stories while we lay in the dark, barely able to breathe under the heavy load of blankets. It was through these stories that she instilled the values and beliefs that would inform everything I would do later in life.

'You come from a line of very strong women,' she would repeat over and over again. 'We lead the men. If it wasn't for us, they would never have made it across the Drakensberg or survived the Boer Wars. Always remember that!' She would then go on to tell me how my great-grandparents on my mother's side had settled on a farm called Leeupoort, back when wild lions still roamed freely. She would tell me stories of my ancestors and of my great-grandmother, Helena Gertruida Maria Dreyer, and her marriage to my great-grandfather, Coenraad Jakobus van der Merwe, and how they settled down on Leeupoort, the farm that belonged to my great-great-grandmother. Unconventionally, the women in my family were always the landowners – their husbands joined them on the land.

It was on Leeupoort, in 1915, shortly after the beginning of World War I, that my grandmother was born, the fifth of seven children. She was named after her mother, and was called Lenie for short. But tragedy struck in 1930 when, at the age of 50, my great-grandmother passed away from pneumonia, leaving my grandmother, who was only fifteen at the time, with the responsibility of looking after the family. Her two elder sisters had already left home, so, as the eldest girl, she was expected to leave school and look after her two elder brothers, her teenage sister and her ten-year-old younger brother.

Ten years later, she met my grandfather, Johannes Petrus (Jan) Brandt, at the wedding of her cousin. Unlike my grandmother's family, my grandfather came from the Cape. He was born in the French Huguenot town of Tulbagh on 21 August 1912. His mother, Helena Jakoba Johanna Louw, and his father, Jakobus Johannes Christiaan Brandt, lived on a farm where Jakobus was a foreman or overseer. Like his bride-to-be, my grandfather never went to high school. His parents were extremely poor and there was only money for one child to study. My grandfather went to work so that his elder brother, Grammie, could continue his studies. While his brother became a geologist, my grandfather worked as a labourer. Eventually his brother, who was working as a geologist on the gold mines in the Transvaal, suggested that he join him and become a miner. So he left the Cape and travelled the thousand miles to the north to work underground; it was during this time that he met my grandmother.

They had a small wedding and went on honeymoon to the Cape, but since my great-grandfather lived with them, he went too! 'Well, he wanted to see the sea,' my grandmother would laugh. After their marriage, my grandmother insisted that my grandfather leave the dangerous mine-work. He took up small-scale farming and drove the local school bus as a source of additional income. He subsequently worked at the brick-making factory in the adjacent town, Carletonville, and in his later years he worked in the mills in the closest town, Fochville.

My grandfather was a big, quiet man. He had enormous hands, hardened by years of working the land. But he had a soft heart. He announced one day that he would no longer shoot the pig he used to feed daily to fatten up until the fatal day. He felt it was a betrayal of his bond with the pig, and told my grandmother that she could do it if she felt that strongly about eating pork. From then on, they bought their pork from the local butcher. No one ever left my grandparents' house without bags of vegetables, and if anyone knocked on their door, they would be given food. Needless to say, the word spread, and my grandfather made very little money from farming!

As I got older, I would follow my grandfather around while he worked in the vegetable fields or with the animals. He taught me how to milk cows and drive a tractor. He tried to teach me to shoot a gun, but I was hopeless at it. I hate guns with a passion and I have never, nor will ever, own a gun. So every time I had to aim, I would close my eyes and of course hit everything except the tin target. My grandfather gave up in exasperation one day after I nearly hit him.

My grandparents had two children. My mother, Helena (also called Lenie), was born in 1943, and her brother Hannes was born in 1949. Like most Afrikaners at that time, my grandparents were extremely poor. The house was basic, without running water or electricity. I was already at school (in the 1970s) when they finally got running water and no longer had to collect it from the river every day. Even better, they had a water-borne sewage system installed, which meant that the long walk to the pit toilet and night pots under the beds were at last things of the past. It took many more years (until the late 1980s) before they got electricity.

Despite these difficult circumstances, it was extremely important to both my grandparents, and in particular my grandmother, to ensure that both her children got a university education. From early on, she instilled in them the ambition to strive for something more, and to get an education. At night, by candlelight at the kitchen table, they studied for hours.

It paid off. My mother passed her Matric with flying colours and went on to Potchefstroom University to do a Bachelor of Science and an Honours degree in mathematics. She would later become one of the first women in South Africa to get a Masters degree in computer science, at a time when a computer took up most of a room. My mother's brother received a degree in pharmacology and is a very successful pharmacist. Until her death, my grandmother regarded the fact that she had put both her children through university without incurring any debt as her biggest achievement.

My mother met my dad, Johannes Hendrik Philippus van Niekerk, at university. Bennie, as he was known, was a very attractive pharmacology student and, like my mother, was ambitious and full of dreams for a better future – which was part of the attraction. His father, my grandfather, was a teacher who later became a big commercial farmer on the northern border of South Africa, close to Zeerust. In 1963 my parents got married, and in 1965 they moved to Pretoria. The move was a source of bitterness for my mother, who had been offered a teaching position at her university – an extraordinary achievement given her background and the fact that she was a woman. But my dad insisted on going to Pretoria, where he opened a pharmacy in the suburb of Menlo Park. My mum joined the Atomic Energy Board, where she continued to work as a computer programmer until shortly before my birth in April 1967.

I was born into what was, according to all accounts, a deeply troubled marriage. My dad was an alcoholic and struggled with addictions all his life. My mum was ambitious and determined to make a better life for herself and her children. In December 1969 they separated and a final divorce came through in May 1970. I was only three years old and cannot remember any of the troubles. I have a vague recollection of the big swimming pool and sandpit, as well as our two boxer dogs, Lady and Sir, but nothing more.

Following the divorce, my mum returned to her job as a computer programmer at the Atomic Energy Board. She and I moved from our very big, comfortable house in the suburbs to a one-bedroom apartment in the centre of Pretoria, where we lived until I was almost five years old. I have a few recollections of the time in the apartment. They are happy memories of times with my mum, which would lay the foundation for the very close relationship we still have today. I remember the crèche – in particular the food and naptime, as well as outings to the nearby park to look at the bridal parties, who often had photos taken there. A less happy memory is of my tonsils being removed. I can clearly remember the surgeon's face and surgical cap, as well as the big operating lights. I also have a vivid recollection of waiting for my dad to visit after the operation. He never came – a pattern of disappointments he would repeat until his death almost 25 years later. During the period following my parents' divorce, I spent an increasing amount of time with my grandparents in Leeupoort.

Despite what must have been tension-filled times at home, my days on the farm were happy and carefree. I would run around barefoot, loving the feel of the deep-red soil – particularly when it was wet – under my feet and between my toes. Like all farm kids, I quickly learnt to keep an eye out for snakes and scorpions – and the enormous thorns from the African thorn trees. At night I would collapse, exhausted but exhilarated.

A less happy part of life on the farm was the complex relationship my grandparents had with their farm workers. They were, like the majority of white South Africans at the time, racist. It was a racism born out of a sense of superiority on the one hand, and fear on the other. Yet at the same time there was a close and almost loving relationship born out of Christian values shared with their workers.

As it was a small farm, they only had one domestic worker, called Johanna. She and my grandmother would work side by side, talking like friends for hours. Yet at night Johanna would go home to a little shack on the farm. When I saw Johanna's shack for the first time, I was almost seven years old. I was upset and had an argument with my grandparents, telling them how I would change everything one day when I inherited the farm. They laughed at me, which drove me to angry tears, made worse by my being forbidden to go near Johanna's house again.

Yet, ironically, it was my grandparents who laid the foundations that would lead me to enter liberation politics later on. Through my relationship with them, I learnt early on that education, wealth and status told you little about a person. My grandparents had almost no formal education. They were extremely poor and were not regarded as movers and shakers in society. But they were dignified, humble, caring and cultured people who were wise beyond any 'book knowledge'.

Years later, when I was a political activist, I felt completely at home in townships and with farm workers. Not only did the sound of the animals and smoke in the air remind me of Leeupoort, but the caring, simple nature of the people reminded me of the deep bond I shared with my grandparents – even though they were disgusted with my political beliefs.

In 1971, my mum remarried. Philip Fourie was a colleague of hers at the Atomic Energy Board – and the polar opposite of my dad. An intellectual with a doctorate in physics, he was far more introverted and, thank God, stable than my father. I had no objections to the wedding, although I was livid when my mum insisted that I wear a white-and-baby-blue knitted pant suit to the wedding! Even though it was the seventies, I was furious that I could not wear a dress and, according to my grandparents, I tried to boycott the wedding. It is obvious from my grumpy face in the photographs that I was there under duress.

Thankfully, my and Philip's relationship improved dramatically over the years from the low point of the wedding day, and he became a father to me. A year after the wedding, we moved to a bigger house in the suburbs, which they built just in time for my sister Melissa's birth in April 1972.

I was five years old when Melissa arrived, and it was a happy change to my life. I was overwhelmed with joy at having a sibling, even though Melissa was an extremely unhappy baby who screamed most of the day. I stayed with my grandparents on the farm while my mum was in hospital. Shortly after the big day, my grandparents and I made the two-hour drive to Pretoria, to the same hospital I had been born in, so we could see the new little arrival. However, it was hospital policy not to allow children in, so I had to wait outside. Already grumpy after getting sick in the car, I was extremely upset when I could only wave at Mum and my new baby sister, who were standing at a window two storeys up. Philip brought me a gift to keep me busy while my grandparents were inside. It was a little ironing board and iron. I was disgusted! I still hate ironing to this day.

At the end of 1972, Philip got a post at the University of Stellenbosch and we made the thousand-mile move to the Western Cape. I found it traumatic to leave my beloved grandparents. My mum also resented the move and in particular hated living in the Strand, where my parents decided to live. During this time I also had to start visiting my dad, as per the divorce agreement, which meant a two-hour flight on my own to Bloemfontein, the closest airport. My dad, or his new wife, Dawn, would pick me up, and we would make another two-hour journey to Welkom, the mining town where they lived.

Alcoholism and addiction would remain a life-long struggle for my dad, which made these holidays treacherous and unpredictable. I never knew whether I would find the loving, doting dad or the aggressive, emotionally unstable dad, or indeed if he would even be there. Thankfully, Dawn was a lovely person who looked after me and tried to buffer the emotional outbursts as much as she could. The annual five-week-long summer holidays were very difficult times for me.

Like any child, I grabbed onto any promise or gesture of a loving relationship, but quickly learned never to trust that it would last. Like most children who grow up in alcoholic families, I learned to control the parts of my environment and life that I could, and having control became more and more important to me. This is of course not necessarily a good thing, since life cannot be controlled – which is something that continues to scare and frustrate me. On the positive side, I learnt to become independent and self-sufficient at a very young age, and through the long holidays, without any friends my own age, I became comfortable with my own company. Through necessity, I learned to go deep inside myself when I was sad or emotionally in trouble. 'Disappearing' into myself is something I still do when I am having a really hard time, even though I now know that talking to others (if they can be trusted) can make life easier and help with healing.

What I hated most about these holidays was being separated from my mum and sisters. Yet legally I had no say, and continued to go until I was thirteen. I knew I had a say by that age, and following an especially disastrous holiday, where the alcohol abuse led to very erratic and painful behaviour by my dad, I decided not to see him again. It would be six years before we saw each other again.

In the meantime, I started school in Lochnerhof Primary in the Strand. I remember my first day vividly. Having had enough practice of going to visit my dad, there was never even the slightest option of tears. I was nervous, but in control. I was a bit disappointed in the first day's schedule and could not understand why we did not have more academic work. But I settled in fast and from the second day I cycled to school on my own, even though I was not quite six years old.

In January 1975, my second sister, Nadine, was born – while I was on my annual holidays with my dad. I was almost eight and was beyond myself with excitement for months. Not being able to be at home during this time upset me bitterly. Philip collected me at the airport a few days after the birth and took me to the hospital, where my mum was recovering after a Caesarean section. At least this time I could go into the room – although the babies were kept in a separate baby room, so again I could only see my little sister behind glass. My sisters and I were always, and remain, very close, even though I am quite a bit older than them.

Shortly after Nadine's birth, we moved to the nearby town of Somerset West. My mother finally got her escape from the Strand, which she so despised, and built a beautiful house on a hill overlooking False Bay in a new development called Heldervue. At that time there were only about 30 houses in a very big area and there were still guinea fowl, chickens, snakes and the occasional fox.

I started going to De Hoop Primary School, a dual-medium school – which meant that all assemblies and announcements were in both Afrikaans and English. Of course it was all-white, which did not strike me as strange at all. The dual-language policy helped to improve my English at an early age, which was a huge gift.

Something else that improved my English was ballet lessons. I had started ballet two years earlier, in the Strand. For two years, once a week, I would go to the stern and very English Ms Liz Millington. I immediately loved ballet and practised non-stop. When we moved to Somerset West, I was more worried about finding a new ballet school than anything else. Luckily we found a lovely, warm and creative woman, Beverly Luyt, who was an extremely talented teacher, and I would go to her two or three times a week for classes.

Living out in Heldervue was lovely, but being a bit outside the town meant taking a school bus and then walking twenty minutes from the bus stop. This was fine in winter and I never cared about walking in the rain, but in the scorching summer heat it was terrible.

I did well at primary school and was elected prefect in my last year. I was very proud when I won the cup for best bilingual student at the prize-giving. I never did much sport, focusing on ballet instead. I tried out for netball, but gave up after a teacher laughed at me when I missed a ball. After over-hearing her comments, I believed for years that I had no ball sense. I played recorder and socialised with friends. I also became involved in church ac-tivities. Like most Afrikaners, my parents belonged to the Dutch Reformed Church and we went to church on Sundays. After the service I would join other children in Sunday school, where we would get more lessons. We also had youth groups in the week.

Fortunately, the one thing my mother resisted was 'Voortrekkers'. An Afri-kaner version of the Boy Scouts and Girl Guides, it was at that time ideo-logically driven, race-conscious, nationalist and religious. My mum flatly said no, arguing that she had no intention of ironing silly brown uniforms or driv-ing us around on Friday evenings (which was when meetings took place). It was only later that I realised that she had far bigger political concerns, but protected us by not expressing them.

During these years, the political situation in South Africa started to pene-trate my world. We had a lovely coloured lady who helped with cleaning once a week. Sometimes we would drive this very dignified older woman home. Going into the Coloured areas was like a different world, even though, as I would discover years later, conditions in the coloured areas were gen-erally better than in African townships. On the drive back to our house, my mum would become upset and talk about how wrong this was. It made a deep impression on me. We also had an African man, Ernst, who helped in the garden once a week. Ernst and I would chat for hours, and when I dis-covered that he could not read, I was shocked.

One rainy night, our doorbell rang. It was late and I heard urgent and upset voices at the door. I went to have a look and saw Ernst and a woman, whom I assumed was his wife, standing in the door with a baby in a blanket. They were drenched and looked very distressed. My mum did not see me behind her, but when she pulled the blanket back to look at the baby, it was clear from everyone's reaction that the baby was dead. I must have gasped in shock, since my mum turned around and rushed me back to bed. I was upset for days about what had happened. My mum explained that the baby had died from a chest infection. Nadine, who had croup a few weeks earlier and had to be hospitalised, was now fine, so I could not understand why Ernst's baby had died. My mum explained that they had no money for the hospital and that, as they were living in a shack, it was too cold and wet in the winter for small babies. I was struck by the injustice of it all. I kept remembering the little lifeless bundle and could not sleep properly for weeks. *Maybe if I can teach Ernst to read, it would make things easier,* I thought. I quietly gave Ernst all the money from my piggy bank, but I still felt infuriated by the fact that I could not do anything about the situation.

A similar but much bigger sense of injustice was to result in a turning point in South Africa's history during this time. On 16 June 1976, thousands of schoolchildren in Soweto marched in protest at the enforcement of a long-forgotten law requiring secondary education to be only in Afrikaans. The protests were peaceful, but when they met a large police presence on the way, some children threw stones. One policeman, a Colonel Kleingeld, drew his pistol and fired a shot, causing panic. The police then opened fire, and hundreds of young people were killed. These killings sent shockwaves through South Africa, and large-scale riots broke out everywhere.

The army was deployed, but the military presence only escalated the anger and violence. Even though I was only nine years old, I was aware that something was going on. I would hear anxious conversations between my parents and their friends. Philip was asked to join the local community watch, and would leave at night to stand guard. I did not know where he went or what he did, but I knew that my mum was always anxious at night, and we became more security-conscious. I felt a deep sense of insecurity and found it difficult to sleep; the slightest sound woke me. Luckily, things calmed down towards the end of 1976, although it took a lot longer for my sleeping patterns to return to normal.

By 1980, my mum was also working at the University of Stellenbosch as a computer programmer. Between the music lessons, ballet lessons and working forty-five minutes away from home, all the driving became too much for my mum. Reluctantly, she agreed to move to Stellenbosch, even though she loved Somerset West and would never really settle in our new home. I was about to begin high school, Melissa was also in school, and Nadine was about to start school.

Stellenbosch is a very different place from Somerset West, even though the two towns are geographically close to each other. It is more class-conscious and snobbish. Stellenbosch was largely Afrikaans. Politically and ideologically, Stellenbosch was strongly nationalist, and with the help of the university, which would provide an intellectual justification for apartheid, it became the bastion of Afrikaner nationalism.

This was evident in the high school I attended. Bloemhof Afrikaans Girls' High is the oldest Afrikaans girls' school in the country. Even though it was a state school and therefore had no tuition fees, it was steeped in the traditions associated with exclusive British private schools. The impressive buildings were surrounded by even more impressive gardens, sports fields and, of course, an Olympic-size swimming pool. There was a strong sense of exclusivity, reinforced by the fact that we only rarely engaged with the boys' school across the road, Paul Roos Gymnasium, and never had any interaction with the adjacent English girls' school, Rhenish Girls' High.

The principal of the school was Miss Coetzee, an elderly spinster who ran the place with an iron fist. It was her goal in life to develop Christian ladies who would become upstanding citizens, even if it was just to support their husbands. Frequently, we would be reminded of successful former Bloemhof pupils, such as Mrs Annetjie Marais, whose claim to fame was that her husband, Piet Marais, was a member of parliament. In years to come, when I became an MP, this would make me smile, even though Bloemhof was not impressed with my activities.

And yet, perhaps inadvertently, Miss Coetzee and Bloemhof helped me search for more from life. The fact that we were a girls-only school and had only female teachers meant that we had to do everything. There were no boys to carry things, nor were they given preference in speaking orders or glorified in sport. There were no romantic or sexual distractions. Miss Coetzee would frustrate us endlessly with her little sayings in assembly, such as:

'Always fill your mind with beautiful thoughts' or 'Remember that CL [the car registration code for Stellenbosch] stands for "Christian Ladies".' Yet some of her frequently repeated quotes embedded themselves into my subconscious. Years later, I still remember: 'Even a dead fish can swim with the stream' and 'There is not enough darkness in the world to destroy the light of one little candle.' Wise words.

I focused on academia and ballet. I was now doing up to three hours a day of ballet lessons, and I would get up at around 5am to practise for two hours before school at the barre my parents had installed for me in the playroom. From an early age, my sisters and I had a Calvinist approach to work and life instilled in us. If you wanted to get somewhere in life, you had to work hard. To work harder than anyone else was the only way to get anywhere, and in addition, it was virtuous. To be idle was no good.

I still find it difficult to watch television without doing something else at the same time. Television time was strictly controlled; even at high school, we were not allowed to watch TV after 8pm. So we practised and worked hard. These teachings were reinforced by the church, where I spent most of my free time. The doctrine of the Dutch Reformed Church was based on fear and was fervently anti-Catholic. I did my best to follow the instructions and teachings.

Naturally, being in an all-white church, school, ballet group and neighbourhood isolated us all to a great extent from what was going on in the rest of the country. The only impact we felt from the unrest elsewhere was the regular drills at school in case of a terrorist attack, which we all knew really meant a 'black attack'. In such an event, an alarm would go off, and on the teacher's command of '*Val plat!*' we would have to get down under our desks or hide in cupboards or storerooms. We practised this drill frequently. We were also taught to identify terrorist explosive devices, with examples of various bombs and limpet mines exhibited throughout the school. There was a weekly instruction of 'Jeugweerbaarheid' (Youth Preparedness), which, depending on the teacher, could be more or less ideologically driven. As instability grew and riots became more frequent in the 1980s, we were rarely aware of them, since the media were tightly controlled. Apartheid was very successful in what it set out to do – namely, to keep us apart.

During this time, however, Miss Coetzee gave a long lecture in assembly against 'the black terrorists who were causing all the riots in the townships in Cape Town'. Even though I knew very little about what was going on, I instinctively revolted against her racist language and crude generalisations. As we left assembly, she called me aside and asked me why I had frowned during her speech. I said I did not like the way she had spoken and was sure that things were more complicated than she had made them out to be. I thought I could see the smoke coming from her ears as she turned red with anger. She pointed her long-nailed, crooked finger at my face and poked at my nose while rhythmically saying, 'Be very careful [poke] young lady [poke]. Very [poke], very [poke] careful [poke, poke].' I became equally annoyed, and turned around and walked away.

If any of the teachers did not agree with the school's philosophy, they kept it to themselves, fearful for their jobs. But there was one teacher who made a big impression on me and my fellow students. Letitia Snyman had spent many years in England before returning to South Africa to be close to her elderly parents. She taught English and was in a different league from the rest of the teaching staff. Although she never explicitly voiced any political opinions in class, we all knew she thought differently. She gave us additional English texts to read, like *Animal Farm* and *Lord of the Flies*, and insisted on us expressing opinions on difficult and moral questions.

She did not judge our conclusion as long as it was well thought through and well argued. She must have had a difficult time at Bloemhof, but later became the principal of the adjacent English Girls' School: she guided that school through a process of racial integration, and also turned it into a top all-round school. She made us think, and, contrary to the rest of our education, insisted that we were not only allowed to question things around us, but in fact had an obligation to do so.

In my final year of school, I was elected chairperson of the Christian Student Association. This was not of much consequence, except that I invited a well-known theology student, Wilhelm Verwoerd, to address us at our annual meeting. He brought his girlfriend along. Apart from thinking that he had appalling dress sense, I was quite impressed with the talk, although I was completely unaware that he was a grandson of the former prime minister.

I had two boyfriends at school, but being very religious, we only ever held hands and kissed. In fact, even dancing was frowned upon, so although I

34

loved ballet, I never danced socially until the school's farewell ball, with my boyfriend of the time.

I continued to be completely absorbed by ballet. I was good at it, and danced the lead in many performances. I wanted nothing more than to become a professional dancer. The teachers felt I had enough talent to make a success of it, but my mum was completely opposed to it. Given her personal history, not getting a degree was not an option for me. She made that clear for years, although, when she saw how ecstatic I was every time I came off stage, her position gradually softened. Eventually she gave in and agreed that I could go to the University of Cape Town to study ballet. But as soon as she agreed, I started to have doubts of my own, and one day, after taking the bandages off my bleeding toes, I had had enough and decided to go and study at Stellenbosch. For years I would wonder if I did the right thing, and I still miss the thrill of doing a perfect arabesque or landing a pirouette.

2

In January 1985, I enrolled at Stellenbosch University. Having only recently decided not to do ballet, I was not sure what to study. I knew I liked children, so enrolled for primary school teaching. Within a week, I knew it was a mistake: I was completely bored.

  On my mother's suggestion, I decided to attend various different lectures. I enjoyed psychology and philosophy. I had thought about studying theology before, but since women could not be ordained, I thought it was impossible. Then I heard of a woman a few years ahead of me who had studied theology. On investigation, I was told: 'You are welcome, and you will get a degree, but nothing formal regarding the church.' I was delighted. My poor parents despaired. Having finally agreed to ballet, they (correctly) thought that primary school teaching was not a good choice for me. But now I had decided on a degree with absolutely no career prospects. As a compromise, I promised to study psychology as well, so that I could potentially become a clinical psychologist. So along with psychology, I would do three years of theology, two years of Greek and Hebrew, and three years of philosophy.

  I was the only woman in the class of nearly 50 men. Coming from the girls-only school and having only sisters, I thought this might pose some problems, but I quickly made friends and discovered that I often enjoyed male friends more than female friends. Herman Nienaber, Robert Vosloo and a few others became close friends, and together we had great fun. They, more than I, would get into endless mischief. During boring lectures, they found various ways of entertaining themselves and the other students. One trick nearly caused serious injury.

  We had Ancient Hebrew on the ground floor of an old building. As the building had no air-conditioning, the windows would usually be open. We would be bored to death while our lecturer enthusiastically wrote long sentences of Hebrew on the blackboard. The lads thought out a mischievous plan. One of the guys would jump out of the window, walk around and enter the classroom, apologising for being late. He would then take his seat, only to repeat the process a few minutes later. This would be repeated a few times, with a rather confused lecturer never quite understanding what was going on. This silly, but hilarious, stunt went on for weeks, until one day our lecture was moved to a first-floor lecture room. This must have slipped my classmate's mind, and to our horror we saw him making his hasty escape through the window. A loud yell followed, and we all rushed over to the window, only to see the escape artist stuck in a rather thorny tree below the window. The poor lecturer still had no clue what was going on.

Outside of class, there was also lots of fun. Although my home was in Stellenbosch, I decided to live in one of the residences on campus. This was the norm, and I was allocated to a big residence called Heemstede. The residences were single-sex, and the tiny rooms were shared by two students, with big communal bathrooms on each floor. There was a dual − and to my mind very unjust − system when it came to the female and male residences. No men were allowed in the women's rooms. If they wanted to visit anyone (this was of course in a time before mobile phones), they had to announce themselves to a person on duty at the front door, who would state over the intercom that so-and-so was there to see you. There were sitting rooms, which were monitored by residence staff, where you had to 'meet'. But it was the curfew that irritated me most. In your first year, you had to be signed in at 8pm, and in subsequent years at either 10pm or 11pm. None of these rules applied to the male students.

At a welcome meeting for first-years with the rector and vice-chancellor, Professor Mike de Vries, I raised the unfairness of the system. He gave me a patronising smile and said it was for our own safety, since 'we all know what men are like'.

'Well, then it seems to me that you should rather lock the men in at eight in the evening and we will all be safer,' I shot back − to a cheer from some of the women and cat-whistles from the men. I heard afterwards that the rector wanted to know who I was, since I was 'clearly a troublemaker'.

Years later, the rector must have been relieved after my sisters and I finally graduated, all in the same academic year (Nadine received her Bachelor degree in law, Melissa a postgraduate law degree, and I received my Masters). Apart from my political activities to come, Nadine became the second female president of the student council, and Melissa the editor of the student newspaper, *Die Matie*. We all challenged the institutions, which were archaic, racist, sexist and intolerant of freedom of speech. Not only did different rules apply to the female and male residences, but the (very) few nonwhite students stayed in a separate residence slightly off campus. Organisations such as the End Conscription Campaign were banned. When *Die Matie*, with Melissa as editor, exposed some very harsh initiation rites, all copies of that edition were stolen and publicly burnt. There was no punishment for those who were involved. So, not surprisingly, our activities did not go down well.

Back in 1985, I shared my tiny room with a lovely young woman, Nicolene Burger. Being the child of a church minister in the small, rural Free State town of Zastron, she struggled to adapt to the liberal arts department, where she studied fine arts. When they had to do drawings of nude males the first week, she came back to the room in tears and was physically sick. Even though we were politically very different, we became good friends and spent two years together as roommates. Being locked up during the long evenings, we also made many other friends, like Elsa Jute, a brilliant science student.

Like most of my fellow students, I was extremely religious, and we would often attend Christian camps during weekends. In September 1985, I camped at Betty's Bay, about an hour away from Stellenbosch. On the Saturday, a few of us piled onto the back of a pickup to buy snacks at the local convenience store. On the way there, we made an unexpected stop at a group of houses. Wilhelm Verwoerd, one of the leaders of the camp, whom I knew from when he had addressed us at school, was sitting in the front and now hopped out. There had been a big storm the previous week and he was checking for damage at what I assumed was their holiday home. Staring out at the three houses on a fenced-in piece of land, I asked my friends: 'What strange people have a flagpole in their yard?'

There was a moment of silence while they looked at me with amazement.

'Don't you know who he is?' one finally asked.

'No. Who?' I responded.

'He's the grandson of Hendrik Verwoerd,' another replied. 'It was the prime minister's holiday home and now belongs to the family.'

Like most South Africans, I knew the name Hendrik Verwoerd, even though he had been assassinated the year before I was born. I knew he had been prime minister and was known as the 'architect of apartheid'. As a child I would hear my parents and grandparents speaking of him in glowing terms, and my grandmother treasured her copy of an HF Verwoerd photo book published after his death.

I looked at Wilhelm with interest, but still mumbled that I thought it was ridiculous to have a flagpole in your yard. That night, around the campfire, Wilhelm struck up a conversation with me. We chatted about religion and philosophy, and various moral questions. Wilhelm, who was four years older than me, was completing his Honours degree in philosophy, having graduated the previous year with the same theology degree I was studying for. He was also a part-time lecturer in philosophy. It was clear that he was highly intelligent, but I gave the conversation no further thought.

Three days later, there was an announcement at the residence that I had a visitor. I went down to the front door to find Wilhelm waiting. He explained that he had enjoyed our chat and that he had to attend a black-tie event a few weeks later.

'Would you please accompany me?' he asked. I agreed, and we spoke a while longer before he left. As I walked up the stairs back to the third floor I had a very clear, slightly unsettling thought. I entered the room and found two of my friends waiting. 'Well? What happened?' they asked excitedly.

'It was Wilhelm Verwoerd,' I said. 'I don't know how to explain it, but I'm almost certain this is the guy I'm going to marry one day.'

'Wow! That was fast!' laughed Nicolene.

'No, I'm not even sure if I like him very much,' I said in a daze. 'I just can't shake this feeling.'

This was the first of a series of what some would call 'premonitions' (I prefer the term 'clear thoughts') that I would get throughout my life, all of which would lead to dramatic changes and take me down roads that would be life-altering.

The event was fun. Wilhelm was charming and entertaining, and by the end of the evening I liked him a lot more. But I was worried about his family connections. When I had phoned my mum to tell her he had invited me to the ball, she responded: 'You have to be very careful. His family are extremely conservative.'

So when Wilhelm called next, I confronted him: 'Look, before we talk any further, I need to know where you stand politically.'

I could hear that Wilhelm was slightly taken aback, but he responded that he was to the left of the National Party. I could live with that. After the ball, we saw a lot of each other and grew increasingly close. Yet it was clear to me that Wilhelm did not want to get into a serious relationship. Eventually he confided in me that he had applied for a Rhodes scholarship to study for three years at Oxford, starting the next year. He felt it would be unfair to start a relationship if he was about to leave. We agreed to wait until December, when he was due to hear if he had been awarded the scholarship. We were also a bit worried about the fact that he was one of my tutors in philosophy.

In December 1985, to his delight, Wilhelm was awarded the prestigious Rhodes scholarship. Knowing how much this meant to him, I was happy for him and accompanied him to deliver the good news to his parents. Wilhelm's parents lived in the Stellenbosch neighbourhood of Uniepark in a rambling family home dominated by large pictures and busts of HF Verwoerd. I had met his parents briefly before and liked his mother, Elise, in particular. She came from the small farming town of Sannieshof in the North West Province. A soft-spoken, very religious woman, she was (and remains) totally dedicated to her husband and family. Wilhelm's father, Wilhelm senior, is the eldest son of Hendrik and Betsie Verwoerd. Until his retirement a few years ago he was professor in the Geology Department at the University of Stellenbosch. As the eldest son of the family he is very much the patriarch of the extended Verwoerd family and since his father's assassination had taken on the role of protecting not only HF Verwoerd's legacy, but also the 'good' name of the family.

Even though I was of course aware of the Verwoerds' political background, I was still shocked when his father reacted with disappointment and disgust at Wilhelm's proud announcement that he had won a Rhodes scholarship. Wilhelm senior made it clear that he did not want the Verwoerd name associated with the British colonialist Cecil John Rhodes. He also said Wilhelm would be corrupted by the liberal English attitudes at Oxford. I could see how this hurt Wilhelm. It was to be my first glimpse into how ideologically driven Wilhelm's family was, and I did not like it at all.

Yet I liked Wilhelm – in fact, we were in love – and despite our earlier agreement, we started a serious relationship. A few months later, however, a revelation from Wilhelm nearly ended our relationship. One evening Wilhelm was very late for an appointment we had. When he finally arrived I asked where he had been, but his answers were vague and evasive. Under pressure from me he eventually 'confessed' that he had been at a Ruiterwag (junior Broederbond) meeting at Professor Tom Dreyer's house. I was furious.

'Are you a member?' I wanted to know. Wilhelm said that he was. I exploded and bombarded him with angry questions and accusations. I could not understand how he could be part of a secret, Afrikaans, male-only organisation with such dubious political motives. I also made it clear that I could never be with anyone who belonged to the Ruiterwag or Broederbond. Even though he argued passionately with me on the night, I think Wilhelm had started to doubt the wisdom of belonging to the organisation even before our conversation. A few days later he resigned his membership.

In July 1986, Wilhelm left to start his studies abroad. He went first to Utrecht in Holland for three months, and then to Oxford to study politics, philosophy and economics for three years. Before he left, we agreed that we would get married at the end of 1987, when I had finished my first degree, if we were still together then. The period he spent abroad was traumatic for Wilhelm, especially his time in Holland. Not only was it his first trip outside South Africa, but he ended up in a house with ANC members and gay couples – all former South Africans – who were very hard on this 'naive' white Afrikaner who carried the Verwoerd surname. He wrote long letters to me daily and spoke on little cassette tapes that he sent me. The certainties of his youth were being undermined and it was clear that he was having a difficult time. He became confused and even depressed.

At the end of 1986, I decided to visit him in Oxford. We spent three weeks Inter-Railing through Europe. It was not my first trip abroad, but we were badly prepared for the extreme cold of the European winter. Things became even more challenging when Wilhelm lost all his money and his passport. Given that this was during the apartheid years, no one was very keen to help us and, as it was close to Christmas, the embassy officials just shrugged their shoulders. Yet we survived.

Back in England, we met a young South African in exile, Tshepiso Mashinini. Tshepiso's brother Tsietsi had been one of the leaders in the 1976 Soweto uprisings. Tshepiso was a brilliant man and we talked for hours. He challenged our political views and told us about the other side of life in our country, which we had not known existed. He introduced us to other exiles, who did the same. For hours they talked about their living conditions in South Africa, the struggle to get an education, and the police harassment they endured. Some even showed us the scars they carried from being tortured by the security police. They were our age and had grown up in the same country as us, yet our lives were worlds apart.

Meeting Tshepiso had an enormous impact on me. I returned to South Africa a month later with my whole perception of reality changed. I looked at everything and everyone around me with new eyes – and with growing suspicion. I felt as if everyone in authority – the church, teachers, lecturers, and even my parents – had lied to me for years. I watched the TV news with disdain, thinking how none of it was the truth.

Back on campus, I started questioning and challenging many of the ideological and political statements the lecturers made. This resulted in furious exchanges between the lecturers, my classmates and me. I had been warned that there were one or two students in every year who were paid to feed information to the security police, but I could not have cared less. One day, I arrived home to find one of my lecturers having tea with my parents. I could see that my mum was irritated, and she told me the lecturer had come to warn them of my 'revolutionary' ideas, which he felt were not only dangerous but also anti-Christian. I eyed the professor furiously.

'Isn't that what they said of Jesus as well?' I asked coldly.

Before he could answer, I left the room, but I heard the professor say: 'There you have it! Need I say any more?'

Even though my parents must have been concerned, they did not say anything to me afterwards. They had always encouraged debate and free thinking, and the dinner table would often resemble a debating society. I gradually sought out more of the (very few) left-wing students on campus. Wilhelm, meanwhile, kept sending me books and articles that were banned under the draconian censorship laws in South Africa. In order not to be caught, he would include photocopies of, for example, Donald Woods's book *Biko*, about the life of Steve Biko, or Mandela's speech from the dock, between copies of philosophy articles. These books gradually opened my mind and broke down the intellectual walls my apartheid education had put up.

After a few months apart, we agreed that we would get married a year later, in December 1987. We were still very young, but adored one another. We shared a powerful intellectual connection and value system, and above all we wanted to contribute to positive change in South Africa. We did not want to spend another two years on different continents, but believing that sex before marriage was wrong, we felt that we had to get married before I could move to England and we could live together. With the wisdom of hindsight, this was not very smart. We barely knew each other, having spent so much time apart. We were both rapidly becoming disillusioned with religion, so we should have overcome our no-sex-before-marriage belief. To make matters worse, I would be only twenty years old and would need permission from both my parents to get married.

I was concerned about how my dad would respond to our decision. Since the disastrous holiday when I was thirteen, I had not seen him, apart from a brief visit to get him to sign a passport application the year before. Yet he would cause endless problems for me over the years, frequently phoning the residence at university in a drunken rage. One night towards the end of 1986, he called again, this time about money. He wanted me to agree that he could stop paying for a life insurance policy, with me as the beneficiary, that he was legally obliged to maintain. He rarely paid any maintenance, but now that he was in financial difficulty he wanted the life insurance to be paid out to him. On the spur of the moment, I said: 'I'll sign that, if you agree to sign your parental rights over to Philip and don't hassle me any more.'

There was a moment of silence before he said: 'Okay!' No questions, no fight, just: 'Okay!'

A few days later, my father phoned to say he was in Stellenbosch. We met for tea and he told me that we had to go to court the next day, where he would sign me off and I would be formally adopted by my stepfather. My mum offered to come with me, but as always when I have to face something very difficult, I preferred to do it on my own, going deep inside myself for strength. The judge asked a few questions before agreeing to the order. I then asked if he could tell my dad not to bother me any more. The judge looked at my dad and said: 'Mr Van Niekerk, I have never dealt with something like this before, and I don't like it at all. I'm not sure what is going on here, but you'd better behave and do what is right.' He then signed the order. It was all over in ten minutes.

How could it be this easy to get rid of your child? I wondered, as he dismissed us. My dad (who was legally not my dad any more) and I left the courtroom together. We walked down the rose-lined path outside the magistrates' court in silence. At the end of the path, we paused.

'Bye,' I said softly. My dad did not respond. He turned to his right and walked away. I watched him, hoping he would look back and give me a little wave or even just a final look. He didn't, and as he disappeared around the corner I turned to my left to go to the car park, in tears.

That evening, my dad called. He had clearly had too much to drink and he screamed at me. He raged about what a failure I was and would always be. He assured me over and over that I would never succeed at anything I did. Instead of seeing this as drunken meanness stemming from his own sense of failure, I desperately tried to convince him otherwise. At some point he threw down the phone, after which I went to find my mum. I rarely involved her in my troubles with my dad, but it had become too much for me. She was furious, and I overheard her calling my father, and then his sister, to ensure that he would leave me alone in future.

This awful conversation at the end of an awful day was the last time I spoke to him. I have no doubt that the legal signing-off was the right thing to do for me to have some normality in my life. Yet it left me with deep emotional scars for a long time, particularly when it came to developing trusting relationships, especially with men. I also became more driven to be successful. I had always worked hard, and these increased efforts brought further results, but at a high emotional and physical price.

In 1992, I got a call from my dad's wife saying that he had died suddenly from cancer. I was too far pregnant with my second baby, Wian, to attend the funeral. Even though I did not shed a tear, I will forever regret that I did not have a relationship with him and that he never saw my children or experienced my entering parliament. Irrespective of all the pain he had caused me, he was still my dad.

3

Wilhelm and I were married on 29 December 1987. We rented a beautiful little Presbyterian church and invited about a hundred guests. By now, we had many friends from across the racial spectrum. Wilhelm's mother did the flowers, and we used Wilhelm's father's antique German DKW as the wedding car. Wilhelm had arrived only a few days earlier from Oxford, so I made almost all the arrangements on my own.

Two days before the wedding, a crisis erupted. We had asked Anton van Niekerk, one of our philosophy professors who was also a theologian, to lead the service, but since he was no longer a practising minister, he could not conduct the legal part of the ceremony. So we asked a friend, Sydney Davis, a minister in the nearby coloured area, to officiate. He said he was honoured, and to our delight agreed. When Wilhelm's father found out that a 'coloured man' was to be part of a Verwoerd wedding, he exploded. He said that he would not attend, and would not allow Wilhelm's mother to attend either. I was livid! I felt that, out of principle, we should not cave in. Yet, for his mother's sake, Wilhelm convinced me otherwise. Sydney immediately understood, and graciously still came to the wedding. It was an early-morning wedding, and afterwards we had tea for the guests on a veranda on the Neethlingshof wine farm. It was a glorious summer day and thankfully everything went smoothly.

After the wedding, we moved into a flat the local council provided for low-income white families – for which we qualified, being students with almost no income. We were due to return to Oxford, but Wilhelm had agreed to take a break for a year and do some part-time teaching, so that I could complete my Honours degree in philosophy. (I had graduated a few days before the wedding.) Even though a recent synod of the DRC church had finally agreed to the ordination of women, I had no interest any more in going to the seminary school to study for another three years. I was deeply disillusioned with the church on political and gender grounds. I had lost all respect for its leaders and was seriously questioning my faith. Instead of taking the safer route of studying for a postgraduate degree in clinical psychology, which I had also considered, I decided to follow my heart and study philosophy.

In between studies, Wilhelm and I were settling into married life. In the middle of the year, Wilhelm was invited to join a group on a clandestine trip to meet the ANC in Lusaka, the capital of Zambia. Similar trips had previously resulted in the participants' passports being withdrawn and them being held up to public ridicule, so the trip was to happen quietly. Originally I was also going, but then it was decided that women could not attend. When I asked why, I was told that they were not sure what living conditions would be like, and that women might not cope. I felt patronised and insulted, and vowed never to be excluded from political discussions again.

On his return, Wilhelm became increasingly withdrawn, and the arguments with his family increased. Even though our political activities were very limited at this stage, it became apparent that the government was aware of us. In 1987 Wilhelm and I dropped Wilhelm's grandmother, Betsie, at the airport in Cape Town. As the wife of a previous prime minister, she was entitled to use the VIP lounge for life. While we were waiting for her flight to depart, the door of the lounge opened and FW de Klerk, who was at the time the minister of National Education and Planning, walked in with a few staff members. He spotted Ouma Betsie and came over to greet her. She in turn introduced us to De Klerk. His eyes narrowed slightly when he heard our names.

'Yeees,' he said with a sigh, looking at us knowingly. 'We know about these two.' Then he leaned forward and said in a threatening tone: 'Be careful, you two, very careful!' He turned and left to board his plane before we could ask any questions.

We returned to Oxford at the end of 1988, after I had graduated with an Honours degree in philosophy. I had enrolled for a Masters in philosophy at the University of Stellenbosch, and was planning to do the research for my thesis while at Oxford with Wilhelm. My thesis was on the work of various feminist theologians who questioned how the masculine language used for God was impacting on society and patriarchal structures. I quickly discovered that Oxford was not the best place to do work on feminist theology.

Wilhelm found Oxford a lonely and challenging place. Not being under the same pressure academically, I loved it. The first apartment we were assigned was dark and dreary, but when we subsequently moved to a much brighter ground-floor apartment close to University Park, I was much happier. We had very little money, since we were both living on the Rhodes scholarship. Eventually I took a job delivering newspapers to bring in a bit more cash. I bought anything we needed second-hand from Oxfam or at the university club, where foreign students would sell their belongings when they left Oxford. I would cycle into the city centre daily to have lunch or dinner with Wilhelm at Corpus Christi College. I loved the big old dining hall, with its long tables and benches. Sometimes we were invited to high table, which meant sitting at the top table and getting much better food. Afterwards we would have coffee in the senior common room; it was all very civilised.

On my first day in the common room, I met a lovely Scottish man. 'Hello! I'm Eddie McKenzie,' he said in a strong Scottish accent.

I introduced myself, then asked what he was doing at Oxford.

'Oh, I kill frogs,' he responded.

'Why?' I asked, surprised.

'Because I like it!' Eddie said without the slightest tone of irony. 'Actually, I prefer South African bullfrogs. They croak less when you kill them.'

Slightly perturbed, I told Wilhelm about the conversation. He just laughed and told me that Eddie was doing a doctorate on genetics in frogs.

We made many good friends from around the world, such as Todd Breyfogle from the United States and Graeme McLean from Australia, who would later become godfathers to our children. Together we would play croquet and spend long hours in the pub (even though I never drank alcohol). During the summer, we spent leisurely afternoons punting on the river; in the evenings, we would frequently go to evensong in Christ Church College.

During our first year at Oxford, Wilhelm and I made two big trips. First, we decided to backpack and camp through Israel. I had always wanted to see the holy sites. It was an extraordinary three weeks during which Wilhelm and I were very close. I will never forget waking up on the banks of the Sea of Galilee, watching the sunrise through our open tent flaps. In between visits to the holy sites, we made time to float in the Red Sea and snorkel in Eilat. Although it was a magical time, we were disturbed by the political tensions

47

in the country. Even coming from South Africa and its succession of states of emergency, we found the military presence in Israel and the animosity between Palestinians and Jews unsettling. It was clear that peaceful co-existence between the two communities was very far away.

In retrospect, Wilhelm and I seem to have been drawn to conflict areas. Having seen Israel, we decided to visit Ireland. In the weeks before we left, I was amazed to discover how few British people – and in particular how few Oxford students – had ever been to Ireland (North or South). Despite – or perhaps because of – the centuries-old conflict there, no one seemed particularly interested in the country. A good friend of ours, Edward Peters, who worked for a Christian organisation called Moral Re-Armament (MRA), with which Wilhelm was very involved, joined us.

We drove to Stranraer in Scotland, from where we took the ferry to Belfast. We stayed with two other lovely MRA people, Peter and Fiona Hannon, in Coleraine. Lady Fiona is the daughter of the Duke of Montrose, a title her brother inherited. She and Peter had spent many years in South Africa, and I was good friends with their daughter Catherine. Peter and Fiona were well connected in Northern Ireland and arranged various political meetings for us.

One of the most memorable of these events (for all the wrong reasons) was a lunch with the Reverend Ian Paisley in his home. After passing through security, we were asked to wait in a sitting room. Shortly afterwards, Ian Paisley arrived, greeting us warmly. He asked Wilhelm and Edward what they did, and he then turned to me. He clearly assumed that I was a housewife, but I corrected him, saying that I was also studying.

'Oh? And what do you study?' he wanted to know.

'Theology,' I responded.

'Oh good!' he smiled. 'What type of theology?'

Now I was getting a bit nervous. 'Well,' I started hesitantly, 'feminist theology.'

Ian Paisley locked a stern gaze on me. He snorted slightly. 'In my church, that will not be allowed. In fact, women still wear hats!' he said, while spitting slightly as he emphasised the 'ts' of hats. He clearly had no interest in continuing the conversation with me, and his wife invited us to the dining room. It was not a good start.

After saying a lengthy grace, Ian Paisley engaged Wilhelm and Edward in political discussions. I was listening with interest and was struck by the similarities between his arguments and those of conservative whites in South Africa. After our earlier interaction, I kept quiet. However, when Ian Paisley laughingly told us that he always knew when there were Catholics on a plane, as he could smell them, I was shocked. As I have never been good at keeping a poker face, it showed. He wanted to know why I looked so shocked.

'Well, with respect, Reverend Paisley, I think it's deeply offensive – and exactly what racist whites would say about blacks in South Africa,' I responded.

A silence fell around the table. Again he looked at me with a stern gaze. There was a tense pause before he said: 'No, no. We Protestants associate ourselves with the cause of black South Africans.'

'How is that?' I wanted to know.

'We are a majority, who could soon be oppressed by a minority,' he responded, much to my surprise.

A far happier meeting, on the opposite side of the political spectrum, was with a wonderful Catholic community worker called Paddy Doherty from the Bogside in Derry. He did extraordinary, inspiring work developing cross-community links between young people.

So many aspects of Northern Ireland were similar to what we were going through in South Africa. The restrictions on the media and on political activities, prejudice and suspicion between people, security concerns – even the metal detectors at shopping malls were familiar. Yet people in Northern Ireland looked basically the same, and spoke the same language; the conflict clearly was not really about religion any more. *Why can this conflict not be resolved?* I wondered, once we had left Northern Ireland and were driving through the green hills of Connemara.

Thankfully, the rest of the trip was more relaxed. I was seduced by the peaceful charm and beauty of the west of Ireland. We stayed at B&Bs and loved the charm and humour of our Irish hosts. We crossed the country and drove east to Dublin, where we visited the tourist sites and strolled around Trinity College, before taking a ferry back to the UK.

During our first year back in Oxford we also made a trip back to South Africa. We wanted to see our families, but also had something special to do.

We had kept in contact with Tshepiso Mashinini (the younger brother of Tsietsi Mashinini), whom I had met during my first trip to Oxford in 1986. Over a cup of coffee one day, Tshepiso remarked how sad he was about the complete lack of contact with his parents. Knowing that any communication might be picked up by the South African security police, he did not want to expose his parents to any possible harassment or put his own life at risk. However, this meant that his parents did not even know for certain that he was alive. Wilhelm and I offered to visit his parents in Soweto, when we were in South Africa. On our suggestion Tshepiso made a tape recording which we took with us.

Given that there was still a state of emergency, we knew it would attract attention if we just drove into Soweto, and since we did not know the area we asked a friend to take us there. He asked us to hide under blankets as we drove past the military presence at the entrance. Feeling tense, but also exhilarated, we were very happy to meet Tshepiso's parents and to bring them greetings from their son. They were overwhelmed with joy to hear that he was not only alive and well, but had succeeded in getting a scholarship to study at the Oxford Polytechnic. Their relief and pride was visible. Over refreshments one of Tshepiso's younger brothers, who was sitting quietly next to Wilhelm, suddenly asked loudly: 'So what do you think of your grandfather?'

A shocked silence followed before his parents berated him in Zulu. But Wilhelm did not mind and took some time to engage with this young man, who was clearly very politicised. After an hour of intense discussion and being fed endless cups of tea, we left, leaving the little tape recorder and tape with them to listen later.

It was our first visit to Soweto. We were deeply moved by what we saw and by the time we spent with this remarkable family that had sacrificed so much in the struggle. Years later Tshepiso and I would work together on the White Paper on Local Government, before he died of a heart attack at the very young age of 32.

Back at Oxford, Wilhelm and I decided to start a family. It seemed like a good idea, since I had a lot of free time. We felt it would be good to have the children young, so we would still be relatively young when they were teenagers and young adults. We planned things carefully, since we did not want the birth to happen before or during Wilhelm's final exams, but our visas ran out at the end of July 1990 and I would not have been able to fly back to South Africa if I was too far pregnant. This gave us a window of three weeks in which everything had to happen. Fortunately, I became pregnant easily, and we quietly congratulated ourselves. Little did we know what was about to happen.

I have a condition called porphyria variegate, which runs in certain Afrikaner families. I inherited it from my dad. The condition results in a faulty liver enzyme which can, in some cases, cause great difficulties with certain medication, dramatic hormonal changes, and sensitivity to sunlight. You can live with porphyria without ever showing any symptoms, and the only reason I was tested was because my dad had the condition. I had never had any difficulty with it before (or since) the pregnancy, although I am always extremely careful with medication.

In October 1989, I developed kidney infections, and after weeks on antibiotics I woke up one morning in agony. The doctor diagnosed a kidney stone and I was taken to hospital by ambulance. There I warned all the doctors that I had porphyria – and told them that I might be pregnant. Since porphyria is extremely rare outside South Africa and Scandinavia, the British doctors knew very little about the condition and, as I realised afterwards, paid little attention to it for the first few days. An ultrasound showed a kidney stone in my right kidney, and a little white flicker confirmed that I was indeed about six weeks pregnant. I was delighted – with the pregnancy, if not the kidney stone! Of course, my pregnancy meant that the doctors could do nothing apart from pain management for the kidney stone. I was also vomiting frequently, which was put down to morning sickness, and I was becoming dehydrated.

On the night of 8 November, I started to get severe stomach aches and my urine turned dark brown. Within hours I was fighting a losing battle to remain conscious and was having breathing difficulties. I was afterwards told that doctors had no idea what was happening to me. Then a doctor from South Africa overheard them discussing the case and suggested that it might be a severe porphyria attack. He was right: the moment they treated the condition correctly, I improved, but I was semi-comatose for a few days.

I eventually woke up to find the South African doctor who had saved my life next to my bed. He reassured me in a strong South African accent that everything was going to be fine. He then told me that the Berlin Wall had fallen while I was unconscious! I stayed in hospital for ten days before flying home to South Africa (on the suggestion of the doctors in Oxford) to recover. This gave Wilhelm, who was trying to study for his finals, a much-needed break. We were of course very concerned about the impact my illness had had on my tiny foetus, but a scan in Cape Town showed all three centimetres of her moving around happily.

The rest of the pregnancy was challenging. I returned to Oxford in January, but had to be admitted to hospital on three other occasions. I had no further difficulties with the porphyria, but had three more kidney stones. I was looked after by a high-risk team in the John Radcliffe Hospital and got world-class care from the NHS.

In between all the hospital visits, on 11 February 1990, we sat with a few college friends in their kitchen watching for hours a tiny TV screen showing the gates of Victor Verster Prison in Paarl. Finally Madiba appeared on the screen – a free man. We wept and hugged each other, overwhelmed with joy and wishing we were home. We knew it was time to go back to South Africa, but there was one more momentous event that had to take place before we could leave Oxford behind.

Shortly after Wilhelm's finals, at the end of June 1990, Wilmé was born. It was agreed that I would be induced, but after sixteen hours of labour, Wilmé went into distress and an emergency C-section was performed. Thankfully, I was awake during the birth; I'd had an epidural earlier. Just before midnight, they lifted Wilmé over the screen covering my tummy. It was the most magical moment of my life. She did not cry, but a little tear ran down her left cheek. I had a strong sensation that I recognised her – that I would have recognised her among other babies as my child. Before I could hold her, my blood pressure suddenly dropped dramatically. Feeling that I was about to lose consciousness, I said to the anaesthetist: 'I'm going, I'm going!'

'Where?' she asked.

'Heaven, I hope,' I managed to joke, before everything turned black.

A while later, I woke to the voices of doctors urging me to look at my baby. This had the necessary impact and I regained consciousness – and held

Wilmé for the first time. I stayed in hospital for a week, watching the World Cup in Italy (where both England and Ireland progressed to the final stages), in between recovering, and of course doting on my beautiful new baby.

4

Three weeks after Wilmé's birth, Wilhelm and I returned to South Africa. Although we were excited to go back, for me it was a sad farewell to Oxford. Apart from the usual hormone-driven days after the birth of my first baby, I was also unsure about what was waiting for us back in South Africa. Mandela had just been released, but violence was escalating daily. Family and friends were anxious about the future (if any) for whites, and the economy was on its knees.

To make matters worse, conscription was still in force. Wilhelm had so far avoided doing military service by studying, but we knew that the moment he returned to South Africa, he would have to do his time (which had recently been reduced from two years to six months) or face six years in jail. Politically this posed a huge dilemma, since much military activity was in the townships, directed against the struggle – a cause we believed in.

On a personal level, I was unhappy about being left on my own with Wilmé while trying to adjust to life back in South Africa.

In the weeks before we left, Wilhelm received various calls from headhunters for British companies, but in the end we both knew we would not stay in Britain. We wanted to go back to our roots. We wanted to make a difference, however small, during the transition. Above all, we felt that we had received much from a country with a system that benefited us while discriminating against others, and that we had a duty to give something back.

In the end, we nearly did not make it back to South Africa. For some bizarre reason, between packing, breastfeeding, saying goodbye and recovering from the birth, I never thought about the fact that Wilmé might need a passport. I just assumed that the birth certificate would be sufficient for her to travel with us. Two days before our planned departure, I went for my last postnatal check-up at the John Radcliffe Hospital. In the waiting room, I chatted to a mum next to me about our imminent departure. She mentioned something about a passport for Wilmé, and it dawned on me that we might have a problem. This set off a wild panicked trip to London, and after a lot of begging at the South African embassy on Trafalgar Square, we got a travel document for Wilmé.

Back in South Africa, we settled into an apartment around the corner from my parents' home, and about ten minutes away from Wilhelm's parents. I found being back very difficult. While Wilhelm went to work every day – he quickly got a job as a lecturer in the Department of Philosophy at the University of Stellenbosch – I was at home with our little baby. Even though I was besotted with Wilmé, I was bored and claustrophobic – not only in the flat but also in South Africa. I found people's attitudes very small-minded and I missed Oxford. I wanted at least to try and finish my thesis, but between household chores and not sleeping, I did not make much progress. This caused a lot of conflict with Wilhelm. It shocked me how happy he was to accept the traditional gender divisions – reminding me that he was the breadwinner and needed to prepare for the next day's lectures in the evening, and rest during the night. I was deeply unhappy.

Fortunately, the South African parliament finally put an end to conscription just weeks before Wilhelm was due to report for duty. Although I was thankful for this, I sometimes wondered if I would have noticed if Wilhelm had not been at home. I needed something to do – a challenge. So I decided to build a house. Since Wilhelm's job was not well paid and we did not have a lot of money, we bought at an auction a plot of land in a beautiful new development called Paradyskloof. We designed a simple house with the idea of extending it later. We did not have the money to employ a builder, so I took charge of hiring labourers and ordering all the supplies. We were building during the hottest time of the year, and with six-month-old Wilmé on my hip it was hard going. Wilmé thought it was the funniest thing in the world to spit her dummy into wet cement and then wait for the shocked 'yo-yo-yo' cries of the African tradesmen, who would run to rinse it off. I had wanted a challenge, and I got one.

Despite keeping the budget extremely low (I think I built the house for the equivalent of just over R100 000), it soon became clear that we would not survive on Wilhelm's salary. Having grown up in an academic household, I knew that a lecturer's salary was not huge but that you could live comfortably on it. But Wilhelm's was very low, partly because he was at

entry level and had not finished his doctorate, and also because a more dis-
cretionary system was now in place. I felt Wilhelm should at least ask for
more money, but he would not. Our different attitudes to money would become a major source of tension throughout our marriage. I had to find a
job. In principle I wanted to work, but between looking after the baby,
planning to finish my thesis and building the house, it was difficult to see
what I could do.

Eventually I found a part-time position as an assistant in the university
library, a post I shared with another mother. I hated the job. I found it mind-
numbing dealing with grumpy students, and packing and sorting books. To
make matters worse, I was paid the minimum wage (R5.60 per hour). Day
after day, I would watch the clock and count the few cents I was making as
the time ticked by. I knew I could not do this for long, and a frustration and
determination grew in me. *I will not do this for the rest of my life*, I kept
thinking. To make matters worse, Wilhelm seemed to be moving forward,
researching, lecturing, publishing and going to conferences. In everyone's
eyes, he was the next generation of Verwoerds: hyper-intelligent and destined
for big things. I, on the other hand, was Mrs Wilhelm Verwoerd.

Luckily, there were some lighter moments. One day, after dropping
Wilmé with Wilhelm's mum, I rushed to the library. Already late for my shift,
I searched for my security tag to get through the security gate, but could
not find it. I knew it was somewhere in my messy handbag, so I started un-
packing the bag on the table next to the gate. Out came a baby bottle, a
night nappy, a few biscuits, a squashed banana, a few dry diapers for Wilmé,
two dummies, my wallet and keys – all covered in traces of baby hands and
something sticky. At some point, I heard a giggle behind me. Turning around,
I saw a group of students looking at me and the contents of my bag in
amazement. I was only 24 years old and looked very young, but this was no
regular student bag! At least the baby experience gave me some practice in
dealing with the 'demands' of the job.

A year or so later, I was on counter duty in the library. Yet again, some
stressed-out student was losing his cool because the book he needed was
already out on loan. Having dealt with the beginnings of a two-year-old's
tantrums at home, I inadvertently slipped into my 'mummy' mode. Using a
slow, well-verbalised, over-calm voice, I bent forward and said: 'Now, I can-

not help you if you shout, because I do not understand you. Take a deep breath – go on, in and out – and when you have calmed down, tell me what you want, and if I can, I will give it to you. No need for this.' I heard the suppressed laughter from the other staff next to me, as well as the giggles from the other students behind him. But it did the trick.

The one part of the job I did enjoy was the interaction with the coloured and black workers. They were in the very low-paid positions, but we quickly connected and would have long political discussions. We were careful not to be overheard, since the mostly female, all-white Afrikaner librarians were extremely conservative. Political discussions like the ones we were having would have been frowned upon.

This was a time of great upheaval and uncertainty on the political front. In the early 1990s, the multi-party negotiations started. The violence was widespread and increasing, and at this stage it was mainly black-on-black. It filled our TV screens night after night. In fact, more people died in political violence between 1990 and 1994 than in the preceding ten years. Right-wing white politicians and church leaders were instilling more and more fear, and neo-Nazi movements such as the AWB (Afrikaner Weerstandsbeweging), with the charismatic (in Hitler-like fashion) Eugène Terre'Blanche at its head, gained momentum.

Wilhelm and I were watching the situation closely. I was part of a feminist discussion group and through one of the members, Wina du Plessis, the dynamic wife of Professor Lourens du Plessis, I heard that there was an ANC branch in the 'white' part of town. I knew that I wanted to do more, become more involved, so I cautiously made contact through Wina.

To say that it was a branch is perhaps something of an exaggeration. At any stage, there were never more than eight to ten white members. I first wanted to see if I would fit in, and quickly became close to the driving forces in the branch: Annie Gagiano (a dynamic professor in the English department), Wina du Plessis (a great feminist), Zelda Dalling (who was married to an independent MP) and Rudolf Mastenbroek (head of the student organisation NUSAS). Wilhelm supported my investigations, even though he was cautious. The ANC town branch met frequently in Zelda's comfortable house, but I was not quite ready to sign up yet. This was about to change, thanks to two extraordinary Africans.

I had met Nomajoni (Emily) Makwena in 1988. Wilhelm and I looked after the three children of one of Wilhelm's colleagues while the parents went overseas for three weeks. Emily (as I knew her then) was their live-in domestic worker. We immediately hit it off and would talk for hours. She is an exceptionally bright, caring and charming woman. We kept in touch afterwards, and when Wilhelm and I were in Oxford we wrote letters. On our return to South Africa, she begged me for some part-time work. I was reluctant because of the power relations and the trap of racial stereotypes, but Emily was clear: 'That's your problem, not mine. I need a job, I know you will pay me well, and we will stay friends. Deal with it!' As always, she was right.

Emily (and her son Luthando) gradually became an inextricable part of our family. Even though she started with only one afternoon a week, she gradually worked more and more, and by the time our second baby, Wian, was born, she was with us full-time. At times, when she had personal problems, she and Luthando would live with us. She quickly became my children's other mother, and they adored her (and still do). She in turn would talk of them as her children and would scold me if she thought that my parenting was not up to scratch.

Far more importantly, Emily became my bridge to the political world and the other South Africa that I did not know. Through her stories and explanations, I started to gain an insight into the lives that millions of Africans led in South Africa. She took me into the townships and showed me around, introducing me to the women. Through her patient education, my eyes were opened to the brutal realities of life in the townships, and of being black in South Africa.

In particular, the lives of the domestic workers distressed me. When I was growing up, we were the exception to most white South African homes in that we never had a full-time domestic worker. My mum, despite being a professional woman who always worked, did almost everything herself. From time to time we had someone come in for a few hours once a week to clean, but even that made my mum uncomfortable. When she designed and built our various houses, she never included a 'maid's room', as was the practice, and begrudgingly had an outside toilet, only because it was a legal requirement. So the world of the live-in domestic worker was a shocking new discovery for me.

As I met more of Emily's friends, I could not believe the conditions in which they were living and working. They had no formal hours and had to be on call 24 hours a day. Their average salary was less than R200 per month, and if anything broke, it was deducted from their pay. They rarely had leave (and often had to go with the family on holiday, to cook, clean and mind the children) and were not allowed to have partners or husbands stay over. Their rooms had no hot water, sometimes no electricity, and just a toilet (with no basin or shower). Often there was only a mattress on the floor. The most distressing thing was that, if they became pregnant, they had to send their baby away to their family in the rural areas – they rarely saw them afterwards – while they were raising the white family's children. I was appalled. It was the early 1990s, not the 1700s!

What I found most baffling and infuriating was that I knew many employers personally. They were mostly well-off, educated, middle-class women, well known in Stellenbosch, who pretended to be defenders of human rights. These experiences caused more and more arguments between me and these women at social functions. The problem was that domestic workers, like farm workers, enjoyed little, if any, protection under the law. Something had to be done.

Emily and I decided to set up an organisation to defend the rights of domestic workers in Stellenbosch. I would negotiate a contract with the employer and monitor their conditions. Emily would be the head-hunter and trainer. Emily quickly had a list of competent women. We drew up their curricula vitae and I advertised our service. I started receiving calls from white women, but found the negotiations a sobering experience. I insisted on contracts, and that we would inspect the living conditions first. We also demanded decent wages, as recommended by the domestic workers' union. We had a few successes, but for the most part our venture did not go down well, and word quickly spread that I was involved in Communist activities with 'the blacks'. I was conscious that I was increasingly being pulled away from 'my community' and, like quicksand, sucked into the arms of another. But it was only after a meeting with one of the most exceptional men ever to live that my life took a radical new turn.

About a year after his release, Nelson Mandela was invited to a private meeting with some progressive Afrikaners in Stellenbosch. The cocktail party was to be held at Jannie Momberg's house. Jannie was a very affluent Afrikaner. A former wine farmer, he had sold his farm, Neethlingshof (where Wilhelm and I had had our wedding reception), and gone into politics. He had truly done the rounds. He originally joined the right-wing Conservative Party, then switched to the governing National Party, but as things progressed he crossed the floor to the Democratic Party. (He later joined the ANC and became one of the senior whips in the new parliament.) Wilhelm and I knew the family through their children, who were our peers, and I was pleased – although slightly apprehensive – when Oom Jannie invited us.

The meeting caused a stir in Stellenbosch. On the night, various members of the press were present. Mandela, with his amazing charm, quickly put everyone at ease, and people started to talk to him. Being academics, they tended to keep their emotions under control and engage more intellectually.

We hung back, but at some point Oom Jannie spotted us. Never a very discreet diplomat, he pushed everyone away and pulled us closer, then introduced us to Mandela. The moment Mandela heard the surname, his eyes lit up. 'Ah, I am so honoured to meet you,' he said in a sincere, warm voice. My heart was racing. I had no doubt that we were in the presence of greatness. How could he be honoured to meet us – especially with the surname? After all, it was Wilhelm's grandfather, the architect of apartheid, the symbol of oppression, who had banned the ANC, and it was during his time as prime minister that Mandela had been incarcerated.

Wilhelm started to talk politics, and then tried to apologise for his family's role in Mandela's personal suffering.

But Mandela stopped him. 'No,' he said, 'you only need to remember that with the surname you both carry, you have a voice. People will listen to you. So you have to think carefully what to do with that power.' He paused for a moment, then said: 'By the way, how is your grandmother?'

Slightly taken aback, Wilhelm explained that she was well, even at 92, and, slightly embarrassed, admitted that she had moved to Orania, a whites-only enclave in the Northern Cape.

Mandela looked at us earnestly and said: 'If she will not get angry at you, please send her my regards. Tell her from an old man that I am happy that she has reached such a great age.'

By now I was shaking. What an extraordinary man: no bitterness, no anger.

After 27 years of being unfairly imprisoned, he did not seek revenge. In fact, the opposite: he sent his sincere regards to the wife of the man who was behind his incarceration. How could we have been fed such lies all our lives? Mandela the terrorist. Mandela the dangerous, evil monster. Mandela who hated everything white. I vaguely registered that a photographer took a photo and that journalists were eavesdropping.

That night I could not sleep; over and over I heard Mandela's words: 'You have a voice. People will listen. Think carefully what you do with that power.'

The next day there was a piece on the 'Verwoerd–Mandela meeting' in the Afrikaans newspaper *Die Burger*. Before long, we were summoned to the Verwoerd house. Wilhelm's father took Wilhelm into his study, where they remained for hours. As the wife, I was not to be involved in the political discussion, which was seen as men's business. When Wilhelm finally emerged, I could see that he was tired and shaken, but also angry. His father had lectured him on his naivety, the danger of people such as Mandela, the need for separation of the races, and of course the need for loyalty to the family. Wilhelm felt patronised, but also misunderstood, and remained in an angry, introspective mood for days.

Having been excluded from the conversation, I took note of it, but did not reflect on it too much. I tried to speak to Wilhelm, but, as was his usual practice, he withdrew into his own world of reflection. I continued with my work in the library and, on my free days, with the domestic workers. But Mandela's words stayed with me.

Two days after our meeting, I drove home after yet another infuriating meeting with a potential employer. It was around 5pm, and as I drove into our neighbourhood, Paradyskloof, I watched the regular exit of black women to Kayamandi township on the outskirts of Stellenbosch. These women did not 'live in', but worked during the day in the luxury houses of the white women. At night they left to go home to their little tin shacks. Many recognised me by now and waved and gave me big smiles, shouting: 'Kunjani sisi?'

Mandela's voice rang in my ears: 'You have a voice, you have a voice.' A deep sense of sadness and tiredness came over me. 'Sikona, mama, enkosi!' I replied, waving back. But I knew that, even though they called me 'Sisi' and I respectfully called them 'Mama', it was still 'us' and 'them'. *Us* whites, *them* blacks. *Us* in the affluent neighbourhoods, the good schools, the good churches. *Them* in the shacks, the overcrowded schools, the outdoor church-es. Even my R5.60 an hour at the university library was a fortune compared to what they were earning.

'I am so tired of these divisions,' I said aloud. And then I knew I had to do something big, to step across this divide. I loved these women; they had become my friends; they were kind, caring and gentle. They were politically skilled and informed, even though very few of them had formal education. These were the people I felt at home with – in contrast to the women I worked with in the library or met at the mother-and-baby groups. The women from Kayamandi talked about Mandela, economic oppression, and their hopes for their children's future – while always singing and laughing. The white women complained about their maids, the horrible possibility that the blacks would take over, and how we all had to emigrate, for our children's sake.

I wanted to cross this us-and-them divide, and the only way I knew how to do that was to join the ANC, the only truly non-racial party in South Africa at that stage. I had for years read their policies and met with their members and leadership. I knew I would feel at home there. I also knew that joining the ANC would probably cause more trouble with Wilhelm's family, but being 'the wife', they probably would not notice – and we cer-tainly would not be drawing it to their attention.

Back home, I discussed my plan with Wilhelm, who was fine about it. He would not join yet, because of his fear about his family's reaction, but he agreed – not that anything would have stopped me. So later that evening, I drove over to Zelda's house, filled in the yellow membership form and paid my R10 fee. With these few simple actions, I became a member of the ANC. I asked them not to say anything about it, not that they intended to. After all, I was not a true Verwoerd, so no one would be interested – or so I thought.

For the next six months, I regularly went to ANC meetings at Zelda's house, where we were briefed on political developments. I was still working at the library but, increasingly, I was leading a double life, with ANC meet-ings and domestic-workers business at night and serving white Afrikaner students by day. Passing some of the black or coloured workers in the library or on campus, they would now quietly say 'Hello comrade', but nobody said anything openly. I was also pregnant with our second baby and dealing with morning sickness and tiredness; but thankfully, this time all was going well.

On 17 March 1992, President FW de Klerk called for what was to be the last white referendum. The question (asked of the white voters) was whether he had a mandate to continue negotiating with the ANC. I was working that day and the atmosphere was tense, with more than the usual irritable and racist comments about where the country was going. The 'comrades' kept passing me little notes on the way to the bathroom with information they had received from various places around the country. After work, I went down to the town hall to vote. I met Wilhelm and Wilmé there. Wilmé had on a little sun hat that some campaign worker had given her, with the word 'Ja' on it. A photographer took a shot, and she was in the local paper the next day. As I left after casting my vote, I bumped into Annie Gagiano. She was on her way to the annual general meeting of the ANC in Kayamandi and insisted that I come with her. I agreed.

In the township, it was of course business as usual, since the referendum was only for the whites. I was met by the now-familiar smell of fires and the sight of raw, fly-covered meat being sold at the side of the road. Radios were blaring everywhere, and people shouted greetings and news to one another – sometimes from several blocks away. There was a buzz and liveliness, and a sense of community in the townships that is hard to describe.

We parked the car on the road and wove our way through the rows of shacks. It was dark, so we had to step carefully to avoid the raw sewage running between the shacks. We finally came to a spot where a few shacks were put together, with a sign proclaiming 'Community Hall' above the door. Inside, it was spotlessly clean. There were rows of benches and the place was packed. Annie, Rudolf Mastenbroek and I were the only white people there.

As always, the meeting was opened with prayers (so much for the ANC being anti-religious, as we were always told by the government) and the singing of 'Nkosi Sikelele'. I had heard it sung many times before and knew most of the words, but I had never stood among a hundred or more African people, all singing it with deep emotion. I had goosebumps and felt tears in my eyes. After the chants of 'Viva ANC!', 'Long live Nelson Mandela!'

and 'Amandla!', we settled in for various speeches and reports. We all sat tightly squeezed on the backless benches with rain pelting on the corrugated-tin roof. Every fifteen minutes or so, the light coming from a single bulb hanging from the roof would go out. Exasperated exclamations would follow, and a child would be sent out to fix the problem.

Kayamandi was linked to the electricity grid, but only a handful of older houses, the municipal building and the police station had electricity. Frustrated, people would hack into the mains supply; the area above the shacks looked like a spider's web of wires, all connected in an amateurish fashion. This was of course extremely dangerous, and people were regularly electrocuted. The community hall's light was hooked up to five extension cords that were running outside on the wet ground to a comrade's shack, which was in turn illegally hooked to the mains supply. But every time the owners wanted a cup of tea, the supply to the community hall was disrupted.

The child would report back that the comrade said that he, or someone else, needed a cup of tea and would be done in five minutes. Everyone would murmur understandingly, and then wait quietly in the pitch dark until there was light again. Then the meeting would continue as if nothing had happened.

This was a completely different world for me. I thought how all the people I knew, including my family, would react if they knew I was sitting shoulder to shoulder in the pitch dark in a big shack in Kayamandi. They would be sure that I would be killed. But I felt completely safe – and indeed thrilled by it all. In fact, it struck me that no one took much notice of me or Annie or Rudolf. That was the essence of the ANC: it was truly non-racial. If you joined, you were a comrade, and that was all that counted. Of course, you had to be loyal, but I had expected that, as a white with the surname 'Verwoerd', I would have to deal with many questions and suspicions. But there never were any.

Towards the end of the long evening, the elections for the new executive were held. Annie was nominated, but declined because of work pressure. She then nominated me. Before I could protest, the nomination was seconded, hands flew into the air in support, and I was elected. Rudolf, who was secretary, and would become a very close friend, came over and said: 'Welcome. This is going to be interesting.'

As we drove back through the quiet, wet, oak-lined streets of Stellenbosch, I thought about the contrasts of the day. The results of the white referendum suddenly seemed so irrelevant in the light of the evening I had just experienced. I was now a member of the Stellenbosch ANC executive!

After my election onto the executive, my life became very full. Briefings, organising marches, consulting with our members and signing up new members took much of our time. There were also frequent meetings in the ANC's little office close to Du Toit Station. The chairperson was Patrick Xegwana, a messenger at the university. He was a strong but quiet leader with a big heart. He lived with his wife and children in a tiny shack in Kayamandi. I had enormous respect for him and was distraught when he drowned a few years later while trying to save his child's life. Other members were Mpumi Hani (a relative of the Chief of Staff of MK, Chris Hani), Malcolm Ncofe (a teacher), Oom Tom Ncungwa (a trader who sold meat in an open stall on the street in Kayamandi) and Franklin Adams (a fiery coloured guy, who had many small-business ventures). We were later joined by the deeply religious, but equally fiery Faghrie Patel. And of course Rudolf Mastenbroek and I were there too.

Meetings usually started 30 to 45 minutes late ('African time' being the excuse), but were extremely structured and organised. There were a few rules: 1. You always spoke through the chair and were not allowed to make personal attacks; 2. Smoking was allowed, but only one person at a time; 3. Everyone got a chance to speak for as long as he or she wanted. But then the meeting decided on the issue at hand – preferably by consensus. And once the meeting had decided, that decision had to be respected. This was equally true of the small meetings of the executive and of the big community meetings. Even though this approach meant that meetings could go on for hours, it taught me valuable lessons about leadership, decision-making and the power of the collective.

We frequently held executive, subcommittee and big community meetings where not only political issues, but also some of the everyday challenges of our members were discussed. I was then sent to do battle on behalf of residents of Kayamandi with the local council, to sort out various concerns such as the lack of water, sanitation and housing. The executive felt that my surname and command of Afrikaans might just help, although I sometimes felt that their anger at this white 'traitor' made the white officials even less cooperative.

All this work meant that I was becoming a familiar face around Kayamandi, as was Wilmé. She would often stay with Emily in her house in Kayamandi, playing with Luthando while I was working. This was a source of great interest to the people of Kayamandi. Very few whites ever went to the townships at that stage, and to leave your young child with someone there was simply never done. But I knew that she was safe and that she loved the endless attention from the curious and doting African women. Later, Wian would stay there too: as soon as he could walk, he could not wait to run around the shacks with all the boys and play soccer in the street. Often, when I drove back into the township to pick them up, I would stop the first person I saw and ask them if they knew where my children were. The person would shout to someone a few blocks away, who would shout to others, and within a few seconds we would know where the *mlungu* children were. Far more efficient than cell phones!

When Emily was busy, Wilmé would come with me to meetings. This usually went well, since most of the women would have their little ones there too. One night, however, things became a bit crowded. We had a small subcommittee meeting, but the person with the key to the office never arrived. The wind was howling so we could not hold the meeting outdoors. Our only option was to have it in Rudolf's car, so six of us (and Wilmé) squeezed into his car. The meeting went fine, but Wilmé, who was two years old, was getting restless. She spotted Rudolf chewing bubblegum and 'whispered' loudly that she wanted some too. I did not have any, so I interrupted the 'meeting' to ask Rudolf if he had any more. He did not. I explained to Wilmé that there was none, but she insisted: 'Ludolf [as she called him] has some!' She was getting upset, and no amount of explaining would help. Eventually Franklin said: 'For God's sake, Rudolf, spit out the gum and give it to the child.' Rudolf looked at me, I nodded, and Wilmé sat quietly for the rest of the meeting chewing away on 'Ludolf's' recycled gum.

Wilmé's political exposure meant that she quickly imitated some of aspects of the meetings. She knew how to throw her little fist into the air and shout 'Amandla' or 'Viva Mandela'. This she did with gusto, not only at meetings, but every time she saw Mandela or ANC images on TV. She quickly mastered the toyi-toyi, and during the rolling mass action that Mandela called following the breakdown of negotiations, she often came with me on protest marches. She had a standard 'survival kit' that always came too. It consisted of at least three dummies (one in her mouth and one for each hand), a teddy bear, and of course her sippy cup with juice. But as soon as the toyi-toying started, she would hand me the dummies, teddy and juice and jump like a pro. One African man once said to me: 'That piccanin is almost black!' There were never more than a handful of whites in our marches, so between the dummies and teddy, and my daughter jumping around like a mad thing, we were a sight to behold. To top things off, by this stage I was heavily pregnant with Wian.

Wilmé's political fervour nearly exposed our involvement in the ANC to Wilhelm's parents. By now I was truly living a double life. During the day, I was working at the university, but at night and weekends I was Comrade Melanie, and I would spend all my time working for the ANC. Up to this point, no one in the white community, apart from a few ANC members, knew about my involvement in the organisation, and we went to great lengths to hide it from Wilhelm's parents.

One evening I took Wilmé for a visit to my mother-in-law. I was preparing some supper for Wilmé while she was playing on the carpet, close to her grandparents, who were watching the news. From the kitchen, I suddenly heard the reporter giving an account of an ANC protest march that had taken place that day, and images of toyi-toying young people flashed across the screen. Through the door, I saw Wilmé's head turning sharply towards the TV. I knew what was coming. I saw her get up and her little fists forming, ready for a big 'Viva the ANC!' Even though I was heavily pregnant, I flew into the room and grabbed Wilmé just as she was taking a deep breath. She was so amazed by my swinging her into the air unexpectedly that, thankfully, she lost interest in the TV, and my in-laws were none the wiser.

Although this was a close call, I was silently hoping that they would never find out. I knew they would not approve, but I never anticipated what was about to happen. About a month before Wian was born, the political journal *Die Suid-Afrikaan*, edited by Chris Louw, had a short paragraph on its back page under the heading 'A rose by any other name'. The author said that he had heard a rumour that there was a Verwoerd on the Stellenbosch

ANC executive. 'Could it be true?' he wondered. 'And is this an effort to clear the Verwoerd name?' *It would take a lot more than my involvement to do that*, I thought. Even though I was concerned about the reference, I knew that Wilhelm's parents would never read this magazine.

A few days later, the *Sunday Times* phoned. This would be my baptism of fire with the media, and set in motion a series of events that would change my life. The journalist said he had confirmation of my membership and gave me an ultimatum: either I give him the interview and we work together, or he would write the story without me. He gave me an undertaking that he would not approach Wilhelm's parents if I gave him a brief interview. Today I would never believe such an undertaking, but I was young (I had just turned 25), and desperate to avoid conflict with Wilhelm's parents, so I agreed.

We met in a coffee shop in Stellenbosch. The interview went well, but as we left, the journalist said: 'You know, as part of my journalistic integrity, I have to ask Wilhelm's parents for a comment.' I was furious. I told him he had broken his word, but he did not care. He eventually agreed to give us a few hours to tell the Verwoerds first. Although the interview was about my involvement in the ANC, he then phoned Wilhelm to check if he was a member too. Wilhelm had quietly joined a few months earlier. At first he would not comment, but the journalist insisted that he would then write that Wilhelm was not a member, which was not true. The cat was out of the bag. Wilhelm went over to his parents to talk to them, but somehow they did not fully understand (or he did not make it clear) that he was also a member. So thinking that it was just me, they expressed their disapproval, but Wilhelm was relieved that it all turned out reasonably well.

The article appeared two days later. His parents would not take the journalist's call, but of course bought the paper, which they otherwise never did. We had gone for the day to my parents, who by now were living in Gordon's Bay. My parents did not agree with our decision to join the ANC, but felt that it was our choice to make. They had raised me and my sisters to be free-thinkers and to raise questions, and they knew I would not easily back down once I had carefully analysed an issue and decided on a position. Ultimately, they believed that family and personal relations were more important than any ideological position – a belief I share.

Early that afternoon we got a call, and just like a year earlier we were summoned to the Verwoerd house. We were told not to bring Wilmé. The reception was icy. This time I was included in the conversation, as was Wilhelm's mother. Wilhelm's father was furious. He raged for what seemed like hours. Although he largely ignored me, it was clear that he felt I had misled Wilhelm. He called us traitors to the Afrikaner nation and a shame on the family name. Wilhelm tried to reason with him, but he would not listen. Wilhelm's father was the patriarch – not only of his own family, but also, as the eldest son, he was the guardian of the Verwoerd legacy. We were now a threat to that legacy, he insisted, and had no right to be in the fold any more. He told Wilhelm that, since he no longer regarded him as his son, we had no right to the surname any more. We would no longer be welcome in 'his' house, and were disinherited. Wilhelm's mother, who was in tears, asked him what this meant in terms of the grandchildren. He was clearly a bit troubled by this and said that they were welcome as long as we were not with them.

Of course, this was a deeply distressing conversation, and over the next few days we tried repeatedly to talk to him, but nothing would help. Over the next ten years, Wilhelm's father would shun us. We would quietly visit his mother when he was not home, or I would drop off the children, waiting in a nearby restaurant for the call to come for me to pick them up.

To add to the stress, the media, both in South Africa and around the world, had got hold of the story, and would not leave us alone. The phone was ringing non-stop. The ANC asked us to do as much media as we could, because it was great publicity for them. I do not think I quite understood the shock waves this episode sent through the anti-apartheid movement. It was only years later, when I overheard a fellow MP, Salie Manie, telling a US governor about me, that I got some sense of what our joining the ANC meant. Salie explained how the news spread and how so many of the ANC activists felt that if a grandson of Verwoerd could join, it was the ultimate validation of everything the ANC stood for.

So we did literally hundreds of interviews. This was exhausting and stressful – not helped by the fact that I was almost nine months pregnant, and still working and trying (unsuccessfully) to finish my Masters thesis before the baby arrived. With all the media coverage, which focused more on Wilhelm than on me, Wilhelm's father decided to denounce us publicly. He did so in a letter to the big Afrikaans newspaper *Die Burger*, which was quickly picked up by some of the other Afrikaans publications.

Almost immediately, letters threatening to kill us were sent to our house. These were distressing but I could deal with them. What really disgusted me was that people would call our home phone and when Wilmé picked up, tell her that they were going to kill us. She was only two and a half and became distraught. After this happened a few times, I made sure that she could not get to the phone and eventually I changed our number. This helped for a while, but the new number got out and the threats started again.

I was now also not welcome in Stellenbosch any more. None of our friends would talk to us, and I was asked not to attend the mother-and-toddler groups. In town, people would hiss 'traitor' when they saw me, and I was frequently spat on. We got a call from a professor at the university to warn us that he had reliable information that we were on the hit-list of a far-right organisation. He told us that we were third on a list that included Chris Hani.

In the next year, we received information that the two above us on the list had been assassinated. The ANC offered us protection, but I knew that if anyone really wanted to kill us, nothing would stop them. I did not want the incredible invasion of privacy that protection would entail, with armed men in and around my house. Intelligence sources felt that the children were not at risk, so we decided against any security. We kept to this decision although I would later, during the election campaign, agree to security at public events, when the ANC felt there was a specific threat.

In the midst of this chaos, I gave birth to my beautiful son, Wian Brandt. At 36 weeks, he must have got a bit claustrophobic, according to the doctors, and miraculously flipped around into a breach position. The doctors decided to do an early Caesarean section, but for the week before his birth I would be suddenly breathless when he headbutted me. Despite his early, backwards entry into the world, he still tipped the scale at just under nine pounds. All went smoothly, apart from Wilmé, who got a peanut stuck up her nose the night I went into hospital. I again had an epidural. Wilhelm recorded Wian's entry into the world on video camera with the help of an enthusiastic anaesthetist, who completely forgot about me while directing Wilhelm.

As was the practice with babies born by Caesarean section, Wian had to be 'warmed up' for a few hours in an incubator. The nurses reluctantly agreed that I could keep Wian in an incubator next to my bed in my room, as I had arranged with the paediatrician beforehand since I wanted to have as much contact with him as possible. Wian was restless and crying in the incubator. I eventually took him out and, knowing that he had to stay warm, I fed him and then covered him up completely under the duvet, before we both fell asleep. I woke up with panicked nurses, doctors and security men next to my bed. Someone had spotted the empty incubator, assumed that Wian had been stolen and set off a mad panic. When I lifted the duvet to reveal him peacefully sleeping, there was a sigh of relief. The nurses were not impressed with me, though.

Wilmé visited later that morning, and brought Wian a panda bear. For months she had been excited about Wian's arrival and had spoken to him through my tummy. Every night, she repeated the same words in a little sing-song tone: 'Hello, Wian. I'm Wilmé. I love you.' When Wilmé arrived at the hospital, Wian was fast asleep, as only a newborn can be. I propped Wilmé up on the pillows and carefully placed the sleeping baby in her arms. She looked at Wian intently and then said, in the same sing-song tone: 'Hello, Wian. I'm Wilmé. I love you.' A split-second later, Wian's eyes flew open and he stared at Wilmé, wide awake and alert. She was thrilled and I was in tears. They were – and remain – very close. From the start, Wilmé wanted to take on the parental role. Just before she left the hospital at the end of her first visit, I changed Wian's nappy. She watched closely, and when Wian started squirming a bit, she gently pushed me aside. 'Excuse me, Mummy. I'll do that,' she said.

Wian was a more restless baby than Wilmé. He had colic and I had many sleepless nights. Of course, my political activities got the blame. Thank God for Emily, who would arrive in the morning and put Wian in a blanket on her back. Wian loved this and would quickly fall asleep. As he grew older, Emily would swing him onto her back, then throw the blanket over him and tie it tight in the front. And, Pavlov-like, he was often asleep before she'd tied the blanket.

In the meantime, I went back to work, and continued to attend ANC meetings. One comrade said afterwards: 'You were at one meeting with a tummy and at the next meeting without a tummy. So we assumed the baby came in between?'

As with Wilmé, I was determined to breastfeed Wian exclusively until he was six months old. Since there were no cell phones yet, I got a pager, and Emily would page me when Wian needed to be fed. I hated expressing milk and fed him on demand, so I was dashing between work, breastfeeding and ANC meetings. It was exhausting.

5

In May 1993, Allan Boesak, the head of the ANC in the Western Cape, asked Wilhelm to speak at an ANC rally to be held in the Parow Civic Hall. We discussed it for a few days before Wilhelm agreed.

His participation in the rally was announced at a well-attended press conference. Immediately, the death threats increased. A few of the threats suggested that we would not make it home alive after the meeting. We were warned by intelligence sources that things were 'extremely hot'. I was worried, and asked friends around the world to keep us in their thoughts.

The afternoon before the meeting, Wilhelm was outside in the garden with Wilmé in his arms. The sun was shining brightly on both of them – both father and daughter had very blond hair – creating a halo effect. Wilhelm was whispering in Wilmé's ear, and she was quietly listening with a serious expression on her face. It dawned on me that Wilhelm was saying goodbye, in case something went wrong that evening. It shocked me, but I knew we had to go to the meeting. Once you give in to the threats of bullies, you will never stand up for what is right. There will always be those who hate others who are different and do not share their views. But if we allowed hatred to paralyse us with fear, there would be no Mandela, Tutu or Gandhi, and no struggles for freedom.

On instructions from the organisers, we left the house early. As we got closer to the venue, we noticed that the police and military presence increased dramatically. Around the venue it looked like a battlefield, with armoured vehicles, ANC marshals and mobile medical units. No one could get into the meeting without going through metal detectors and being searched. People were already filling up the hall two hours before the meeting was due to start.

Allan Boesak was chairing the meeting and he was joined by ANC spokesperson Carl Niehaus, an Afrikaner who had spent seven years in jail for his membership in the ANC. I sat in the second row on the stage, behind Wilhelm. Allan is a fine orator and could get a crowd going in minutes. He introduced the people on stage and there were many 'Viva's'. When he introduced Wilhelm, the audience exploded. 'Viva Verwoerd, viva!' they chanted. 'Long live Verwoerd, long live!'

Hearing those words said together was like a bolt of electricity through all of us. I became aware of Wilhelm shaking in front of me. I bent forward to ask if he was okay and realised he was overwhelmed with emotion. I was concerned that he would be unable to make the speech, but he did. At the end of his carefully crafted words, the audience exploded again. Suddenly someone shouted: 'Verwoerd for president!' There were a few seconds of shocked silence, before laughter – and a huge cheer – erupted.

In contrast to the happy scenes inside, things were tense outside. The AWB had arrived, fully armed and in uniform. There was a huge crowd of ANC supporters who could not find space inside the hall; they were furious and impatient. To make matters worse, word spread to the townships that the AWB was trying to break up an ANC meeting. People piled into minibus taxis armed with sticks, petrol bombs and whatever else they could find, and rushed to the venue. The police, peace secretariat and army found it difficult to contain the situation.

At some point, the AWB broke through the police cordon, and from inside the hall I could see them beating against the glass doors to get access before the police regained control.

In the end, we made it home safely. We only heard weeks later that the peace secretariat had had to position people on the roofs of the buildings in the area to calm down AWB snipers.

After the Parow meeting, Wilhelm was frequently asked to speak at ANC rallies. I was happy working at grass-roots level. A few months later, Allan Boesak's wife Elna asked if we would participate in a video they were producing. We agreed and went to their Bishopscourt home to be interviewed for the video. Most of the questions were directed at Wilhelm, but then Elna asked me a question. Allan had just entered the room and was quietly watching the interview. I could see that Elna was impressed with my answer. She asked another question, and Allan walked forward to hear my answer better. I saw him and Elna exchange glances. Afterwards, they both said how impressed they were, but I did not think much of it.

A few months later, while I was at work at the university, I got a call from someone in the ANC provincial office. She explained that Mandela was going to have an election tour in Cape Town and that they were putting together a list of speakers for the closing rally of his visit. Conscious of the disapproving looks of my co-workers, and assuming that they were actually looking for Wilhelm, I impatiently told her to phone Wilhelm directly.

'No, no!' she said. 'Comrade Boesak wants you. He thinks you will be fantastic.' I was dumbstruck. I had never done any public speaking. What would I say? Would I cope with the big crowd that was bound to be there, given that Mandela would be present? But how do you say no to Mandela? You can't. So I agreed.

On the day of the meeting, I had to fly to Johannesburg to participate in a TV recording on feminism, and then back to Cape Town. I went straight from the airport to the rally. I had written the speech over a few days and thought it was fine. What I had not anticipated was the size of the audience. The meeting was indoors in the Civic Hall Concourse in Cape Town. It was estimated that there were more than 4000 people present: the place was packed to the rafters. Of course, the press was also there in full force. When I was introduced, loud cheers went up. Wilhelm (who was this time sitting behind *me*) was also introduced, and Mandela turned around to shake his hand. When it was time for me to speak the huge crowd became quiet; you could hear a pin drop.

'Comrades,' I started. The crowd erupted. 'Viva Melanie, viva!' I waited for the noise to die down, then began again. I told a few funny stories to lighten the mood, and they went down well – especially this (true) story about Wilmé. A few weeks earlier, I was keeping a watchful eye over Wilmé and a few of the Afrikaans children from the neighbourhood playing outside our house. I heard three-year-old Wilmé announce loudly: 'I am Mandela!' There was a stunned silence from the other little Afrikaans children. Expecting some negative reaction, I stood ready to intervene. But then the little boy from next door, whose parents were very conservative, announced defiantly: 'No! I am Mandela.' A huge argument developed, with all four children demanding to be Mandela. Eventually, it was agreed that all four could be Mandela, and then the four little Mandelas marched around on the grass, singing the traditional Afrikaans song 'Aanstap rooies, die pad is lank en swaar.' Out of the corner of my eye, I could see Mandela shaking with laughter.

At the end of the speech, I was astonished when the crowd jumped to their feet and gave me a long and boisterous ovation. As I turned to go back to my seat, Mandela was standing behind me. He gave me a big hug. Enfolded by his arms, all I could think of was how tall he was. 'Baie, baie dankie,' he said in Afrikaans. 'You are very loved and will make a big difference.'

As I left the stage at the end of the meeting, various ANC branch chairs from across the Western Cape came to ask if I would speak at their branch meetings. Still bewildered by all the attention, I agreed. Allan Boesak came too. 'There's something special in you,' he said. 'Please think about making yourself available for the regional executive.'

Despite the positive feedback, I was still unsure about my speech. I often felt intellectually inferior to Wilhelm, and, as we drove home, I asked him if it was okay. He said it was, but I could see that something was bothering him. He would not say what, but I assumed he felt that my speech had not been intellectual enough.

Over the next few months, I spoke at meetings almost every night of the week. At first it was only in the Western Cape, but gradually I got invitations from branches all over South Africa. It was an exhausting schedule. I mostly drove in our battered Volkswagen Golf, which frequently broke down, often late at night and on isolated roads. Despite my exhaustion and the occasional danger, I loved it. Passing through towns that I had visited numerous times before, I would end up in the 'other' part, the 'non-white' area. I felt as if I was reclaiming my own country and its people.

Towards the end of 1993, the ANC Western Cape had its annual provincial conference at the University of the Western Cape. I attended as part of the Stellenbosch branch delegation. There were hundreds of delegates, and nominations took place for the provincial executive, after which there was a secret ballot. As I stood in line to vote, it struck me that this was the only place where 99 per cent of the people present were able to vote. It was a sobering thought.

On the Sunday, at the final session, the newly elected officials were announced. My name was among them. Now, apart from raising two children under three years of age, working part-time at the university, doing ANC branch work, still trying to complete my thesis, and talking at branches all over the country, I would also have to attend frequent meetings in Cape Town. I thought it was impossible to be busier than I had been up to that point. But I was soon proven wrong.

During this time, I was asked whether I would be available to stand for parliament in the upcoming first democratic elections in 1994. Wilhelm was also asked, but he declined. He felt that we could not both do it and he preferred a more reflective life whereas I was the natural activist.

At the lengthy Kempton Park multiparty negotiations, where the Bill of Rights and interim constitution were negotiated, it was agreed that South Africa would have a proportional list system. This meant that all the parties taking part in the election had to draw up two lists of candidates for the national parliament of 400 MPs: one national list and nine provincial lists. Then 200 MPs would be elected from the national lists, based on votes the party received nationally, and a further 200 from the provincial lists based on the votes the individual parties received in each of the nine provinces. This was a far more representative system than the traditional first-past-the-post constituency system – in particular for the parties that represented minority groups. Every vote counted. It was up to the parties to decide how they compiled the various lists.

The ANC had an extensive process that was deeply democratic. The branches made nominations to their provincial executive. In order to get onto the internal ballot, you had to be nominated by at least seven branches. The branches would then all send delegates to a provincial electoral conference and vote. The candidates with the highest number of votes for the national list would then go through to a national electoral conference. There, all the provincial nominees would be put on the ballot, and delegates from all over the country would vote on them. The names would be ranked according to the votes received, and a list of 200 candidates would be compiled out of the thousands of names. It may have been democratic, but it was stressful for the candidates.

There were only two exceptions to the democratic nature of the process. Should Mandela not top the list after the vote, he would be put there, since he was the presidential candidate. Needless to say, there was no need for concern about that. The second issue related to the representation of women. For years, the ANC Women's League had insisted that there should be a quota for women in parliament. The ANC executive had agreed to a quota of one-third. So when the election results were known, they carefully checked to ensure that there were enough women high up on the list. As it turned out, they did not have to change any position on the first hundred names and only a few in the second hundred names. Clearly, the years of insisting on equitable representation for women had resulted in comrades naturally voting for women.

I was not at the first national list conference, but when the names were announced, I was astonished. I was number 84, which meant that I was almost guaranteed a seat in parliament. (The ANC was expected to win close to 60 per cent of the vote, which would have meant that the first 120 names would get seats.) I was delighted, but now life became even more hectic, with electioneering and increased media pressure.

I still found it strange to see my name and face on election posters, some of which were quite clever. Since both Ella Gandhi – a granddaughter of Mahatma Gandhi – and I were on the list, the ANC designed a poster that read: 'Only the ANC has Gandhi and Verwoerd in one party.'

6

The next few months were filled with the peculiar madness typical of any election campaign. But there was something special about this election. For the first time, millions of South Africans would be able to vote. After years of fighting for this most basic right – years in which thousands of people died and thousands more were unjustly incarcerated and tortured – freedom was finally on the horizon. There was such energy and a sense of anticipation, as well as fear that everything might still fall apart. Of course, all of this was happening under the watchful eye of the world's media, which had flocked to South Africa to report on the campaign and on election day.

One of the many logistical challenges was how people were to be identified as legitimate voters. It would be impossible to compile a legitimate voters' role in time for the election so it was agreed that everyone who wanted to vote should have a bar-coded identity document or a bar-coded voter's card. Although almost all white South Africans had the little green ID book, only a small percentage of black South Africans had one, so it became a mammoth task to ensure that as many as possible received them in time.

It was challenging for the Department of Home Affairs to deal with the millions of applications, and there were many other stumbling blocks. The majority of Africans, especially those who were over 40, did not have a birth certificate. Many of them had been born in the rural areas with the help of traditional midwives, and the births were never registered. In addition, even though the application process was free for the election period, many could not afford the two passport-size photographs required. To top everything off, there were literacy problems, the forms were complicated, and, given the history of oppression, people were deeply suspicious of filling in any form issued by the government.

Determined to make sure that our ANC voters would be able to vote, we arranged free photographers on certain days, helped people fill in forms, and tracked down baptism certificates and affidavits from teachers and priests. Job well done, we thought.

A few weeks later, however, I got a call from the post office in Stellenbosch. They complained that, in their depot, there were thousands of ID books with incomplete addresses that could not be delivered. Almost all the people of Kayamandi lived in informal squatter areas that did not have any street addresses. The residents would informally name sections, but there was no way the postman would know where to go. Even if he did, he might refuse to go into certain areas.

I agreed to take responsibility for delivering these ID books. For the next few weeks, I spent hours every night walking between shacks asking for people and handing over their ID books. It was time-consuming, but the joy that was evident when people finally received their ID document made it all worthwhile. Now, at last, they existed in the eyes of the state.

The rest of the time was spent canvassing. I divided my time between the Stellenbosch ANC branch, the provincial executive work, and canvassing across the country. There were not many Afrikaans-speaking candidates, so I was in high demand in the coloured areas. By now, I could deliver the speeches about reconciliation and why people should vote for the ANC in my sleep. As the election drew closer, I would make up to eight speeches some days. I spoke so often that I lost my voice and was told I had damaged my vocal cords. But I loved it, and along with all the hard work we had a lot of fun as well.

On one occasion, the ANC asked if I would spend some time in the Northern Cape, where the majority of the potential voters were Afrikaans-speaking. I flew to Kimberley and for a few days a group of comrades and I crisscrossed this vast, semi-arid area, speaking in hundreds of places. The poverty was on a scale I had not seen before, and truly shocked me.

One Sunday, a meeting was scheduled at a place called Grootdrink. It was lunchtime, and the temperature was over 40°C when we stopped under a tree. I looked around, but could not see anything.

'Are you sure this is it?' I asked the organiser.

'Yes, just wait,' he said, sliding down against the tree, tipping his hat over his eyes, ready to take a nap.

I was dubious. The heat and sun were unbearable, the sun beetles were screaming, flies were trying to get to the liquid in our eyes, and I spotted a snake sliding past a few feet away. Who would come to a meeting here, and at Sunday lunchtime?

But then I saw it. On the horizon, against the heat haze, various coloured umbrellas were moving towards us from all directions. The farmworkers from the area were on their way. Many had walked for hours to get there. It was one of the most moving and rewarding meetings I have ever spoken at. Watching their leathery, tanned faces, I knew that I had far more to learn from them than they from me, so in the end we just talked about where they felt the country should go, and their hopes for the future. This was true democracy in action. I promised myself I would forever remember and serve the people of Grootdrink once I was in office.

In one of the towns, we stopped at the home of the local ANC organiser. He was a deeply religious coloured man and we said prayers before his wife served us tea and cake. After discussing local ANC matters, he announced that he had a gift for me. He presented me with an almost life-size bust of Hendrik Verwoerd. The ANC leader told me how he had been so shocked and upset the day Verwoerd was killed that he had gone into the mountains to get clay to make this bust in honour of Verwoerd. The likeness was very good and, appropriately, it was made from white clay. I could see the amused but uncomfortable smiles from my other ANC colleagues. I complimented my host on his handiwork, and he insisted that he wanted me to have it and pass it on to my children. It would have been rude to say no.

Since it was too big to fit in the boot of the car, we left with the bust sitting between me and my ANC colleague on the back seat. There was a tense silence in the car, and I saw my colleague repeatedly glancing over at the bust. Eventually, he could not take it any more.

'I'm sorry, comrade,' he said, 'but this is freaking me out. I don't want to be disrespectful, but I can't relax with Oupa Hendrik sitting here!'

I had a thin scarf with me to protect me from the sun. 'Will it help if I cover him up?' I asked.

Everyone in the car agreed that this would help, and there was a sigh of relief. Then someone said: 'F**k! This would only happen in the ANC!' and everyone burst out laughing.

Wilhelm was also canvassing, which meant that we rarely saw one another, and when we did we were exhausted. One night we stumbled into each other when we both got up to attend to the children, who had woken up. Wilhelm sleepily stretched out his hand and introduced himself . . .

To spend some time with the children, we often took them with us, when we knew the meetings would not be dangerous.

As well as these smaller community meetings, there were many huge rallies. My initial shock at the crowd of 4000 at the Cape Town Civic quickly passed as I spoke at rallies in stadiums filled with thousands more. On the last MK Day (the day celebrating the ANC military wing) before the election, we organised a rally in Stellenbosch. It was to be held on the sports ground in Cloetesville, in the coloured area across the road from Kayamandi. We built a podium for the speakers, installed a powerful sound system, organised refreshment tents and laid on transport. To our annoyance, from early morning, the police were monitoring our movements with a helicopter flying low over the venue, kicking up dust.

An hour before people were due to arrive, there was a sudden panic. We had forgotten to organise a flagpole and the raising of the ANC flag was a vital part of the day. What to do? 'Leave it to me,' Franklin Adams said, waving over a few of the ANC marshals in full uniform. They drove off in Franklin's old bakkie. About 30 minutes later, we saw the marshals marching over towards us in military style, with the flagpole above their heads.

'Where . . .?' I started to ask.

'Better if you don't know,' Franklin said with a smile.

I learned later that they had 'borrowed' the flagpole from the much-hated municipality in Kayamandi. (The flagpole was later returned.) The pole was mounted on the wall, so the marshals had climbed onto the roof and then lowered one of their number down by the legs. The flagpole was unscrewed and then proudly marched over to the field. The municipal building was right next to the police station in Kayamandi, but all the police stationed there were ANC members, so they were at the rally.

The rally was a great success. Among others, Winnie Mandela attended, in full camouflage. She spoke charismatically, as only she could. She was and remains enormously popular – beyond being the wife, or former wife, of Nelson Mandela. Ordinary people around South Africa have endless stories of acts of kindness done by her, and how brave she was. She endured enormous suffering while Mandela was in jail. She and her children were constantly harassed and then put under house arrest in the tiny town of Brandfort in the Free State. Clearly, she was deeply damaged by all of this, and increasingly things went wrong. The well-documented death of Stompie Moeketsi and the corruption convictions, as well as her appearance at the Truth and Reconciliation Commission, were shocking. I had met Winnie Mandela before and later when we were in parliament. Her seat was close to mine, so we spoke often. She is one of the most charismatic people I have ever met. Even at an advanced age, she is stunningly beautiful, and she listens intently to everything you say, with a piercing look. Of course, much of her life remains hugely controversial, but I believe it is too easy to demonise her, as often happens.

7

For the first time in the history of our country, on 27 April 1994, all South Africans, whatever their language, religion, culture, whatever their colour or class, will vote as equal citizens. Millions who were not allowed to vote will do so. I, too, for the first time in my short life, will vote.
Nelson Mandela

26 April 1994. The ringing of my cell phone woke me. I groaned; it was 4.50am, just two hours since I had gone to bed after watching, on television in the election office, the old South African flag being lowered and the new one being raised. I was exhausted after three days of no sleep, but today was the big day. Finally, election day had arrived. 'Please Lord, let it all go well,' I prayed silently as I answered the phone.

'Comrade Melanie!' shouted one of my fellow executive members. 'Wake up and get down to Kayamandi. You have to see what's going on!'

Before I could ask if everything was all right, he hung up. I dressed quickly and sped through the sleepy streets of Stellenbosch. As I crossed the railway bridge leading to the entrance of Kayamandi, I spotted lines and lines of people, barely visible under the few streetlights. Had there been an accident? But something else was going on. The lines stretched for miles. People stood quietly in the darkness and rain, waiting. Old people were sitting on oil drums, and those who could not walk were wheeled over in wheelbarrows. Babies were tied to women's backs, with plastic shopping bags made into little hats to keep their heads dry. Even sleepy teenagers were there to see what was going on. They were all there, in line, waiting to vote.

Overwhelmed with emotion, I got out of my car. Together with the other election organisers, we went up and down the lines, explaining that the polling booths would not be open for several hours, that there were three days of voting, and that everyone could go home and come back later. There was no need to stand in the rain. But no one moved. One old man said to me: 'Comrade, it is my first and possibly only chance to vote. I will not move until I have done so.'

This was to be the beginning of an extremely emotional few days. All over South Africa, long queues formed. People waited for hours, some sleeping outside overnight. 'Madams' and 'maids' waited in line together, sharing food and drink, all watched over jointly by MK and South African defence force soldiers. A few short years earlier, they had been engaged in bitter military battles against each other. Now they were jointly guarding the birth of a new country. It was hard to imagine what it must have felt like for those who had fought so hard and sacrificed so much, to vote for the first time. An emotional Archbishop Tutu said: 'It is like being asked to describe the colour red to someone born blind – impossible!'

Emotional stories were reaching us from all over the country. One of them had us in tears. In the Eastern Cape, a frail elderly gentleman was wheeled by his grandson into the voting station in a wheelbarrow. He could not read or write, but was assisted by the independent election monitors. He smiled broadly as they marked his finger with the indelible ink. As they left the venue, he collapsed and died. His final act was to vote. His family believed that he had 'hung on' so that his lifelong dream of voting could be fulfilled.

Having experienced this election, I will never take my right to vote for granted. I get furious with voter apathy, especially among young people.

Of course these were also very emotional days for the white population. Writer Antjie Krog described the election as a cathartic experience for everyone in the country. Tutu echoed her words, saying he believed it liberated blacks and whites equally. He said the whites entered the voting booth as oppressors, but exited it free of those shackles.

I also felt something of this liberation when Wilhelm and I voted in the morning in the Stellenbosch Town Hall – an event captured, of course, by the media. After everything, it seemed to go too fast, and yet, as I drew my cross next to Nelson Mandela's photo, I reflected how much my life had changed since the previous time I had voted at the same venue only two years before, in the last white referendum. Perhaps not everyone felt liberated, but as the first day of voting drew to a close, everyone gave a huge sigh of relief that things had gone well.

At around 6pm the Stellenbosch election committee congregated in the office to take stock of the day and send our reports through to the provincial office. We knew from the numbers that almost all the eligible voters had already voted. So what were we going to do for the next two days?

'What about the homeless shelters?' someone asked.

'Brilliant!'

Faghrie Patel was given the job of rounding up the homeless in his delivery van. Rudolf and I would ensure that they got temporary voting cards, Franklin would do some voter education on the way (of course, no canvassing was allowed during the election days), and then they would be delivered to the voting station. All was going well until an official who was issuing the voters' cards questioned why so many people had their birthdays on Christmas Day. Apparently few of the homeless people knew when they were born and Faghrie suggested that they just make it up. Christmas Day seemed as good a day as any – until the official became suspicious.

When the polls finally closed on the last day of voting, almost 20 million South Africans (19 726 579) had cast their votes. Remarkably, despite all the concerns about literacy, only 193 081 (less than 1 per cent) of votes were declared invalid. The only thing that remained outstanding was the result.

Three days later, the sun was setting over the blue peaks of the mountains surrounding Stellenbosch, turning them pink. I was taking a much-needed break. I had been monitoring the vote count for two days, and after months of electioneering, my body was starting to complain. As I stretched out on the slightly damp grass, my cell phone rang. 'Hey, how are things going?' It was Faghrie Patel.

Faghrie was a deeply religious Muslim man in his late forties who had joined the ANC executive about two years earlier. He owned a small fruit-and-vegetable shop in Cloetesville, one of the coloured areas of Stellenbosch. From behind the vegetable stands, he helped us run the election campaign with a passion. He had a big heart, but a fiery temper.

'It's not going well, Faghrie, we're losing badly,' I told him.

'What the hell are you guys doing?' Faghrie replied. 'They must be cheating and you're just too tired to see it! I'll be there in five minutes. Get me some accreditation.'

Before I could protest, the line had gone dead. True to his word, five minutes later Faghrie came speeding down the road in his little delivery van, smoke and dust flying behind him. Like most of our cars, the vehicle was barely roadworthy, a real *skoro-skoro*.

The unease on the whites' faces was clear when he marched into the sports hall. A big man, with a beard, a large tummy, and an Arab-type scarf tied around his neck, he was well known by the whites – and cut an impressive, and scary, figure. He planted himself wide-legged at one of the tables, leaned forward and said: 'Right, every time there is an ANC vote, I will shout "Amandla!" and every time there is one for the ACDP [African Christian Democratic Party], the brother here on my right will shout "Hallelujah!"' He winked at me and fixed his eyes on the ballot papers, ready to do the necessary shouting. Unfortunately, even though there were few Hallelujahs, there were even fewer Amandlas.

For some reason, we had not believed the opinion polls that had predicted the Western Cape would stay with the National Party. How could this be? Our world was changing. Surely everyone could see the sense of voting for Mandela, the ANC and the new South Africa?

One of the problems facing the ANC in the Western Cape was that it had little idea how coloured voters, the largest cultural group in this region, would vote. It soon became clear that most coloured people had chosen to vote for the NP, maybe arguing that it was better to stick with the devil you know.

It would take a couple of days before the final results were known, but it was clear early on that we were going to lose badly in Stellenbosch. So, while the rest of the country was preparing to celebrate, we felt pretty low. Franklin, who taxied a group of regulars to work from their homes in the coloured area in his little minibus, felt particularly aggrieved and 'embarrassed' that 'his' people had let him down. The first morning after we realised that we were going to be overwhelmingly defeated, Franklin waited until everyone had got into the minibus, as usual. He then turned around and said:

'Right! Which of you f**kers didn't vote for the ANC?'

There was silence, but then two women said slightly snootily: 'Our vote is our secret.'

At this point, Franklin opened the door and said: 'Out you get! And never get into my taxi again.'

As he drove away, one of his passengers wanted to know how he could be sure the two women were National Party supporters.

Franklin responded: 'If you're ANC, you say it! Only the National Party has this secrecy bulls**t.'

When Franklin told us the story, we all laughed, but it was indicative of increasing tensions and fear in the coloured community.

Four days after the final day of voting, on 2 May 1994, Nelson Mandela made this announcement in the Carlton Hotel:

> My fellow South Africans – the people of South Africa: this is indeed a joyous night. Although not yet final, we have received the provisional results of the election. My friends, I can tell you that we are delighted by the overwhelming support for the African National Congress.

With these words, joy erupted throughout South Africa, particularly in the townships. I was watching Mandela's speech on television at home, and immediately my phone rang. 'Comrade!' someone shouted. 'Get down here. The people are moving.' In the background, I could hear the jubilant cries of masses of people.

At the entrance to Kayamandi I was met by a huge crowd of people moving towards town. People were laughing and hugging and playing loud music on big radios held on their shoulders. They were ecstatic and wanted to celebrate with everyone. It was later reported that similar marches happened all over South Africa. We marched Mardi Gras-style, first through the coloured areas. The crowd grew every few minutes as people joined along the way. Then, after about 45 minutes, we entered the white areas. No one was on the streets; clearly they were afraid. None of the marchers seemed to notice or care, but things were about to change.

As we reached the town square, Die Braak, we were surrounded by a huge military presence. The reservist army of all-white volunteers had been called out as news of the march spread.

Inspired by Mandela's words of reconciliation, we were all in celebratory mood. This changed in an instant when we were confronted and stopped by white, heavily armed men in armed vehicles. It was the ultimate symbol of the apartheid oppression. There were angry whistles and shouts. Stones were being picked up. It was clear that the situation was going to get ugly.

I was annoyed, but also worried. I saw a young man on top of an armoured vehicle pointing a machine-gun at me. I saw him smirking in disgust. I hate being verbally or physically threatened. I do not get scared, I get furious. This was the ultimate threat, and I saw red. Before I had thought about it properly, I climbed onto the armoured vehicle and grabbed the barrel of the automatic weapon. 'Go on!' I shouted at the young man in uniform. 'If you want to shoot me, shoot me, you coward. But I have just been elected as member of parliament for the ANC, so I hope you are ready for what happens then!'

The crowd behind me had gone completely silent, watching us. The young man in front of me was shaking and I could see the fear in his eyes. Knowing that fear is far more dangerous in these situations than anger, I knew I had to calm down and defuse the situation, or I might end up dead. I lowered my voice so that the crowd could not hear me, and said in Afrikaans: 'Look, this can only end badly for both of us. If you lower the gun, we will get the people back into the township. Okay?'

Our eyes locked for a few seconds, and then he nodded and lowered his gun. There were loud cheers as I climbed off the vehicle. Together with another ANC executive member, we got onto the back of a parked car and encouraged the crowd to move back to Kayamandi. People were not happy but eventually agreed, although a few shop windows were kicked in on the way. Thankfully nothing was looted. And so it was that our first night as a democratic South Africa was not much different from the old South Africa. But still we partied until dawn.

A few days later, on 8 May 1994, all the elected ANC members of the national parliament and senate were called to our first caucus meeting. I arrived at the front door of parliament and was swiftly waved through by security guards. I walked into the lobby, where a few years earlier Wilhelm had had to borrow a jacket from one of the staff when we went for lunch with a former MP. In the apartheid era no one was allowed to cross the lobby without a jacket and tie. But things had changed. The lobby was alive with noise, children running around, and people loudly and happily greeting each other. Ties and jackets were nowhere to be seen, as most people had dressed in their finest traditional outfits.

Eventually we filed into the Old Assembly Hall. The symbolism and significance of the moment were not lost on me. The venue of the former white apartheid parliament was now the caucus room of the ANC. I found a space on one of the green leather benches to the left of the old Speaker's chair, across from where the National Party prime ministers had sat for decades. Mandela entered through the front door, to loud cheers and ululating. He lifted his fist triumphantly in the air and beamed at all of us. Then he took his seat on the bench with the copper plate that read 'Prime Minister'.

As he sat, I thought back to my first visit to the Chamber. A few years earlier, Wilhelm and I had taken some friends from Australia on a tour of parliament. Realising who Wilhelm was, the staff had insisted on a private tour. When we reached the Old Assembly Chamber, the woman 'kindly' pointed to a piece of carpet, which had a slight but distinct brown stain. 'It's from Hendrik Verwoerd's blood,' she said in a strong Afrikaans accent, looking almost proud. She then turned to Wilhelm and, to the horror of our friends, said: 'I don't know what you heard, but I heard that he had to stab your grandfather quite a few times. That's why there was such a lot of blood.'

Back in the caucus room, I craned my neck. The stain was still there, but now, sitting on the bench where Verwoerd had died was his former archenemy. Except now, Verwoerd was dead and Mandela was a global hero, and about to become president of South Africa.

I realised that Mandela was looking at me across the floor. Our eyes locked and for a brief moment he held my gaze. He smiled and nodded at me. Emotions were starting to overwhelm me and I was not the only one. Thabo Mbeki was chairing the meeting and, as was the practice, we were asked to stand and sing the anthem. More than 200 people rose to their feet and slowly lifted their fists into the air. There was a moment of silence and then, spontaneously, a woman started the prayer 'Nkosi Sikelel' iAfrika'. She was joined by her comrades, the newly elected government of South Africa. Slowly the sea of voices filled the hall. It was as if people, through their voices and their prayer, wanted to cleanse the place where so much evil had been conceived and brought into law. I swallowed hard not to cry, but I saw tears streaming down many faces.

As we came to the end, there was an emotionally charged pause. Then Mandela threw his fist in the air and said loudly 'Amandla!' To which everyone responded 'Awethu!' And as if a bubble of joy had suddenly burst, people chanted repeatedly: 'Long live Nelson Rolihlahla Mandela! Long live the spirit of Chris Hani! Long live the spirit of Oliver Tambo! Long live the ANC! Amandla!'

After we all settled down, it was time for Mandela to speak. But first he wanted to address two issues. 'Comrades,' he said in his slow, deep tone, 'you are now leading this country. As leaders, you have to lead by example. So this concept of African time must stop!'

There were a few suppressed laughs, but a stern look from Mandela quickly stopped them. 'Secondly, "Nkosi Sikelele" is not the national anthem. After today, you must all learn, and sing, the full anthem.' There were a few uncomfortable shuffles and the sound of people clearing their throats. Apart from the few people like me, who were taught 'The Call' and 'Die Stem' at school, nobody in the ANC would have sung the much-hated apartheid anthems. But Mandela insisted.

After Mandela's address, Thabo Mbeki led us through a series of practical and housekeeping matters. I was thankful that I could just listen, hiding away at the back, partially hidden behind the Speaker's chair. Then we came to the question of who should nominate Nelson Mandela as president. This was a formality that was to happen the next day, after we had all been sworn in as members of parliament. There was a moment of silence. Ronnie Kasril's hand went up. Ronnie's Jewish grandparents had fled from Latvia and Lithuania to South Africa at the end of the nineteenth century. He had been radicalised by the Sharpeville massacre and became a key member of the South African Communist Party. He was also a founding member of uMkhonto weSizwe (MK) and, through his military activities, became known as one of the main enemies of the apartheid state. Ronnie was popular and widely respected in the ANC ranks. He was called on to speak.

'Comrade chair, comrades,' he started, 'I wish to propose Comrade Melanie Verwoerd.'

I nearly swallowed the peppermint I was sucking. Hundreds of eyes turned towards me. So much for hiding away in a corner.

Ronnie went on, 'The comrade has proven herself, the symbolism would be significant in terms of her surname, race and gender – and the fact that she is the youngest woman ever elected.'

I was getting anxious. I did not think this was the right thing to do at all. Here I was surrounded by the giants of the struggle and liberation movement, people I admired. How could I be asked to perform such a historic and important task? I saw Mandela giving me a tiny smile. I tried to attract Thabo Mbeki's attention. He looked over at me.

'I don't think it's right,' I said in a loud whisper to him. 'Let me just withdraw.'

He whispered back: 'No! Let's see what the meeting feels.'

There was a short discussion about the pros and cons of the symbolism. I was starting to panic. Thankfully, Gill Marcus, who later became the governor of the Reserve Bank – and a woman I admire deeply for her intelligence, strength and courage – rescued me. 'I can see that Comrade Melanie is deeply uncomfortable with this discussion,' she said, looking over at me. 'Even though I agree with the symbolism, I am sure she would like to be more than just a symbol. Let us rather go with Comrade Albertina Sisulu.'

Thank God, I sighed with relief. It was much more appropriate for 'Ma' Albertina, wife of Walter Sisulu, both stalwarts of the struggle and close friends of Madiba, to take charge of the nomination.

The next day, I got up early. The press wanted to follow me for the day, but I insisted that they meet Wilhelm and me at parliament. I got dressed in the olive-green linen suit my mum and I had bought a few days earlier. Having lived in ANC T-shirts and jeans for almost two years, I had nothing appropriate to wear to parliament – never mind the opening of parliament. In a panic, I had called on my mum for help. Thankfully, she offered to pay for the suit: I had not yet received a parliamentary salary, and my hourly university rates were not going to go far in the dress department. In fact, my new salary had caused problems from an unexpected front earlier that week.

Up to that point, Wilhelm and I had had a joint bank account. We had no use for separate accounts, and mostly lived on overdraft anyway. After I was elected, all the banks sent me (and the other MPs) letters touting for our business. My local bank in Stellenbosch sent me a letter, offering the top package, with all the related benefits. I made an appointment and went to see my personal banker. She confirmed the offer and I filled in the forms and signed on the dotted line. As a last step, the official informed me that she had to look at our current file. She went off, only to return a few minutes later looking gloomy. 'I'm sorry, Mrs Verwoerd, but your husband does not qualify for the top package on his income,' she said with a sigh.

'Yes,' I said, 'but I'm not applying for him, I'm applying for me.'

The woman gave me a patronising look. 'Of course, you can't apply for him. He can apply for you, but not the other way around. I'm sorry, you'll have to stay on the lower package.'

'Why?' I demanded to know.

'Well,' she answered earnestly, 'we know that it's not good for marital relations if a wife has a better package than her husband, so it's against bank policy.'

At first I could not decide whether to laugh or give in to my growing fury. The fury won. I insisted on seeing the manager. He confirmed that it was indeed the bank's policy – unless of course my husband gave his permission. Now I was really furious. 'I'll call him right now!' I said, and grabbed the phone on the manager's desk. 'Wilhelm, the bank won't give me the gold package unless you tell them that your ego can manage with me getting a better package than you,' I fumed.

'Oh my God!' Wilhelm exclaimed.

'I'm not asking your permission,' I said angrily. 'Just tell these idiots that the fragile male ego can manage.'

The two bank officials looked uncomfortable, but after the conversation they reluctantly agreed to make an exception. On investigation, I realised that most banks had the same policy at that stage.

So I had a 'gold' bank account with nothing in it, and two new dresses: one for the swearing-in, and a lovely cream suit for Mandela's inauguration the next day. What more could I possibly want?

On the inauguration day, Wilhelm and I drove from Stellenbosch to Cape Town in our battered Golf. Wilhelm had had the car converted years earlier to diesel, so a thick cloud of black smoke followed the rather noisy sound of the engine. In the back were the children's food-covered car seats, and to keep the sun out of their eyes, we had fixed two cloth nappies over the windows. This was the way we always drove and it did not cross my mind to change a thing.

A Japanese camera crew had been making a documentary about us and was planning to film us as we drove through the gates of parliament. Expecting a luxury car, they missed us as we drove past them in a cloud of smoke, with nappies stuck in the window.

This story had a funny twist a few weeks later. All MPs got a car subsidy after they were inaugurated. After much soul-searching and looking around, I decided to buy a Volkswagen Golf GTS. It was a lovely car. It had air-conditioning (bliss) and a CD player. I was thrilled. Most MPs went well over their allowance and bought expensive BMWs or Mercedes Benzes. I felt that it was important, as an ANC representative, not to have these visible signs of an affluence which most of our supporters could only dream of. However, shortly after I bought the car, ANC members at a community meeting in Stellenbosch confronted me. 'What is this?' they asked disapprovingly, looking at the Golf.

'It's my new car,' I said proudly.

'Why did you not buy a proper car, like a BMW?'

I explained my reasoning. To my surprise, this went down like a lead balloon. 'You insulted us!' an old man said angrily. 'You are now our representative, and we want to be proud of you, like the whites were of their MPs. How can we be if you drive a Golf?' He walked away and spat in disgust. You could have knocked me over with a feather.

Back on inauguration day, when we emerged from our old smoke-spitting car, we were surrounded by the masses of media from around the world. We spoke briefly to some of them, then rushed inside. The bells rang and we filed into the spacious National Assembly. It is an impressive hall, built in the PW Botha era, when he created the Tricameral Parliament. Even though the three houses were strictly separate on most matters, they convened jointly from time to time. The National Assembly was built for that purpose.

But now it housed the first democratically elected parliament of South Africa. What a change. A few times in the past, I had attended a session of the white parliament, in protest. It was of course all-white and mostly men (there were never more than five female MPs at any given time) wearing dark suits. They were either Afrikaans or English-speaking. Now the hall was filled with people of all races, speaking in different languages, wearing brightly coloured outfits. Actually, some men wore very little: they were dressed in traditional loincloths, with beads and elaborate headgear. There were more than 100 women and, thanks to an ANC quota for people with disabilities, there was a deaf person, a blind person and several people in wheelchairs.

As Mandela entered, the people in the packed public gallery jumped to their feet and applauded loudly. The ANC MPs started singing and dancing. I looked up at the gallery and it struck me that the only person sitting was Marike de Klerk, wife of FW de Klerk, now deputy president. Sitting in the front row on the left of the gallery across from her husband, her angry protest was very visible. She would repeat it in the months to come.

FW divorced her in 1998 after meeting Elita Georgiades. Sadly, Marike de Klerk was murdered in a brutal attack in her home in 2001. Back in 1994, I heard one of the MPs shouting at her: 'Get up, Marike, you are rude!' She glared down in the direction of the voice but stayed put. Nothing was going to dampen our spirits, though. In small groups, in alphabetical order, we were called to the front, where we swore that we would faithfully serve our country and its people.

After the swearing-in, Ma Albertina nominated Nelson Mandela for president of the Republic of South Africa. No objections were made and the gallery and chambers erupted once more. We were told afterwards that the whole country seemed to come to a standstill as people watched the proceedings on television or huddled around radios. When Nelson Rolihlahla Mandela was formally accepted as president, car-horns beeped, people hugged each other in the streets and many tears were shed. We were all transported in buses the few blocks to City Hall. Tens of thousands of people had come together on the square facing the building to welcome their new president, as they had done in the same place four years earlier after his release from prison.

An emotional Archbishop Tutu acted as MC. From the back, we heard him encouraging the crowd: 'Everyone hold hands and say after me: we are free, we are free! We are the rainbow nation of the world!' The crowd was ecstatic. Then came the moment that Tutu would later describe as the second-happiest of his life (the first was the birth of his first child). 'I now introduce to you your new president, Nelson Mandela!' Madiba walked slowly up a few steps to appear on the balcony. The crowd went mad. They cheered and cheered, and chanted 'Madiba! Madiba!' I wondered what Madiba must have felt, after 27 years in jail (and four years after his release), to be welcomed by his nation with so much love as their president.

Afterwards I was standing with a cup of tea when Tutu spotted Wilhelm and me and stopped. He clasped his hands together and said in his high-pitched, excited voice: 'Aah, the Verwoerds! Thank you, thank you. God bless you!' He gave me a big hug and shook Wilhelm's hand before rushing off again.

The next day, we all flew up to Pretoria for Mandela's inauguration. I had a sinus infection, but I was not going to miss this historic occasion. Special flights were arranged for very early in the morning from all over the country. We were taken by bus to the Union Buildings. Despite the early hour and the freezing cold, crowds were already congregating on the grass below the building.

The Union Buildings are an impressive sight. Sir Herbert Baker designed them, and construction took three years, between 1910 and 1913. Even though they are not in the centre of the city, they are the highest point of Pretoria, and from the amphitheatre, where Mandela was to be inaugurated, the view over the city is breathtaking.

Not only was this the venue for the inauguration of apartheid presidents and prime ministers, it was also the place where, on 9 August 1956, 20 000 women marched from all over the country to protest against the pass laws, which would enforce the carrying of passbooks by women. It is recorded that as the big clock chimed at noon, the crowd stood in complete silence. Not even a baby cried, and when the clock stopped, the women chanted: 'Whathint' abafazi, whatint' imbokodo!' (Strike the woman, strike the rock!) JG Strijdom, who was prime minister at the time, apparently got such a shock that he ran from the building and the women threw the thousands of petitions around his office.

But this day was going to be happier. We were shown to our seats while dignitaries from across the world arrived. Presidents and prime ministers from 140 countries attended, as did film stars, UN diplomats, sports stars and church leaders. Some caused a bigger stir than others. When Fidel Castro arrived, the ANC ranks erupted in spontaneous chants of 'Fidel Castro!'

A few hours later, with a gentle winter sun warming us, the ceremony began. Mandela had arrived, beaming with joy and waving at the thousands of people who had gathered on the lawn below the Union Building. The ceremony was shown there on big screens and of course broadcast around the world too. It struck me that De Klerk looked a little less happy, but I suppose that was no surprise. Always the reconciliator, Madiba acknowledged De Klerk and his contribution, saying: 'He has made for himself a niche in history. He has turned out to be one of the greatest reformers, one of the greatest sons of South Africa.' He then added, in Afrikaans: 'Wat is verby is verby.' (What is past is past.)

In the rest of his emotional speech, he promised his continued commitment to reconciliation and the enforcement of basic human rights in South Africa. Following Mandela's speech and swearing-in, we all settled down again. Suddenly, over the koppies in the distance, black spots appeared. We held our breath. The dots were fighter jets from the South African Defence Force. They approached fast, but as they grew closer they visibly slowed. They descended sharply and, with a tremendous roar, flew very slowly over the amphitheatre. They were so low you could clearly see the young white pilots inside. As they flew over Mandela's head, they all looked down and raised their hands to salute him. I could hear the sharp intake of breath all around me from the ANC cadres, many of whom had for years fought in MK. To see these airmen – who had, for decades, been trained to eradicate the ANC and its followers – salute Mandela as their new president and commander-in-chief was almost beyond belief. As I looked around me, I saw tears glisten in many eyes.

There were more aerial displays, choirs sang, and then Mandela and his two deputies, FW de Klerk and Thabo Mbeki, went down to the Botha Lawn to wave to the crowds. As the BBC reported: 'More than 100 000 South African men, women and children of all races sang and danced with joy.'

Then we went to another part of the lawn where big white marquees had been erected. The party of all parties was about to start. Everyone wanted to keep mementoes of the day, and we were encouraged to take the flowerpots and wine. A security guard drew the line, however, when one elderly African woman wanted to put an African pot that was taller than she was on her head to take home.

Late that evening, we were all flown back to our homes. Exhausted, many of us fell asleep on the plane. It was completely quiet on the two-hour flight to Cape Town, as one of the greatest days in South Africa's history came to a close.

8

After all the exciting days of the election and the inauguration, our next task was to get down to governing the country. Of course, there were many obstacles. In practical terms, most MPs had to be trained, since they had never been in parliament before – and in fact had never expected to be. There was no continuity, so everything had to be started from scratch. Apart from the obvious shift in the racial diversity of the public representatives, the other big change was the number of women MPs.

Under successive white governments, there had never been more than five women in parliament at any one point. In the lead-up to the first democratic elections of 1994, however, women across racial, class, cultural and politi-cal divides, in an unprecedented move, formed an alliance and insisted that they would be represented fully in the new political dispensation. Under pressure from the ANC Women's League, the ANC leadership agreed that 30 per cent of those who were elected – as well as those standing as candi-dates – had to be women. As the ANC was the largest political party, this meant that after the April 1994 election I was part of a group of more than 100 women who swore the oath to serve our country and its people faith-fully, under the watchful eye of our new president.

True to his word, Mandela went further, ensuring that more than 30 per cent of his Cabinet consisted of women and that they were not only given the traditional female portfolios, such as health, social welfare and children's affairs, but also occupied positions relating to finance, safety and security. In addition, the Speaker and Deputy Speaker of the House were women, as was the leader of the Upper House, the National Council of Provinces.

As women representatives, we immediately formed a women's caucus across party lines to discuss issues of policy that would affect women in particular. Our male colleagues found this troubling and protested that it was dangerous to step outside party allegiances. For some reason, they did not have the same objection when it came to them forming a cross-party rugby team. Apparently to have a thinking scrum together was far more problematic than actually scrumming together.

We were not representing only women, nor was our work focused exclusively on women, but having a critical mass (i.e. sufficient numbers) meant that we were able to make significant changes to policy and legislation that benefited women, and therefore society as a whole. For example, a committee was formed with the charismatic Pregs Govender as chair to monitor all issues related to women and children, and an Office for the Advancement of Women was strategically placed in the office of the president. Following the Australian parliament's example, we introduced the concept of a Women's Budget, which analysed the percentage of money spent by various departments on the advancement and protection of women and children. On the back of the Women's Budget, a motion was passed in the House that made it obligatory for all departments to reflect in their budget review the breakdown of their actual and planned expenditure on certain gender-sensitive criteria.

You would think that with all these changes, the biggest and most challenging battles had been fought and won, but nothing prepared us for the battle of the toilets. Having more than 100 female members meant that the few toilets allocated to 'Female guests of members' would not suffice. We made a submission to Public Works requesting that a few male cloakrooms be converted for female members. But the wheels of government turn very slowly. After weeks of having to walk down various sets of stairs to visit the guest cloakrooms, and endless memos, we took action. To the singing of 'Sisters are doing it, doing it', we replaced some of the 'Men' with 'Women' signs and, with a few plants strategically placed in the urinals, the battle of the toilets was finally resolved.

Operation Childcare was more protracted, and required more extreme actions. Given the nature and demands of politics, the majority of women entering parliaments around the world are usually older, and past childbearing age. However, in South Africa, a huge percentage of the women who were elected were young and had small children. Also, as is typical of the extended family in Africa, many MPs who were grandmothers were also looking after little ones. Given the long hours of our work, childcare was badly needed – something that would of course also benefit many of our male colleagues who had children. Having been promised a childcare facility on the grounds of parliament before the election, we were annoyed when it did not materialise. After yet more memos that had no effect, we all decided to bring our children to work on a given day. It is hard to describe the chaos that ensued. Children were running everywhere, playing on the stairs and disrupting meetings. But it worked. Miraculously, by lunchtime, rooms had been evacuated in a nearby building, temporary staff were found and the parliament crèche was in business.

Of course, all these victories did not mean that we were working in a sexism-free environment. We struggled, for example, to get a policy for maternity leave. Colleagues often reported being asked to perform certain tasks for male colleagues, such as getting them food, doing typing or – as happened to me – booking them plane tickets. As in the broader society, there were sexual harassment issues, but we tackled it all with passion and with the knowledge that there were enough of us to insist on change.

On the home front, the fact that I was now an MP contributed to my feminist upbringing of Wilmé. After the opening of parliament in 1995, Wilhelm and I arrived home. 'Where have you two been?' my five-year-old daughter wanted to know, looking suspiciously at her father and me.

'In parliament,' I answered.

'I know where *you* were,' my daughter said indignantly, 'but where was my dad?'

I explained that we had gone to the opening of parliament, where Mandela was, but her face just expressed growing confusion and concern. Eventually she asked me to bend down, then whispered anxiously in my ear, looking over at her dad: 'But he is a boy, and boys can't go into parliament!'

Although I loved the new challenges, it was difficult to balance the home responsibilities and work. We were still living in Stellenbosch, which meant a daily journey on the N2. In winter, thick mist often rises from the surrounding wetlands, sometimes making it impossible to see the white lines or exits. I started to dread this daily journey, which, depending on traffic, could take up to two hours.

I would get up at five in the morning to prepare breakfast for the children, who were four years and seventeen months old respectively when I was elected. I would try and leave before 7am to avoid the worst traffic in order to be in parliament for 9am meetings. Meetings and sittings ran most nights until 7 or 8pm, and then there was constituency work to do.

I hated that I saw so little of my children. This situation was made much worse by Wilmé, who would get up at around six in the morning and start a little daily mantra: 'Are you going to work again? Why are you going? Why do you leave me? Don't you love me?' I tried to be calm and loving but firm, as all the books on working mothers advised, but by the time I was in the car I would be in tears, often having to pull off the road to compose myself enough to drive safely.

It was also clear that Wilhelm was becoming resentful of the demands my work was placing on our relationship. Despite his intellectual commitment to equal opportunities, his sense of anger and frustration would continue to grow over the next decade. I was now earning almost three times his salary, which meant that our financial situation was much better than it had been, but Wilhelm found this tricky to deal with. I tried to please everyone, sometimes making the dreaded journey more than once a day in order to spend time with the children. Weekends and constituency weeks were easier, and at least we got some time off around the middle of the year and at Christmas. But it all took a toll, both physically and emotionally – and not only on me.

The one thing I believe none of us was prepared for was the toll parliamentary life took on women's personal lives. Female MPs, almost exclusively, remained the primary caregivers for their children. Trying to balance the long legislative hours, the constituency work, and family life was extremely difficult for most of us. Our health and marriages suffered, and in the first year of the 1994 parliament, it was reported that 38 marriages of female MPs failed (the figure was far lower for male MPs). Some argued that this was a sign that women were simply not suitable for parliamentary life. This is nonsense. What was needed was better support and an understanding of the need to maintain a family life.

Most parliamentary systems are products of age-old systems where privileged men came together in the afternoon and debated matters of state after a relaxed lunch. Why, for example, do most parliaments have committee meetings in the mornings and start their plenary sessions in the afternoon, around the time children finish school? Why not change it around, which would mean that parents could spend some time with their young ones before engaging in the evening sessions of constituency work? When we tried to change this, we were told that it was tradition and that nothing could be done to change it.

Added to our tremendously demanding parliamentary schedule was the constituency work. Having never had any access to public representatives, our constituents now made full use of this novelty. We received an allowance to open an office in the designated constituencies and to pay a staff member. Given the demographics of Stellenbosch, I decided to appoint an African woman called Thandi Molefe and a coloured woman, Hillary Bergstedt, to share the job. I then opened an office midway between Kayamandi, Cloetesville and the town centre.

But nothing was ever simple when it came to township politics. Even though I had advertised the positions and formed a panel to help me interview and to fill the two positions, a woman from Kayamandi was furious that her daughter had not been appointed. She was known for having some dark powers. One day she was waiting for me when I arrived at the office. 'Comrade, be careful, I'm going to curse you and this office,' she warned. The saga had been going on for weeks and I'd had enough.

'Ah, go ahead! You know they don't work on white people,' I said.

Thandi, though, looked ashen-faced. A while later she got a panic attack, which she immediately saw as a sign of the curse working. No amount of rational argument would change her mind.

A few days later, Hillary phoned: 'Melanie, are you okay with this digging up of the garden?'

It turned out that Thandi had gone to a spiritual healer in Kayamandi, who advised her – after parting her from a lot of money – to plant certain bottles of potions in front of the door. I felt that this was harmless enough and told Hillary to let it be.

'What about the thick black oil being burned in the office to drive away the bad spirits?' I could hear that Hillary was not impressed at all. 'It keeps setting off the fire alarm,' she complained.

That had to stop, and I told Thandi so. But the treatments did not help, so Thandi asked for some 'stronger' help.

One day I was sitting at my desk behind the partition when there was a loud bang and a demonic shout. I jumped up and looked cautiously around the partition. I nearly bumped into Thandi, who explained: 'Don't panic, Melanie, it's the local pastor, he is expelling the evil spirits.' The pastor was jumping around in traditional regalia, shouting and waving a smoking stick around. This soon set off the fire alarm again. Sadly, this apparently did not work either (these were nasty spirits) and Thandi then went on a weekend retreat to a sangoma in Cape Town. After various potions and enemas – which of course cost her yet another fortune – she arrived back at work on Monday, pale and barely able to walk. No amount of persuasion by Hillary or me would convince her to go to a Western doctor, so eventually I gave her some time off. During her leave of absence, Thandi fell in love, and miraculously the curse was broken. Love does apparently conquer everything! I am sure that not many MPs around the world have to deal with such 'spiritual' matters in their daily work.

Since most people never had much state help during apartheid, they demanded, with a sense of entitlement, to get assistance with whatever challenges they faced. They appealed to me for help with debt issues, leaky roofs, problems with children's schooling and even medical issues. One day I arrived for a meeting with one of the ANC members. He was a local Rastafarian who had previously brought a petition to me on behalf of the Rastafarian community. They were petitioning the government to be allowed to grow their 'herbs' without harassment, based on the protection of freedom of religion in the new Bill of Rights.

On this day, he had a more personal problem. He settled down in front of me with a depressed look on his face. I asked how I could help. 'Well, Melanie,' he started, in a slow, sad voice, 'the thing is . . . I can't get it up.'

Out of the corner of my eye, I saw Hillary's head popping up over the partition behind the man. She was not going to miss this.

I was not sure that I understood him correctly. 'I don't understand. You can't get *what* up?'

This was a big mistake. The man started to tell me the intimate details of his problem, how it was affecting his marriage – and of course his ego. I did not misunderstand him then. It looked as though Hillary was about to faint, she was trying so hard not to laugh. I was also struggling to keep a straight face, and when I started to smile, the man got very upset. 'Don't laugh, it's a disaster!' he exclaimed.

'Sorry,' I assured him, 'I get that it's a big problem. I just don't understand how I can help. This is a political office, but your problem is clearly not political.'

'You in the ANC promised a better life for all,' he insisted, 'and this is making my life worse and worse. So you have to fix it!'

I always knew that this slogan was going to come back to haunt us, but did not anticipate this argument. 'What about a visit to a doctor?' I suggested.

'No,' he said firmly. 'It's against my faith.'

'A traditional healer then?' He looked more interested.

After he left, Hillary collapsed on the floor with laughter.

A few weeks later, the man insisted on another appointment, which Hillary immediately agreed to. I waited apprehensively, but there was no need for concern. The man arrived with his wife, both of them beaming. They had come to thank me for the advice. Apparently the traditional healer had performed wonders. It's always good to have satisfied voters.

A few months later, I was asked by the *Mail & Guardian* newspaper what type of issues came up in my constituency work. I told them about the debt, housing and education concerns. 'Anything humorous?' the journalist asked. 'Well . . .' and then I stupidly told her the story – which she of course published. For weeks after the article appeared, male colleagues in parliament would sit down next to me in the Chamber to have a 'chat' and ask advice; apparently they also had difficulties 'getting it up'!

The most challenging part of serving my constituency was the work with the farm labourers. Stellenbosch has many hundreds of wine farms scattered around its environs. From the roads it was easy to see the picturesque Cape Dutch-style farmhouses, surrounded by their lush vineyards, but it was impossible to spot the homes of the thousands of mainly coloured farm workers in this labour-intensive industry. Behind the high dam walls or trees there were literally thousands of labourers leading a meagre existence in grim shacks and hovels, secluded from the outside world. These labourers were the invisible machine that pumped out the gallons of wine destined for the tables of the privileged people of South Africa and Europe.

Before the 1994 election, we had tried to canvas some of these workers on behalf of the ANC but made little, if any, progress. Election campaigners had the legal right to enter the farms, but most farmers had simply ignored that and refused to let us on their land. They knew the ANC did not have the resources to go to court to challenge their veto. Theoretically, we could have asked the police for help, but they were all white and hardly likely to stand shoulder to shoulder with us. It was an area where we were up against the apartheid establishment at its most powerful and entrenched. Furthermore, by now there had been a lot of fuss in the newspapers about Wilhelm and me, the traitor Verwoerds, so most farmers knew who we were and many resented us. When I walked through town, these same farmers would spit at me.

So when it came to the election of 1994, there were no votes from farm workers in those election boxes that Faghrie was monitoring with razor-sharp eyes. The only votes the ANC got were from our own on-site election monitors. In truth, this was hardly surprising. The monitors reported that the farmers would deliver their employees to the polling stations in the back of their bakkies. The ballot papers carried photos of the party leaders (many of the voters were illiterate), and the farmers would point to the picture of FW de Klerk, or 'Kaalkop', as he was known in the ANC, and tell their work-ers: 'I will know how you vote, and if you don't vote for him, you won't have a job tomorrow.' They did this freely in front of our monitors: the intimidation could not have been any more blatant. Needless to say, Kaal-kop won.

When I became an MP for Stellenbosch, it was a priority for the ANC and for me personally to improve the lot of farm workers. As an MP, I found it marginally easier to gain access to these workers than before, so I began to visit farms to learn more about the workers' lives and to run educative work-shops – and I immediately discovered a secret world of abuse, exploitation and squalor that was horrifying even by the standards of apartheid-era South Africa.

Traditionally, farm labourers would remain on the same farms for gen-erations, working and raising their families, but despite this they had no legal land-tenure rights. Some farmers treated them as possessions, no more or less entitled than their sheep or cows, and would kick them off the land at any time they felt like it. For years the workers had been victims of the so-called tot system, whereby some farmers would pay their employees in cheap local alcohol in lieu of wages, leading to widespread problems of chronic alcoholism. Farmers often insisted that their workers buy all their provisions from the farm shop – which meant that they were heavily in debt to their boss and trapped in this pitiful existence.

The accommodation given to the farm labourers was mostly a disgrace. Typically, a large family would share one bare room. If they were lucky, it might have an open fire. They would need this, as few farmers saw fit to equip their live-in employees with electricity, running water or a sewage system. When the ANC got into parliament, one of our very first pieces of legislation was a law improving the rights of farm workers. Passing a law, of course, makes no difference unless those rights are claimed – and that was the message I was determined to bring to all those workers.

Most farmers remained defiantly loath to grant me access to their land and staff. I soon became skilled at inventing innovative ways of gaining access. It was generally easier to talk to farm labourers at their places of work at night or weekends. I might now be a South African MP, but even so, Saturdays and Sundays regularly found me donning shabby clothes and a headscarf and blacking up my face with boot polish to fool any belligerent farmer who might spot me.

I almost always made these visits alone, as I had no desire for my colleagues in the ANC to put their lives at risk. I knew that if a farmer found a white woman, and particularly a Verwoerd, on his land, I would get out alive. These good odds would not apply to black ANC members. At election times, many farmers would sit in their bakkies with their binoculars and rifles at the ready to see off our canvassers. One of my coloured colleagues, who was a school principal, was canvassing in the rural areas of the Karoo when a farmer caught him. The farmer had him on his knees for half an hour, pointing a gun at his head and telling him he was going to kill him. He (my colleague, not the farmer) later became an ANC member of parliament.

The night visits were the most nerve-racking. A typically fraught escapade occurred after two workers from a big wine farm just outside Stellenbosch came to see me at my constituency office. They explained that their farmer closed all the gates and access roads to his farm every evening and at the weekend to prevent any visits from 'terrorists', as he called them. The previous week, a young female worker had suffered a ruptured appendix and the farmer had refused to unlock the gate for the ambulance that came to attend to her. The woman had died.

The workers begged me to visit their colleagues on the farm but told me: 'You can't come during the day. If he sees you, even if he does nothing to you, he will kill us.' So a few nights later I drove after dark to a prearranged point on the perimeter of the farm, where one of them lifted the fence for me to crawl under. In pitch black, and utter silence, we stumbled across the field for what was probably half an hour but seemed a lot longer. We walked in silence, but the night-song of the crickets and frogs seemed to get louder and louder as the tension grew. We could not use a torch, and my escort was terrified that the full moon might allow the farmer to spot our silhouettes. It also occurred to me that, as a white woman alone, I had no idea where I was – or how safe the stranger I was with might be.

We headed towards a tiny light in the distance, and as we got closer I saw it was the farm workers' house. The building had no electricity, but was lit by paraffin lamps. I sat there for hours as the distraught family told me about the daughter who had died after the farmer sent the ambulance away. They made me tea and showed me scars on their bodies from where the farmer had beaten them, and bite marks from when he had set his dogs on them while they were working. It was a source of great personal satisfaction to me when that particular farmer was finally brought to justice: a brave journalist from the *Argus* accompanied me on a return night visit and exposed the whole vile story.

I must have visited almost every farm in Stellenbosch during my time as an MP. One recurrent problem was that each establishment had its informers among the workers, who were in with the boss and would go running to tell him we were on his land if they saw us. This happened one weekend when I was sitting talking to a group of labourers about their grievances. Suddenly, the farmer, his sons and the farm manager came piling over in their bakkies, sending gravel flying all around us.

They jumped out, pointed their guns at us and asked what the hell we were doing on their land. I pulled out a copy of the election law from my pocket and read aloud the passage that explained we had every right to be there under the Electoral Act. The farmer was furious and drove off, declaring that he would call his lawyers: I responded that I would call mine too.

The farmer did not return, but my ANC colleagues were rattled by the incident and went home. I remained on the farm, meeting labourers all day, and as night fell I headed out on foot towards a distant worker's cottage. I did not want to loom out of the darkness and scare them, so I called out 'Hello!' as I neared the house. A small girl, who must have been about four years old, appeared in the doorway. Her family only had candles in the cottage, so she could hear me but not see me.

I stepped into the light, and as soon as the child set eyes on me she went absolutely crazy, screaming hysterically and yelling to her mother: 'Mlungu! Mlungu!' I think, in many ways, the horror in that little girl's face haunted me more than all the tales of beatings and maltreatment I had heard on the farms. It was the realisation that she had such a terror of white people and such awful associations at such an early age.

Yet all of this unorthodox undercover constituency work paid off. Slowly but surely, farm workers became more aware of their rights and grew in confidence. My constituency office close to the Du Toit station increasingly saw rows of workers waiting patiently outside to see me. We started taking farmers to court and winning, and I became a real thorn in the farmers' side.

One Monday morning, a labourer came to see me in my constituency office. He complained that he had been kicked off the farm, but he had clearly been drinking – which, I guessed correctly, was why he had been fired.

I phoned the farmer and asked him: 'Did you kick this man off your farm?'

The farmer replied: 'Yes, he's useless!'

I said: 'Well, useless or not, he now has rights under the law. Either you take him back, or we go to the police. But to be fair to you, we will also put him in an alcohol rehabilitation programme. Now, what's it to be?'

There was a long pause, and the stunned farmer asked: 'Who are you again?' I said: 'I'm Melanie Verwoerd, and I'm a member of parliament.'

An even longer silence followed, before he said: 'These f**kers have got friends in high places now, don't they?'

One of the happier tasks I had in my constituency was to organise a public meeting during Madiba's first official visit to Stellenbosch after the 1994 election. As the ANC branch we were pretty annoyed when we discovered that a student organisation had invited him and, after some protests,

Madiba's office agreed that we could host his first meeting in the Stellenbosch Town Hall. On the night, with the Town Hall packed to the rafters, I found it quite emotional to think of all the years of National Party meetings with National Party presidents held there. We had come so far, even in Stellenbosch. Only a few years before there were fist fights between left-wing and right-wing students when Archbishop Tutu gave his first speech at the University. On that night Tutu had defused any further tension by opening his speech with a joke that involved him and Brigitte Bardot. On this night, however, there was no need for jokes – everyone wanted to hear Nelson Mandela speak. In fact, there was a huge crowd outside that could not get in. So after I introduced Madiba and he gave his speech, he went onto a balcony to wave at the crowds below. People cheered loudly and I spotted Professor Sampie Terreblanche getting very emotional. I heard him shout: 'I love you, Mandela!'

9

At the beginning of 1996 we decided to move to Cape Town. The strain of trying to balance children, a marriage, parliament, constituency work and the hours of commuting was taking a serious toll on me both emotionally and physically. I was getting stress migraines up to three times a week and was exhausted. Since Wilhelm's working hours were less onerous and more predictable, it would be easier if he commuted to Stellenbosch than the other way around. We put the house in Stellenbosch on the market and started house-hunting in Cape Town. I wanted to live close to parliament so I could nip home when I had a spare hour or two, but this was going to be difficult. Cape Town house prices were high, and we could not find anything we liked and could afford.

Early one evening, on my way home, I turned into a development on Table Mountain that had been advertised. Wilhelm had been adamant that with the work demands we were under, we could not build a new house again. But when I stood on the piece of vacant land, I knew it was where I wanted to live. Table Mountain was behind me, and in front of me lay the city and the ocean. The view took my breath away. I could not track Wilhelm down, but it was the last plot, and I signed on the dotted line. Luckily, Wilhelm agreed with my reasoning. But the land was expensive, and this meant that we, or rather I, had to be 'owner/builder' again, and organise all the labourers and supplies. History was repeating itself, except this time, I had to work, and I still had to complete my thesis too.

The house in Stellenbosch sold more quickly than I had anticipated, so we had to move into rental accommodation in Cape Town first. On the day before the move, I was busy packing boxes when the phone rang. Wilmé answered and ran back. 'It's Mandela!' she shouted.

'You funny bunny,' I joked with her, taking time to give her a hug before answering the phone.

'Melanie, this is President Mandela's office,' the voice on the other end said. So Wilmé was not joking. The private secretary explained that President Mandela was hosting representatives of 30 Afrikaner women's organisations for tea the next morning in Pretoria. 'The president would greatly appreciate it if you would join him for support. Is that in order?' I looked at the chaos around me. Boxes were everywhere, the kids were in overdrive and Wilhelm had gone to bed. He always struggled to cope with this kind of chaotic pressure. But how do you say no to Nelson Mandela? It just did not seem right to say: 'Thanks for the invite, Madiba, but I'm moving house.'

After a long night of packing, I arrived at the military airbase on the outskirts of Cape Town. I was shown to a waiting room and a few minutes later Madiba arrived, flanked by two bodyguards. Madiba knew all the staff by name and took time to greet them and ask after their families. He gave me a hug and laughed when I told him that I had abandoned Wilhelm for him on moving day. 'This could cause a scandal!' he said, and winked mischievously. We started to make our way in the dark to the small presidential jet across the tarmac. Madiba spotted a man sweeping the grounds in the distance. He insisted that the worker be brought over, so he could greet him. 'This always happens,' one of the bodyguards next to me said with a groan. 'It takes us forever to get anywhere.'

As soon as we were in the air, the bodyguards fell asleep. After my sleepless night I was dying to have a nap as well, but Madiba was bright-eyed and wanted to chat. He also wanted to practise his speech for the morning – which was in Afrikaans – on me. He read it a few times, pausing when he needed help with the Afrikaans pronunciation. I told him how touched I was by the effort he was making. 'Language is important when it comes to reconciliation,' he conceded. 'You know, my only problem is that with my hearing being so bad, I struggle to hear Afrikaans. So please stay close to me, to help me if I need translation.'

At the military base outside Pretoria, we got into the presidential car and it struck me that Madiba had only one security car in front and one behind, and that they kept to the speed limit. His security later explained that he insisted on abiding by all the laws of the country, including speed limits. It was still early morning in Pretoria, and traffic was fairly light. On street corners and at traffic lights, hawkers and newspaper sellers were setting up for a day of trade. At every red light – there was no jumping of lights –

Madiba would wind down his window and greet the traders, who, to the security's exasperation, would rush over to say hello – once they had got over the shock of meeting their beloved Madiba.

At the official residence, Madiba was taken to his office and I was shown to a bedroom by a young Afrikaans man called Jacques Human. He was the housekeeper and chef from the apartheid years, but in typical Madiba fashion had been asked to stay. He told me to have a rest and that he would call me when I was needed. I walked around the room with its dated décor, wondering if it was still the same as in the days of Wilhelm's grandfather, but, too tired to reflect much on the history, I lay down on the bed and quickly fell asleep.

I was in a deep sleep when Jacques woke me. 'You are needed downstairs.' Drowsily I followed him down the stairs into a room filled with women. The smell of perfume was suffocating. I looked around. I don't think I have ever seen so much make-up in one room. The ladies were in their Sunday best. Their hair was permed, there were little neck scarves everywhere.

'Ladies, can I get your attention please,' said Jacques in Afrikaans. 'I would like to introduce you to Melanie Verwoerd. She is a member of parliament accompanying President Mandela today. She is of course from' – he paused for dramatic effect – 'the ANC.' All the blue-eye-shadowed eyes turned to me with cold hatred. 'Good luck!' Jacques whispered, and made a hasty escape.

There were a few seconds' silence before the women resumed their conversations, ignoring me. Then one woman, who was clearly the leader of the group, called them all to order. 'Ladies,' she said sternly, 'before Mandela arrives, I want us to agree on a few house rules. We have to remember that we are here to make a point, to send a message. So can we remind ourselves that we will only speak Afrikaans today. Even if we are asked to speak English, or Mandela speaks English, we will stick to Afrikaans.' There were loud cheers of support, and the leader triumphantly pulled her jacket into place.

Thinking of Mandela practising his speech on the early-morning flight, I felt an anger rising in me. How rude they were to behave like this! Before I could say anything, I spotted Madiba through the window on his way to the room. I slipped out a side door and rushed over to warn him about their intentions. Madiba nodded, and then said: 'Leave it to me. Just stay close if

I need you.' I followed him as he walked into the room to greet the women who had lined up. 'Aaah, goeiemôre! Dis so 'n eer om u te ontmoet,' he said to the first one. She froze slightly, and then went blood red.

'I am so, so honoured to meet you, Mr President. So honoured!' she blurted out in English.

The next one burst into tears. 'I am so sorry what my people did to you,' she cried while Madiba hugged her.

The third woman spoke to him in Zulu!

Out of the corner of my eye I spotted the leader, who had a furious expression on her face. As Madiba invited the women to tea on the stoep, he caught my eye and winked. What a master he is at these occasions, I thought.

The rest of the morning was further proof of this. His speech went down a treat, and during question time he told the most emotional stories of his time in jail. He had all the women in tears, and even though he spoke mainly Afrikaans, they all spoke English. At the end of the meeting, they gave him various gifts, including those Afrikaner delicacies, koeksisters. Madiba loves these treats. There was also an Afrikaans Bible, some Afrikaans music and photo frames for the photos of his grandchildren. It was a hugely successful morning, and in the end, through Mandela's actions, the only point that was made was his enormous capacity to turn the most hardened opponents into admirers.

Back in Cape Town that evening, I went to the newly rented house, where Wilhelm had thankfully already moved everything in and settled the cat, dog and kids for the night. The house move was a huge relief for me. It meant that we now lived less than five minutes' drive from parliament. I could go home to be with the kids in the evenings, and then return if there was an evening session. If an unexpected vote was called, my friends would phone, and I could make it back to my seat in time before the doors closed.

This move meant, of course, that the children would have to go to a new pre-school. At the back of Archbishop Tutu's diocese, St George's Cathedral, there was a small pre-school. It was right next to parliament and facing the big public gardens. Kind, caring women staffed it and given the convenient and lovely location, it was perfect. I could take the children through parliament and then through a side gate, which was for MPs' use only, and be back in parliament in five minutes.

One morning, when we arrived at the gate, it was closed. I was late for a committee meeting. Wian, who hates early mornings and being rushed, was in a foul mood, and Wilmé was anxious about something that was happening at school. I asked the policeman manning the gate why it was closed. He said that he had not got instructions to unlock it yet.

'So you have the key?' I asked.

'Yes, but I can't open it!' he insisted.

The kids were whining behind me. 'Can't you radio someone?' I asked.

'No,' he answered bluntly.

Now I was getting annoyed. 'Look, I'm late. I'm not walking back with these kids just because you won't help. Please unlock the gate, or I'll climb over it.'

The kids were now watching me silently with big eyes. The policeman looked at me, in my black pencil skirt suit and high heels, and then over at the high gate, with spikes at the top. Clearly deciding that I would never dare to attempt it, he turned his head away and ignored me. I was furious. I put the lunchboxes, sports clothes, drinks and teddies down, took my shoes off and climbed over the fence – to the consternation of the policeman.

'Ma'am, I will have to arrest you,' he warned.

'Oh, get a grip. I'm an MP and this is parliamentary ground. I have immunity,' I responded.

The kids were cheering loudly 'Go, Mum, go!' while jumping up and down. A few homeless guys on the other side of the fence were joining in. When I got to the top, I got stuck on the spikes for a few seconds, but luckily got myself disentangled and jumped off on the other side. 'Please pass me the kids,' I said to the red-faced policeman. He was clearly not keen, but Wilmé stretched out her arms to him and he could not resist. He passed Wilmé, then Wian, my shoes, the lunchboxes and the other stuff over the gate.

Having dropped the kids off, I returned a few minutes later to find the gate unlocked. As I rushed into parliament to my meeting, I heard Jannie Momberg, who had introduced us years earlier to Mandela and who was now one of the senior whips, bellowing behind me: 'Verwoerd!'

I turned with a sigh. 'Ja, Oom Jannie?'

'Tell me you did not just climb over the gates of parliament,' he said, trying to keep a stern face.

I looked at him, but didn't answer. Maybe it wasn't such a good idea, I thought, suddenly not so sure about immunity.

Jannie burst out laughing. 'Christ, you are something else! This never happened in the old parliament! You have the whole police force in shock!' He shuffled off, still laughing.

Now that I was closer to the children, I saw a lot more of them. I often picked them up at lunchtime and spent an hour in the Company's Gardens next to parliament, feeding the squirrels and eating ice cream. Of course, it did not mean that everything was stress-free and went smoothly. One day I was at a meeting in Pretoria when the school called. 'You haven't forgotten your children, have you?' the slightly amused principal asked. As it turned out, due to some miscommunication, Wilhelm did not know, or had forgotten, that he had to pick them up. He was still at the university in Stellenbosch. Even though the school included our two 'forgotten' children in the lunch and afternoon nap with the other children who stayed a full day (ours stayed only until lunch), Wilmé has still not forgiven us for the incident. Sixteen years on, she still berates her brother for happily having lunch and a snooze, while she was panicking about 'whether our parents would ever remember us again'. Not one of our proudest parenting moments.

Being so close to my work also meant that I could involve the children in significant events, such as the adoption of the new constitution. For the first two and a half years in parliament we were tasked with writing the final constitution. Even though a Bill of Rights and the interim constitution were adopted before the 1994 elections, we had a hectic parliamentary schedule and were also part of the constitutional assembly, which was tasked with writing the final constitution.

I was part of the committee working on Chapter 7, the local government section. Pravin Gordhan chaired the committee. Pravin is one of the most intelligent people I have ever worked with. A trained pharmacist, he became involved in politics in the 1960s and was detained numerous times. After Mandela's release, he was co-chairperson of the Transitional Executive Council, which prepared South Africa for elections. After the elections, he became chair of the Parliamentary Committee on Constitutional, Provincial Affairs and Local Government that I served on. His office was next to mine, and we worked closely together. I learnt an enormous amount from Pravin.

His clarity of mind and his capacity to think strategically are phenomenal. Up until this day, I use his method of mind-mapping when confronted with a complex problem. It came as no surprise to me when he was later a huge success as the head of South Africa's Revenue Services, and I was delighted when he was appointed minister of finance in 2009. Back in 1996, he played a very important role in finalising the new constitution.

In writing the constitution there was a real sense of being part of making history. After all, how many people get the chance to help write the founding document of their nation? As was also the practice with legislation, it was crucial that the public were involved. The debates were broadcast live, and people were asked to make submissions on various issues. Over a million submissions were received, and the various committees read them all. One of my favourites was from a group of guys who were mechanics in a garage in a small rural town. They said that during a tea break they were listening to the radio broadcast about some issue we were debating in committee. The lads had a chat, felt they had a solution, and wrote to us. The letter was handwritten and signed, with grease and oil marks all over it.

As we got closer to the deadline, which was constitutionally binding, the tension rose dramatically. There were still many outstanding issues, and the National Party was digging in its heels. A charismatic ANC senator, Mohammed Bhaba, was also part of our committee, and was doing most of the talking to the National Party MPs. During the last week, he announced that his 'schmoozing' was not working any more. 'So, time for radical actions,' he announced. 'We have to just exhaust them until they give in.' And we did. There were more of us, and on average we were much younger and fitter. So we just kept going through the nights. The ANC MPs took turns, but the 'poor' National Party guys could not leave, since there were often just one or two of them per committee. The plan worked. Finally, on the Wednesday night, we cracked them and agreement was reached on the outstanding issues.

I left parliament that morning, not having slept at all, as the sun rose over Table Mountain. I went home to have a quick shower, feed the kids breakfast and take them to school, before heading back to parliament for the final outstanding pieces of work. As we arrived at the pre-school, the principal, Mrs Prior, met me. 'Melanie, please remember it's your turn for cupcakes tomorrow.' I looked at her in a daze.

'Cupcakes?' Then I remembered. Every Friday, the children took one rand to school for charity and bought a cupcake that one of the mums provided. My head was filled with the constitutional responsibilities of local government, and the whole cupcake business had completely slipped my mind. I explained that I had not slept in days and that we were in the last day of constitutional negotiations. Was there perhaps another mother who could swap with me?

'No!' Mrs Prior insisted. Apparently I was the only mother who had not taken a turn, and I could not buy something else like popcorn: it had to be homemade cupcakes. I looked down at my two little ones staring worriedly up at me. Of course, at their age, the constitution meant nothing. Cupcakes, and not being embarrassed, were far more important. So of course I agreed. After yet another long day and night at parliament, I stood at two in the morning in my kitchen icing cupcakes, wondering whether any male MP anywhere in the world had ever done this.

The constitution was adopted on 11 October 1996. It was a beautiful, emotive day. Thabo Mbeki, on behalf of the ANC, gave his poetic and dramatic 'I am an African' speech. I got goosebumps listening to his deeply provocative turn of phrase. After his speech, all the other political leaders started their speeches with: 'I, too, am an African.' The big question was what the leader of the far-right, all-white Freedom Front Party, General Constand Viljoen, would say. He was a retired army general with great personal integrity, but his political views were linked to Wilhelm's family's ambition for Afrikaner self-determination and separateness. As he walked to the podium, there was a silent tension in the big chamber. He stood quietly for a moment and looked up at the packed public gallery. Then he said, 'Mr President, I, too, am an African' – to loud applause from both the gallery and the Chamber. How far this country had come in the six years since the ANC was unbanned!

After the session ended, I rushed over to get Wilmé from the pre-school so she could see the festivities. She was delighted. As we walked into the lobby, we bumped into Madiba, who was on his way out. He spotted Wilmé and came over. After greeting me, he lifted Wilmé into his arms. 'Hello, Wilma,' he said, mispronouncing her name.

'It's Wilmé,' she corrected him firmly.

Madiba smiled and apologised. 'It's good to meet you,' he said. 'I am Nelson Mandela.'

Wilmé looked him straight in the eye and said: 'I know who you are. I do watch TV, you know,' before giving him a big hug.

Madiba beamed and then very gently lowered her to the ground. 'See you soon, Wilmé,' he waved.

Watching Madiba's interaction with children over the years always moves me to tears. Wilhelm once sat next to Madiba's great friend and fellow prisoner, Walter Sisulu, on an aeroplane. When Wilhelm asked him what had been the hardest thing to deal with in jail, he responded: 'Not ever seeing any children.' Through all the years on Robben Island, the prisoners were not allowed to have visits from their own or any other children. It is so difficult to think of a life without ever seeing little ones. Another friend and fellow prisoner, Ahmed Kathrada, wrote movingly in his book *Letters from Prison* about his fear of holding a little child for the first time after more than two decades in jail. Amazingly, Madiba had never lost his touch, and Wilmé was delighted – as all the children always were when they met Madiba, even though he frequently insisted on singing a very off-key version of 'Twinkle, Twinkle, Little Star'.

During the constitution-writing process, Wilhelm's uncle Carel Boshoff approached me. Carel was an MP in the Northern Cape Provincial Parliament, representing the far-right Freedom Front. He was married to Wilhelm's aunt, Anna Boshoff, who was a fiery politician with a Margaret Thatcher-like personality. Together with a group of Afrikaners, they lived in and ran a little settlement called Orania in the arid Karoo region in the Northern Cape Province.

Towards the end of 1990, after Mandela's release and the unbanning of the ANC, they had bought a dilapidated and abandoned town which had been the construction camp while a mega-dam was being built. Their aim was to create an independent geographical area where Afrikaans and Afrikaner identity would be protected. Even though they claimed this was not based on race or racist stereotypes, and that anyone who defined themselves as Afrikaner and identified with Afrikaner ethnicity was welcome, it did of course attract only those white Afrikaners who were not comfortable living under a black government. Over the years, they had also bought more than seven thousand hectares of adjacent agricultural land, to seek to become more self-sufficient. In Orania, no 'foreign labour' is allowed, and the principle of self-reliance is central. Large sections of Wilhelm's extended family lived, and continue to live, there. At that stage, it included his grandmother, the wife of the former prime minister. She was to celebrate her 95th birthday, and a big family gathering was to be held.

During a tea break at parliament, Carel Boshoff came over to suggest that we join the gathering. Since Wilhelm's father was not speaking to us, and the rest of the family had made their disgust with us clear, I was not convinced that it was a good idea. But Carel felt strongly that it might be a reconciliatory gesture. Wilhelm and I debated it for days. We eventually decided to go. After all, Mandela had led the way a year earlier.

Shortly after becoming president, Mandela had invited all the wives of the previous prime ministers and presidents for tea. Ouma Betsie was also invited. She politely declined the invitation on the grounds of her age, saying she did not travel any more. In return, she said that if Madiba was ever in the neighbourhood, to drop in for a cup of tea. Knowing that Orania is in the middle of nowhere and very few people would ever have a reason to be in the neighbourhood, she (and the family) felt safe that this would never happen. Of course, they underestimated Madiba. A few months later, with the world's media in tow, he went to Orania to have tea with Ouma Betsie.

While there, Madiba was also shown the statue of Hendrik Verwoerd, which is on the hill overlooking the town. The statue is less than six feet high, prompting Madiba to remark jokingly: 'Well, you made him very small, didn't you?' Senior ANC people had quietly asked me if I wanted to go with Madiba on the visit, but I had felt it would be too provocative and painful for the family. However, a year later, given Madiba's reconciliatory gesture, we felt that it was important to go to the birthday celebration.

During our visit, Wilhelm and I took the children for tea at their great-grandmother's house. Unsurprisingly, the conversation did not flow easily and I felt very uncomfortable with the life-size portraits of Verwoerd looking down at us. To make small talk, I remarked on a beautiful tea set that was in a display cabinet. She replied that it was a wedding present. 'Do you ever use it?' I asked.

'Not often,' she replied. 'I wanted to use it when that other famous man came . . .' She paused, trying to remember something. 'You know, what is his name again? The black guy, that came with all the journalists?'

Wilhelm mentioned one or two film stars' names, but then it struck me.

'You mean Nelson Mandela?' I asked.

'That's the one,' she said. 'He was kind, but the journalists trampled on my flowers.'

'How did you feel about him?' I asked. Wilhelm was looking worried.

'Ah, he was fine. I always enjoy receiving foreign heads of state,' she said.

The weekend was extremely stressful, and was not helped by Wilmé's determination to teach her new cousins ANC freedom songs. To make matters worse, Wian decided to speak only English for the weekend. We never speak English at home, and he has always spoken only Afrikaans to his grandparents. But for some reason that I never understood, Wian insisted on speaking English for the whole weekend. It did not go down well.

At the end of the weekend, I bought a few bars of Orania-branded handmade soap and on my return gave them to my ANC friends back in parliament, who joked that it was guaranteed to 'wash you whiter than white' – the slogan of a famous television ad for washing powder at the time.

I have complex feelings about Orania. Of course I do not agree with the principles it is founded upon. I find the argument that it is not racist or racially motivated disingenuous, and I think that it is damaging to the image of Afrikaners both domestically and internationally. Yet the members of Wilhelm's family who are the driving force behind it are by and large nice people, who only want to get on with their own lives and be left alone to live among those who share their values and ideals. This does not do any harm and happens all over the world, although more organically and less institutionally. We visited Orania again a year or so later on our way to the north. Wilhelm wanted to see his grandmother one last time. He spoke to her at length, and I think they found some accommodation with one another.

Ouma Betsie died on 2 March 2000 at the age of 98. Madiba sent his condolences and despatched the premier of the Northern Cape Province and two other ANC representatives to the funeral in Orania. They held back and winked at me when I took my place with the family at the service. Later, when I went over to thank them for coming, they were very gracious, insisting that I go back to the family and not talk to them for too long.

10

The first five years of the South African parliament was a historic time, and it was an enormous privilege to be part of it. Not only did we write a new constitution, we also passed hundreds of pieces of legislation. Given that all legislation had been written during the apartheid years, everything had to be repealed to be in line with our new, non-racial constitution and Bill of Rights. We also wrote numerous new policy documents and I was closely involved with the White Paper on Local Government. I served on various committees such as those for Constitutional and Provincial Affairs and Local Government, Broadcasting, the Youth Commission, and Surrogate Motherhood.

Above all, of course, we had the enormous privilege of serving under Madiba. He would try and attend our weekly Thursday caucus to address us. It was inspiring. On one such occasion, one of the older ANC women MPs sighed loudly behind me. 'Aaw,' she said, 'I don't understand why he went off with that Mozambican woman, Graça Machel. I would have taken such good care of him. I would have had his supper ready and rubbed his feet.' She clicked her tongue at the thought of the missed opportunity. All of us around her were in fits of laughter – resulting in a stern look from the chief whip.

One thing we did not enjoy was when Madiba came into the Chamber unannounced. During the first few years, the public gallery was almost always packed. If Madiba entered the Chamber, the public would jump to their feet and applaud loudly. If you were unfortunate enough to be at the podium giving your speech, you might as well have given up. How could you compete with such greatness?

I was privileged to be asked to speak in many important debates, especially on reconciliation. During my time in parliament, I learnt the art of making parliamentary speeches. There is a unique discipline inherent in making your point during a strictly timed four- to seven-minute speech. I always wrote my speeches without outside help, working for days on each sentence. I would practise the speech aloud to get the rhythm, timing and tone right. Even though I always found public speaking stressful, I became better at it as time went by, and even started to enjoy it. I was thrilled when I got notes congratulating me on a speech. There are two such notes that I treasure: one from Kader Asmal, and the other from Thabo Mbeki. Given that both Kader and Thabo are very fine orators, these notes mean a lot to me.

One of the most difficult speeches I had to make was during the debate to commemorate the Second Boer War. The Boer Wars are an emotive subject for most Afrikaners. Having fled British oppression during the Great Trek in the 1830s and 1840s, Afrikaners were again faced with British rule 50 years later. Wanting to lay claim to the rich mineral finds of diamonds, the British Empire wanted to annex the Transvaal and Orange Free State. The Afrikaners formally declared independence, and war broke out on 16 December 1880. The combat was short and intense, and the British suffered heavy losses. Peace was declared on 23 March 1881, with the British agreeing to Afrikaner self-government under nominal British oversight.

However, in 1886 another major mineral find was made. This led to renewed British imperial interest and resulted in the Second Boer War of 1899–1902. In contrast to the First Boer War, the second war was lengthy and bitter, with heavy losses on both sides. The British policy of scorched earth and internment of women and children in concentration camps left a deep scar on the Afrikaner psyche, which would play a defining role in the politics of South Africa in the twentieth century. The anger against the British and the determination to achieve self-rule became the focus of the National Party, and led to their victory in 1948 and their subsequent disastrous policies of separate development.

All Afrikaner children grew up with stories of the Second Boer War. My grandmother would get very emotional relating the stories her mother had told her of the concentration camps. In addition, her father had been a prisoner of war, held by the English on St Helena. As a result, my granny, who was a kind, caring and deeply religious woman, had nothing good to say about the English. 'The only good things they ever brought to South Africa were hot water bottles and tea!' she would declare. She understood English and could speak it, but in all the years I knew her she never spoke a word of it.

So to be asked by the ANC to speak in a debate commemorating the centenary of the start of the Second Boer War left me in turmoil. How do I talk about it from an ANC perspective while still honouring my ancestors and their suffering? In the end I spoke about the many black Africans who had died in concentration camps, and had been written out of history. I talked about how important it was to seek peace, and for all South Africans to recommit to reconciliation and never to allow oppression of any sort to exist. I had spent a great deal of time preparing for the speech and delivered it with the passion I felt. Both members and the public packed the Chamber. Mandela was also in attendance.

When the Speaker called on 'the Honourable Melanie Verwoerd', a silence fell. 'Shame on you!' I heard one of the conservative Afrikaner MPs to my left say. I took a deep breath and began. Soon my speech was interrupted with applause and cries of 'Hear, hear' from the ANC benches. I drew to the end of the speech, which was full of emotion, and turned to walk off. I was shaking from the tension and exertion of the address. I walked past Mandela's seat, and he stood up to hug me. 'Thank you,' he said softly. 'You healed many hearts today.'

I suddenly felt tears welling up.

Mandela saw this and said, 'The Afrikaners will not like it, but look, look at what this meant to them.' He nodded towards the Chamber.

I had not noticed, but most of the MPs were giving me a standing ovation. I could not believe it. It was not only the ANC MPs, but also all the African MPs from the opposition parties. As I walked back to my seat, numerous colleagues stopped me to thank me. As I sank into my seat, there were two notes waiting. They were both from Afrikaner MPs in the opposition: 'Shame on you' and 'What a traitor' they read.

My relationship with Afrikaner MPs in the opposition was complex, but mostly cordial and polite. Even though most of them hated that I had joined the ANC, they often wanted a quick chat, hoping that I could give them some inside information – which I never did. In particular on foreign visits, where I was often the only other white person on the trip, they would seek me out for company.

During the first few years, we went on many foreign study visits. They were very informative and gave us invaluable opportunities to study the best and worst of other democracies. The first visit I was part of, in 1994, happened following an invitation from the Congressional Black Caucus in the United States. The purpose of the trip was to study local government, federal government structures and the congressional system. The trip was funded on the condition that only MPs who had not been part of the previous government could take part. In true ANC fashion, the delegation was balanced in terms of race and gender, so I was asked to go. It did not cross my mind until we had landed in America that I might be the only white person on the delegation. This caused huge consternation, and I was treated badly. The organisers could not understand what I was doing there. Time and again it was assumed that I was a secretary, or I was just ignored.

Things became so bad that my ANC colleagues insisted they would cancel the rest of the trip if the situation did not improve.

I learnt a few important lessons during this trip. Firstly, I felt first-hand what it is like to be excluded on the grounds of race. Secondly, I realised that in South Africa we were far ahead of the United States when it came to the principle of non-racialism. We were living and practising inclusivity, whereas the debate in the States was clearly still an us-and-them proposition. I returned to South Africa disillusioned and emotionally bruised.

In the next few years, committees that I served on travelled to the Netherlands, Sweden, Britain, Australia, Chile, Brazil and Argentina. I was also part of a delegation that went to England to support victims of asbestos mining by a British company on the west coast of South Africa. It was heartbreaking to sit in the House of Lords and watch elderly, rural people riddled with asbestos pleading their case in the hope of getting some form of reparation before their painful deaths. Thankfully, after a very long battle and with the help of a young British solicitor, Richard Meeran, they won their case.

The most emotive visit was the one to Cuba in 1997, as part of a trip to four South American countries. Cuba has a particular emotional significance to the ANC cadre. Many studied or received military training there, and some received medical treatment as well. Landing in Havana was like stepping into another world. There were no advertising boards, no shops – in fact no sign of any commercial activities whatsoever. The cars were all original 1950s American models – which made me wonder what happened to all the old cars in the rest of the world.

Pravin Gordhan was leading the delegation. Pravin was a member of the South African Communist Party and I could see that arriving in Cuba was an emotional experience for him. The few days we spent there were mind-blowing. To see socialism at work was fascinating and very liberating.

One of the most significant discussions we had was with the head of the big tertiary hospital in Havana. The hospital was world-renowned for its work in transplant surgery. The professor gave us a tour, and a talk on the impressive services they offered. During questions, someone asked him (rather rudely, I thought) what he was paid. He took no offence and answered: 'About one hundred dollars per month.'

There was an astonished silence.

Taking note of our shock, he added: 'I am a very happy professional.'

'How could you be?' someone challenged him.

'Look,' he answered patiently, 'I received my education for free, and all three of my children, who are doctors, also received their education for free. I get a house and a car from the state; I get food stamps; and once a year I go on a free holiday. And I don't pay for medical services, of course. What more would I want? I can focus solely on the needs of my patients, and serving them. I am not driven by the need to make a lot of money.'

As I listened to him, it again struck me how this represented such a shift from traditional Western, capitalistic thinking. It sounded idyllic and attractive, but we quickly discovered the darker side of the dream. Our Cuban translator told us how she had been forced to start working for the embassy to earn some foreign currency after she and her teenage son, having run out of food stamps for the week, fought over their last piece of bread. That was certainly not a utopian society.

At the airport, we stocked up at the table selling duty-free cigars and rum. We were warned that this could cause difficulties at Customs in Miami. Being all fired up after the visit, we almost hoped we would be arrested, and one MP even drafted a statement just in case. In the end, we were waved through – to the disappointment of some members of our delegation. I fell in love with the natural beauty of Cuba and the unique energy of its people.

On this visit, we did not meet Fidel Castro, who was unwell, but in September 1998 he visited South Africa and addressed parliament. There was huge excitement in anticipation of his speech. As with Mandela's inauguration, the ANC MPs started to chant his name as he entered the Chamber. Castro is known for his beautiful use of words and the deeply philosophical nature of his speeches. This occasion was no different. He started by saying his address was 'the fruit of my imagination, like a love letter to a sweetheart written thousands of miles away, without knowing how she thinks or what she wants to hear, and without even knowing what her face looks like'. He apologised in advance for going off at a tangent if some new idea struck him, since he considered a speech to be 'an intimate and frank conversation', during which, as he put it, he engages in a dialogue 'with my interlocutors while looking at their faces, trying to persuade them'. This is exactly what happened.

At a few critical junctures, he paused and made notes, but the speech was beautifully constructed and thought-provoking. He ended to applause and chants of 'Fidel! Fidel! Fidel!' His parting words were: 'Let us be more generous, more fraternal, more humane. Let South Africa become a role model for a more just and humane world of the future. If you can make it, all of us can.'

About six months before Castro's visit, Bill Clinton became the first American president to visit South Africa. This was shortly after the Monica Lewinsky story hit the media; the trip had clearly been organised partly to give Bill and Hillary Clinton some time away from Washington. The southeaster was howling in Cape Town for days before they arrived, and naturally endless jokes playing on the word 'blow' were doing the rounds. As is the practice, a huge American security contingent arrived beforehand and Cape Town was filled with 'men in black' talking into their shirtsleeves, sealing up manholes and holding up traffic.

The commuters were not the only ones getting annoyed about the impending visit. Some of the ANC MPs who were members of the South African Communist Party were not too enthusiastic about the American visit. Before the parliamentary session where Clinton was to address us started, a few of us were sitting in the parliament bar, where Blade Nzimande entertained us with his misgivings. He declared, to everyone's amusement, that he was wearing red socks as a mark of protest. Little did he know what Mandela had up his sleeve.

Clinton is a great orator and, as always, gave an excellent speech. Afterwards, he walked down the aisle with Mandela, while MPs gave them a standing ovation. Mandela shook hands with MPs and then spotted Blade. It was obvious what was about to happen, and Blade tried desperately to duck behind other MPs. But Mandela walked straight over and introduced President Clinton to Blade. All the MPs were now laughing and cheering on Blade, who was turning red and making signs at us behind his back. Mandela was also smiling, clearly knowing what was going on – even though Bill Clinton looked a bit puzzled.

Mandela then came over and introduced me to President Clinton. Clinton shook my hand, but did not let go while Mandela explained the Verwoerd family connection. This struck me as a bit strange (and uncomfortable). A few years later, I was again introduced to Clinton in Ireland. This time we had a lengthy discussion about AIDS and again, he did not let go of my hand. This is clearly something he does as a sign of engagement with the people (or at least the women!) he meets. My fellow MPs who saw the meeting joked about it for days.

Queen Elizabeth's visit in 1995 was perhaps the most controversial visit by a head of state. It was her second visit to South Africa; she had in 1947 accompanied her father, King George VI, and her mother, Elizabeth Bowes-Lyon. After the National Party came to power the next year, there would be no further visits. In 1961, Wilhelm's grandfather returned triumphantly from a visit to the UK, during which South Africa had left the Commonwealth. Soon afterwards, South Africa became a republic. After the 1994 elections, South Africa returned to the Commonwealth, and it was in her capacity as head of the Commonwealth that the Queen was now paying a visit.

Many ANC leaders, including the Speaker, Frene Ginwala, and the deputy president, Thabo Mbeki, had been in exile in the UK, so there was great excitement in the run-up to the visit. Remembering my grandmother, I was more ambivalent, and objected when we were asked to sing 'God Save Our Queen' (on account of being part of the Commonwealth). I had no problem with singing 'God Save *the* Queen', but not '*Our* Queen'.

On the day of her arrival, the live television coverage showed, for what seemed like hours, the royal yacht nearing Cape Town harbour. The vessel was docked in the bustling Victoria and Alfred Waterfront for the duration of her stay. This restaurant and shopping area is extremely popular and has

Left: My beloved grandparents on their wedding day on 18 May 1940 in Fochville.

Bottom left: With my dad, Bennie van Niekerk, in Amanzimtoti, one of the rare occasions we spent happy times together. This is one of only three photographs I have of the two of us together.

Bottom right: With my mum, Lenie Fourie.

Top left: Me, aged three. The photo was taken in Durban during our first holiday without my dad, after my parents divorced.

Top right: One of many dancing roles during my years at Bloemhof Girls' High in Stellenbosch. I loved ballet and seriously considered dancing as a career until matric, when my bleeding toes got the better of me.

Right: Wilmé and Wian with Santa, played by Archbishop Tutu, at a Christmas party of the Truth and Reconciliation Commission.

Bottom: Our family in Kirstenbosch. Back: Wilhelm, Nadine, Philip. Middle: Melissa, me, Mum. Front: Wilmé, Wian.

Opposite bottom: My wedding day, 29 December 1987. It was a beautiful summer's day and the reception was on the Neethlingshof wine farm. Back: My grandfather, Jan Brandt; Wilhelm's aunt, Martha Rust; Philip's mother, Charlotte Fourie; me; Wilhelm. Front: Wilhelm's grandmother, Betsie Verwoerd; my grandmother, Lenie Brandt.

Top: At my first ANC conference in 1993, with Franklin Adams and Doreen Hani. Willie Esterhuyse, an observer at the opening session, teased me afterwards: 'White people really can't toyi-toyi.' This was the conference where I was elected to the Provincial Executive.

Bottom: After my first ANC speech, Madiba gave me a big hug. This rally, held in the City Council building in Cape Town in 1993, was the start of my political career.

Top: The 'umlungu's' children playing in Kayamandi, Stellenbosch. Wilmé and Wian were looked after by friends in the township while I was busy in meetings. White children were a rare sight in townships and they loved all the attention.

Bottom: My inauguration as an ANC MP. This was the Afrikaans-speaking ANC group, with i.a., Randall van den Heever, Andries Nel, Patricia Coetzee, Dirk du Toit, Danny Olifant and Jannie Momberg.

Top: Presenting my credentials to President Mary McAleese, Dublin, March 2001. During the ceremony, she broke protocol and asked if I had Irish roots, since I 'looked so Irish'.

Opposite top: With Pravin Gordhan on the final night of the constitutional negotiations. The photo was taken at 3am – thus the tired-looking faces.

Opposite bottom: Wilmé (5 years old) meeting Madiba in parliament in 1996. Madiba said to her: 'Hallo Wilmé, I am Nelson Mandela,' to which she indignantly replied: 'Of course I know who you are, I do watch TV, you know.' Madiba thought it was very funny.

Above: Archbishop Tutu and Bono with staff at the embassy. I am on the left, with Wilhelm. Bono had come to tea and received a special blessing from the Arch, who was staying with us. Emily Nomajoni is on the left.

Opposite top: Madiba came to Ireland during the special Olympics, accompanied by Zelda la Grange and Cyril Ramaphosa (here with me, Wilmé and Wilhelm at the airport). We had an eventful few days together, including a funny incident when Madiba met the actor Pierce Brosnan.

Opposite bottom: With Madiba in Cape Town, December 2006. Madiba joked that he was getting old and that young women no longer found him handsome. 'I think you are still very handsome,' I objected. 'Yes, but you are not so young any more,' he teased.

Above: I was very moved to meet Aung San Suu Kyi at an Art for Amnesty event in 2012 in Dublin. This was her first European tour after 15 years of house arrest in Burma without her children and husband.

(Joao Piña for Art for Amnesty)

Opposite top: With Brian May of Queen. Queen supported the 46664 campaign, and after the first 46664 concert in Cape Town, Madiba invited them to a game farm in the Northern Province. One night Peter Gabriel, Annie Lennox, The Corrs and myself were taken stargazing by Brian, who has a PhD in Astrophysics.

Opposite bottom: A kiss from 007! Roger Moore was recruited by Audrey Hepburn to become a UNICEF ambassador. I became good friends with him and his wife, Christiana, during a few trips they made to Dublin to support UNICEF events. Roger is charming, humble and has a fantastic sense of humour. During this press launch for a UNICEF campaign in Dublin, he joked endlessly with the photographers and then mischievously gave me a kiss. It made for great headlines the next day. *(Photocall Ireland)*

Above: With Liam Neeson at a UNICEF photo shoot in 2011. Liam is a gentle, kind man who has no celebrity airs around him. He put all the children at ease during the shoot. *(Photocall Ireland)*

Opposite top: A romantic weekend in Venice, with Gerry. Our hotel was flooded twice and it rained all the time, but we had fantastic fun.

Opposite bottom: In the African bush, July 2009.

Left: My favourite photograph of Gerry, taken at the Jock of the Bushveld camp in 2009.

Bottom: At a New Year's dinner in Monte Carlo in 2010. We laughed so much, I thought the French waiters were going to throw us out.

CASINO

Above: The same New Year's eve. As we left the restaurant, a sting quartet started playing and Gerry started dancing with me. He promised: 'It will be a good year for us'. Little did we know what was waiting.

Right: I needed somewhere I could go to remember Gerry and our time together. A year after his death, I erected a memorial bench for him in our favourite park. A few months later, the bench was burnt down. I replaced it and still go there as often as I can.

For Gerry
(5 June 1956 – 30 April 2010)
"Seasons may change winter to spring, but I love you"
Melinda

Top: At a Community Care Point for children in Swaziland, in December 2010. This was seven days after the inquest into Gerry's death.

Bottom: With the Irish international rugby player Donncha O' Callaghan in Zimbabwe on a UNICEF trip in June 2011. Two weeks after I returned I was fired, despite the fact that we had almost doubled UNICEF's income during that year.

a bustling nightlife, while being part of the working harbour. On the second night of the Queen's visit, someone unwisely made an announcement over the public address system asking people to keep the noise down so that Her Majesty could sleep. A friend of mine who was in one of the clubs said that there was a momentary silence as the message sank in but that, afterwards, the noise levels doubled.

The rest of the official visit was more subdued. We attended a church service led by Archbishop Tutu and had drinks at the British high commissioner's residence in lavish Bishopscourt, where we were introduced to the Queen and Prince Philip. I was shocked when Prince Philip expressed a controversial opinion on AIDS and birth control in Africa to one of my African colleagues, who was standing next to me in the line-up. My colleague was equally taken aback and – perhaps wisely – decided not to respond.

Although all these visits were indicative of South Africa's joyous return to the international community, there was a difficult process happening domestically. The Truth and Reconciliation Committee (TRC) had been set up in 1995 as a restorative justice body to deal with the human rights abuses that took place between 1960 and 1994, from across the political spectrum. There were three committees: the Human Rights Violation Committee, where victims could tell their stories; the Reparation and Rehabilitation Committee; and the Amnesty Committee. Controversially, the Amnesty Committee could decide on whether to grant amnesty to perpetrators of human rights abuses if it could be proven that the deeds had been politically motivated and proportional, and that there had been full disclosure on the part of the applicant. The first public hearing of the TRC was held on 15 April 1996 in East London City Hall. It was broadcast live and was the beginning of an emotional and gruelling journey for our new nation. As Archbishop Tutu warned: 'The truth is going to hurt.'

The last person to give testimony during the first hearing, chaired by Archbishop Tutu, was a former Robben Island prisoner, Singqokwana Ernst Malgas. The dignified elderly man, who was wheelchair-bound, spoke quietly about the three decades of arrest, detention, house arrest, assault, torture and harassment he had experienced, including losing his young son after acid was poured over him. When he described the details of his torture, he broke down and wept. Archbishop Tutu, dressed in his purple clerical robes, bent his head and started crying too. Afterwards, I heard Tutu say he was annoyed with himself for crying, since he felt that this distracted attention from the victim. Watching this on television, I felt that Tutu weeping gave all of us 'permission' to cry, and as the horror of the past gradually unfolded, endless tears were shed. Never again could anyone say: 'We did not know' or 'That's nonsense'.

For most Africans, this was a cathartic time. For whites, it was deeply shocking and confusing – not helped by the fact that those who should have given leadership at that stage, such as FW de Klerk, were fighting for their political lives. Instead of helping the people who had voted for him and his party for years to make sense of what they were hearing, he and other former National Party Cabinet members went into a legalistic defence mode. Although the TRC was not without its shortcomings, I believe that it played a crucial role in the reconciliation process.

Wilhelm decided to take two years' leave from the university to work with the TRC. It was an important change for him. Even though the work was gruelling, he found it very rewarding, and it set him on a new path of work, which he continues today. On a personal level, it was easier for me to have him working in Cape Town too. But we were now both in stressful and demanding jobs, and this was increasingly having an impact on our marriage.

On 29 March 1999, Mandela gave his farewell speech as president. He urged us all to remember that 'The long walk to freedom continues'. His successor-in-waiting, Thabo Mbeki, responded on behalf of the ANC in his usual eloquent style. 'You have walked along the road of the heroes and the heroines. You have borne the pain of those who have known fear and learnt to conquer it. You have marched in front when comfort was in the midst of the ranks. You have laughed to contend against a river of tears. You have cried to broadcast a story of joy. And now you leave this hallowed place to continue to march in front of a different detachment of the same army of the sun,' he said, expressing what so many felt.

Wilmé and Wilhelm were in the gallery. After the emotional session, we went for lunch with my fellow MPs in a big marquee, to celebrate the end of the first five years of the new South Africa. Then we were back into election mode.

11

As in 1994, the ANC had an extensive internal list process for the 1999 election. I was conscious of the role that the Verwoerd surname had played in the first election; this time round, the election would be a test of how well I had done my job. To my great delight and surprise, I moved twenty places up the list – which meant that I was again certain of securing a place in the next parliament.

As in 1994, we worked extremely hard, but during this campaign the reception we received was not always so warm. Many people were disillusioned that their lives had not changed. Of course, the task was huge and it was impossible to eradicate the legacy of decades of neglect in just five years. Nonetheless, people were understandably impatient. I was often told: 'You can't eat the constitution!'

When the results became known a few days later, the ANC had increased its vote nationally to 66 per cent. The National Party experienced a devastating defeat as the official opposition and was replaced by the Democratic Party, which had been the fifth-largest party in 1994. In the Western Cape, we increased our vote by just over 9 per cent (from 33 to 42 per cent), becoming the biggest party in the region. However, since we were not a majority, we had to form a coalition government in the provincial parliament.

I was leading the campaign in Stellenbosch. Even though we improved our results significantly, we were never going to achieve an overall majority. To my joy, however, the ANC won a majority on the farms. Even today, this feels to me like an extraordinary achievement. I will never forget the reaction of one farmer in particular. Best known for his delicious Pinotage, he had formed his own political party in Stellenbosch during the local government elections and had assumed that he had everything sewn up. Instead, the ANC gained a majority. As the result was announced, one of our election monitors phoned me and said: 'Just listen to how he is taking the news.' In the background, I could hear this local big-wig farmer yelling his head off.

He had clearly lost his cool and was screaming: 'This is all Melanie Verwoerd's fault! I will get her for this, if it is the last thing I do!' Ironically, this aggrieved individual was part of a delegation of wine farmers to the South African Wine Fair in Dublin three years later – by which time I was South African ambassador to Ireland.

On 16 June 1999, we flew from Cape Town to Pretoria for the inauguration of Thabo Mbeki as president. As with President Mandela's inauguration five years earlier, the ceremony was held in Pretoria, but, as one would expect, it was significantly more subdued. I took my mother, who loved every minute of it, with me.

We then settled back into the rhythm of parliamentary life. In the second term, I was, in addition to my other committees, now also assigned to the Environmental and Tourism Committee. I really enjoyed the environmental work. I have always loved nature and could finally use my position to protect it. At my request, I was also allocated to a new constituency on the West Coast. My new constituency was huge: it would take me three to five hours to drive from the southernmost to the northernmost point. I was relieved to get away from Stellenbosch, but the driving late at night, after long days spent on farms, was exhausting. Often I had to wind down the windows in the hope that the freezing night air would keep me awake. To this day, I hate driving long distances, especially at night.

One aspect of my new constituency work was rather unexpected. My constituency office was in the grain-growing town of Malmesbury. Towards the end of the first term of office, and during the second term, there were a number of scandals surrounding corruption and political leaders. One of them involved Allan Boesak, who was chairperson of the ANC in the Western Cape during the 1994 election and gave me my 'break'. Allan was accused of misappropriating R400 000 of donor funding before the 1994 elections. He was found guilty of fraud on 24 March 1999 and jailed in 2000, serving just over one year of a three-year sentence in Malmesbury Correctional Facility. Although the incarceration of these important leaders illustrated the new government's commitment to dealing with corruption, it was still sad to see these men, who had survived apartheid, being jailed. Allan received a presidential pardon in 2005, but has never returned fully to politics.

Even though I enjoyed the interaction with the electorate as much as always, I knew something had to change. The long hours in parliament, the hours on the road, and trying to be a good mother to my two small children were starting to take their toll. My health was suffering and our marriage was under tremendous strain. Although I knew and understood the parliamentary system well by then, I felt that the excitement of the first five years had disappeared. We were becoming a 'normal' parliament. This was to be expected, but with the major transformational work now completed, and parliament becoming more of a rubber stamp for the executive, I was starting to feel uneasy and needed a new challenge.

It was not only parliament that was changing. Under the leadership of the new president, the ANC was also rapidly moving in new directions. Thabo Mbeki was born to activist parents. His father, Govan Mbeki, a leader in the ANC and SA Communist Party, had spent 24 years in jail on Robben Island. After his father's arrest, the nineteen-year-old Thabo Mbeki had fled into exile, to return only 28 years later. He was educated in the UK, but later made Zambia his base. When Mbeki was finally able to return home to South Africa and was reunited with his father after decades of no contact, Mbeki senior told a reporter: 'You must remember that Thabo Mbeki is no longer my son. He is my comrade!' A news article pointed out that this was an expression of pride, explaining: 'For Govan Mbeki, a son was a mere biological appendage; to be called a comrade, on the other hand, was the highest honour.'

I have always had a soft spot for Mbeki. I liked his razor-sharp intellect and felt there was a softer side to him that was rarely visible in the day-to-day running of the country. Of course, Nelson Mandela's successor would always be in an almost impossible position. Those shoes were just too big to fill. Mbeki focused on the desperate need for economic transformation of the country and was jokingly referred to as 'Mr Delivery'. He achieved remarkable success, with 4.5 per cent economic growth, massive foreign direct investment and a rapidly expanding black middle class. His vision for an 'African renaissance' led to the creation of NEPAD (the New Partnership for African Development), which in turn played a big role in the creation of the African Union (the successor to the OAU), which would be crucial in repositioning not only South Africa, but the whole of Africa.

Meanwhile, the ANC was rapidly changing from a broad church of people who openly debated topics and issues to what many felt was a more disciplined, fearful organisation. I was never sure to what extent this came from Mbeki or the group of people with whom he surrounded himself and who made it clear that dissent would not be tolerated.

However, many agreed that Mbeki had a tendency to believe conspiracy theories – which would lead to some of his biggest mistakes. Friends have said that the unexplained disappearance of his only son, Kwanda Mbeki, while trying to join his father in exile in 1981, left deep scars. I would frequently play a mental game in caucus to see how long it would take before Mbeki would blame one or other party, such as the whites, the press, the pharmaceutical companies or even evil forces among the ANC, for a particular problem.

It has been argued that this is a legacy of living in exile for so long and having to be constantly alert to infiltrators and informers. Whatever the reason, I believe that his suspicious nature would lead to the HIV/AIDS debate that would tarnish his presidency and, together with his support for Zimbabwe, would unfortunately largely become his legacy.

South Africa has more people living with HIV than any other country. In the early 1990s, the AIDS pandemic was taken very seriously by the ANC. We had a detailed policy in place on the issue for when we were in government. As candidates, we were encouraged to speak about the growing AIDS problem and to encourage safe sex. However, after the 1994 election – as Mandela would years later admit, with great regret – the issues of reconciliation and economic transformation took priority, and AIDS took a back seat.

As the devastating effect of the pandemic became visible, protests on the issue started to grow. In particular, the Treatment Action Campaign, led by a phenomenal stalwart living with AIDS, Zackie Achmat, became vocal in its protests against government inaction on HIV/AIDS.

In October 1999, a few months after his election as president, Thabo Mbeki raised his concerns about the toxicity of AZT (the anti-retroviral drug commonly used at the time) in a speech to the National Council of Provinces. This was the start of a journey that led to devastating consequences for those living with AIDS as well as for the prevention of future infections in South Africa. It signalled the start of the president's expression of his unorthodox views on HIV/AIDS and his alliance with a group of dissident scientists. He raised questions as to the link between HIV and AIDS – and eventually questioned the existence of AIDS as well as the motives and the role of pharmaceutical companies in Africa generally, and specifically in the fight against HIV/AIDS.

This resulted in a radical shift in policy and stalled the provision of anti-retroviral drugs to those living with AIDS, including pregnant mothers. This of course had a devastating effect on the country, and led to a rapid growth in deaths linked to HIV/AIDS, and new infections. For example, in the early 1990s it was estimated that less than 3 per cent of pregnant women at ante-natal clinics in South Africa were HIV-positive. According to Andrew Fein-stein, a former South African MP who wrote the book *After the Party*, by 2005 that figure had grown to 28 per cent. Mbeki's stance resulted in legal and constitutional challenges, but also sparked a huge outcry of disbelief and shock, both domestically and internationally.

Inside the ANC, many of us were also upset and concerned. We tried to influence those around the president, but it fell on deaf ears. Eventually, under growing public and international criticism and ridicule, President Mbeki announced on 26 September 2000 that he would no longer partici-pate in the public debate on the scientific issues surrounding HIV/AIDS. Hoping that this represented a change of heart, many of us breathed a sigh of relief. But two days later, he addressed the ANC caucus on the issue. Many MPs were hoping this would be an opportunity for the issue to be debated at last, and would signal the beginning of change.

In *After the Party*, Feinstein published the detailed notes he took at what would be a disastrous caucus, and a turning point for many MPs. I was sit-ting in my usual spot, across from the president, slightly behind the old Speaker's chair. I rarely took notes at caucus meetings any more, since there was increasing suspicion and paranoia about leaks to the media. But as the president started addressing us, I drew a mind-map of his argument in or-der to be clear about what he was saying.

Mbeki's arguments were often complex and layered, and one usually had to listen carefully not to miss some of the nuances. Not on this occasion, though. Within minutes, it became clear that his position on HIV/AIDS had not changed – in fact, it had hardened. The conspiracy theories came thick and fast: the pharmaceutical companies, the press, the CIA, the USA, whites, the IMF, the West – even the members of the Treatment Action Campaign. He insisted that the HIV virus had never been isolated and therefore that HIV/AIDS did not exist, but was merely an immune deficiency caused by poverty and social circumstances. He argued that that was where the government's focus should be.

As his speech gathered momentum, more and more ANC members started applauding him. As he took his seat, applause broke out and people shouted: 'Viva Thabo, viva!' Then, instead of the anticipated debate, the chairperson, Thabang Makwetla, closed the meeting by saying that the applause clearly indicated that there was no need for any further debate.

I was deeply troubled, and as I left through the door behind the Speaker's chair, I heard a male MP behind me say: 'Thank God, we can now do away with this condom nonsense!' The meeting shook me to the core. I had lost friends to AIDS and had seen babies dying from it. I had visited the orphans in Nazareth House, which was close to my home in Devil's Peak. How could I live with this position?

During that time, one of the government ministers, Alec Erwin, said over a drink in the parliament pub one day that he was sure I would be appointed to Cabinet in the near future. It was just a throwaway comment and he might not have been serious, but it worried me. Walking back to my office afterwards, I knew I had arrived at a crossroads. I was not happy in parliament any more. Apart from being unhappy with the AIDS debate, I was under enormous strain in my personal life. I was not enjoying constituency work and was getting tired of the strain of being in the public eye. All of this was taking a toll on my health. I knew something had to change. I love South Africa and Africa. I believed in what we were trying to do in the ANC and knew that I wanted to keep on contributing to the country. But how?

Soon afterwards, on my way to my constituency office, I was listening to tapes of readings by the Celtic theologian John O'Donohue. John was elaborating, in his soft Connemara accent, on the various elements of Celtic spirituality. Suddenly I had a clear thought: 'Why not become an ambassador?' At first I dismissed the idea. I was too young, Wilhelm would hate it, and where would I go? But the idea became more and more compelling. *Maybe I should go to Ireland!* I had only once before been to Ireland, in the late 1980s, when Wilhelm and I had been on holiday there. I knew very little about Ireland, but immediately felt an incredible sense of peace and excitement. But did we even have an embassy there? Was there a vacancy?

The next day, my friend Carl Niehaus came for lunch. He was now ambassador to the Netherlands, and back home on leave. I casually asked him whether we had an embassy in Dublin. He said we did.

'Who is the ambassador?' I asked.

Carl could not recall, but suggested that I contact the Department of Foreign Affairs. As soon as he left, I did. Bizarrely, the woman in Protocol was not sure and suggested that I phone the embassy directly. When someone in Dublin with an Irish accent answered, I asked who the ambassador was. She answered: 'Oh, we haven't had an ambassador for a long time, but I'm sure we will have someone soon.' My head started to spin. This was starting to sound too good to be true. Now I needed to raise the issue with Wilhelm. Wilhelm had always said that the one thing he never wanted to be was the husband of an ambassador. So, later that afternoon, I cautiously raised the possibility with him. To my great surprise, he reacted positively. He had been frustrated with his work at the University of Stellenbosch, to which he had returned following his time at the Truth and Reconciliation Commission, and wanted a change. He was interested in the peace process in Ireland and wanted to study Celtic spirituality.

My next step was to discuss the matter with the ANC leadership. Wilmé was due to attend the birthday party of the son of the director-general of the Department of Foreign Affairs, Sipho Pityana, the next day. When I dropped Wilmé off, I spoke to Sipho briefly, indicating my interest. He responded that he would be delighted to have me in the Foreign Service and undertook to set the process in motion. I was thrilled.

Following the transition in 1994, the ANC had made various political appointments to the diplomatic corps. The Foreign Service had to be transformed quickly, especially at the ambassadorial level, since it was all white and almost exclusively male. But there were rumours that the president was not happy with the many MPs leaving parliament at that time, so the matter of my becoming ambassador had to be handled sensitively. A few weeks later, Sipho phoned to say things were on track, and to sit tight. A few months later, he phoned again to say that all was well. I was happy and started to work on the logistical arrangements.

A few days later I got another call. 'I'm sorry, Melanie,' Sipho said, 'but the minister won't sign off on your appointment.'

'Why?' I asked, surprised.

Sipho explained that the minister felt I was playing an important role in parliament and that she would invoke the anger of the president if she agreed to my transfer. 'If this is going to work, you'll have to get the president on-side,' Sipho urged. 'Go speak to him.'

The next day I spoke to Charles Nqakula, the presidential liaison in parliament. He was happy to ask for a meeting, but warned me that the president would most probably not agree to it once he heard the reason for the request. However, a few hours later he called back, sounding a bit surprised, confirming that the president would see me the next day.

I was nervous. I knew that it was not a good day to see him. His media spokesperson, Parks Mankahlana, had died a few days earlier. It was widely reported that it was due to AIDS-related complications, but neither the president nor his family would confirm this. The president was on his way to the funeral and the moment I stepped into his office, I could see he was troubled. After a few brief courtesies, he asked why I wanted to see him. I had thought for most of the night about how to address my request. Trusting his deep philosophical and poetic nature, I said what had been on my mind for the past few weeks. 'Comrade President, I feel like I have lost my song.'

The president looked at me intensely. 'Go on,' he said.

'I believe that everyone has a unique song to sing in this life. But I feel I have lost mine. I know in what key it should be: I want to keep working for Africa and its people. But the notes have gone missing and I need to find them again.'

The president looked at me quietly for a while. I was starting to wonder if the metaphorical approach was a mistake. I could hear his helicopter outside starting to prepare for takeoff. 'You know, if you had said anything else, I would have said no to you today,' President Mbeki said. 'But I also believe that we have a song to sing, and it is serious when we lose that song. I will sign the order.'

Our eyes met. Not for the first time, I wondered why the world so rarely saw this other, softer, intriguing side to the man. 'Thank you,' I said, and got up to leave. Then I remembered. 'President, can I please go to Ireland?' I asked.

'Why Ireland?'

'Well, it's the country of Yeats,' I responded, knowing his love for the poet.

A faint smile crossed his face. 'I think they wanted to send you to a bigger embassy, but fine. It is, after all, no country for old men.' He then shook my hand and left through a side door.

After this meeting, things moved fast. A month later, I was called up for a month-long training course in Pretoria. There were a few political appointments at the course, including Priscilla Jana, who would later become my successor as South African ambassador after a posting in the Netherlands. The well-loved singer Miriam Makeba – Mama Africa – also joined us in one session. The training would be my first insight into the slightly bizarre, often pretentious and outdated world of international diplomacy. I was irritated when our first lecturer opened his session by saying, 'A diplomat is someone who is willing to lie for his or her country.' I argued vehemently to the contrary. The international relations and political sessions were fascinating, but when it came to issues such as the finer points of entertaining, I nearly died of boredom. Of course, this section was intended for the wives of ambassadors, but there was no chance that Wilhelm would dream of attending. I bit my lip, taking notes on starching tablecloths, formal place settings, invitation cards and attendance books. But when the presenter started to demonstrate how to roll up individual hand towels for the bathrooms, I reached the end of my patience and slipped away.

The last few weeks of February were a flurry of packing and farewells. In March 2001, Wilhelm, Wilmé, Wian and I boarded the plane in Cape Town to start the next phase of our lives.

PART TWO

Ireland

'When a stranger approaches, and we think he is our brother, and all conflicts disappear, that is the moment when night ends and day begins.'

Shimon Peres as quoted by Paulo Coelho in Like the Flowing River

12

'Ambassador, you are so welcome to Ireland.' With these first words as we stepped off the plane, I fell in love with Ireland. The driver from the embassy and a few staff members met us at the VIP lounge at the airport and took us to the Conrad Hotel. There was no official residence, and the previous ambassador had left almost eighteen months earlier, so until I found somewhere to live, the hotel was home.

Of course, for the first few weeks the children were delighted to be living in a hotel, but the novelty soon wore off and it became cramped. We needed to find a house. We also had to get used to the cold weather. We had left South Africa in the middle of a heat wave, with temperatures well over 40 °C, so it was a shock to land in the freezing temperatures of March in Ireland, complete with snow flurries.

One day the manager at the Conrad Hotel asked if I would mind if they bought some shoes for my children. He explained that they were concerned about my children's lack of shoes in the cold. At first I did not understand, but then it struck me: like many small children in South Africa my children rarely wore shoes in summer. Only under severe duress would they put them on. Having come from the heat, they would run around the hotel without shoes, but of course would wear boots when they went out. I explained this to the manager, who looked amused but relieved.

There were other amusing incidents early on involving cultural clashes. One morning, I took Wian, who was bursting with energy, for a walk to the nearby St Stephen's Green. On the way, we passed a delivery man, who left milk and newspapers outside a small newsagent that was not yet open for the day.

'Mum!' Wian yelled. 'Stop that man!'

'Why?'

'He left his milk and papers!'

I explained that he was delivering them to the shop for later. Wian looked bewildered. 'But it will be stolen,' he insisted. It took some time to convince him otherwise.

Wilmé was more intrigued by the lack of racial diversity in Ireland. She would walk around the streets of Dublin and repeatedly ask: 'Where are all the black people?' One day a shop assistant, hearing her South African accent, asked what she thought of Ireland. With the frankness of youth, she answered: 'You are very nice, but too white.'

Wanting to fit in, the children quickly adopted an Irish accent. About two months after we arrived, I heard Wian asking a friend over the phone: 'Is your dad going to the pub tonight?' This question would never have arisen in South Africa, but I was also struck that he said it in a strong Dublin accent. A few days later I listened in amazement when he placed an order at McDonalds. I could barely understand what he was saying, his accent was so strong. Today, my children sound completely Irish when they speak English, although they quickly adopt a more South African tone and turn of phrase when they are in Cape Town.

After almost two months in the hotel, we were desperate to move into a house. I had looked at numerous houses in the 'Embassy Belt' in the leafy Ballsbridge area, but with Ireland at the height of the Celtic Tiger, I could not believe the cost of rent. One day an agent showed us a property called Ashurst on Military Road in Killiney. Although it was much further away from town than the properties in Ballsbridge, it was spectacular. I was told it had been the retirement house of the late Archbishop John Charles McQuaid. It was only later that I understood the role this former Archbishop of Dublin and Primate of Ireland had played between the 1940s and 1972 in political and social life in Ireland.

A property developer and businessman, Liam Smyth, who had renovated the house and, sadly, turned the little chapel into a gym, now owned the house. The former servants' quarters had been transformed into a pub, complete with beer on tap and the pew benches as seats. The grounds, however, were wonderful. Liam had once spent a holiday in South Africa, so after a bit of haggling, he reduced the price significantly and I got the house for a steal.

We had to find a school for the children. Since it was close to the end of the academic year, we could not find a space anywhere in a state school and had to settle for private schools. Eventually we found a space in Aravon, a small school close to Killiney. The buildings of the school are owned by the singer Chris de Burgh, who went there as a child. The building itself is old and dark, but the grounds are beautiful and there was a big emphasis on sport, which suited my children. In the end, though, it was thanks to the school dog, Zac, a huge white retriever, who came to greet us on our first visit, that we enrolled Wilmé and Wian there.

In the meantime I was also trying to settle into diplomatic life. The first duty of any ambassador to the new country is to present his or her credentials to the head of state, which in Ireland at the time was President Mary McAleese. In all countries the ceremony is solemn, but the pomp and ceremony accompanying the event differs greatly from place to place. In preparation for the event, I met with deputy head of protocol Joe Brennan at Iveagh House, the headquarters of the Department of Foreign Affairs. Joe is a lovely, eccentric man, who has various talents, including playing the piano. The meeting took place twenty minutes after the agent had shown us Ashurst for the first time, so I was very surprised when Joe asked how we liked the house.

'How did you know?' I asked.

'Ah, you will soon realise, Dublin – and Ireland – is a very small place,' he smiled.

He took me through my steps and lines for the next day. I would be escorted by motorcycle riders and then accompanied into a big hall, where the president and my family would already be waiting. 'Now, there is a specific spot on the carpet where you have to stand,' he explained while showing it to me on a photograph. 'Most importantly, you have to speak first. People forget, and then you and the president will stand there in an awkward silence. Really awful!' That seemed odd to me, even a bit rude, but Joe explained that the reasoning is that I am presenting to her. It struck me that it was all extremely formal – in contrast to the otherwise informal and relaxed nature of the Irish.

One thing that was different from the usual running order, though, was that there was no inspection of the guards. There had been a massive outbreak of foot-and-mouth disease a few weeks earlier in the UK, resulting in the slaughtering of up to 93 000 animals a week at the height of the epidemic.

Ireland's response was remarkable. Strict measures were put in place, with disinfectant mats everywhere – even at some people's houses. All public events were either cancelled or postponed, and in the end Ireland had only one reported case of foot-and-mouth. Taking into account that even St Patrick's Day and some of the Six Nations rugby internationals were postponed, I did not complain about the fact that I had no guard of honour to inspect.

On the day, I was nervous. I was wearing the same green outfit I had worn at our swearing-in as members of parliament in South Africa seven years earlier. I kept reminding myself to speak first, and ran through my lines endlessly. We had to be there at an exact time, so our cars and motorbike escort paused for a few minutes in the beautiful Phoenix Park before entering the gates leading to the presidential residence. As we entered the big hall, the president was standing facing me. Luckily, I found the spot on the carpet. 'Speak first, speak first!' I reminded myself.

But before I could say anything, President McAleese said: 'Ambassador, I know they tell you to speak first, but can I just say you are very welcome and you look very Irish. Do you have Irish ancestors?' I immediately knew why people liked President McAleese so much. She is warm, kind and highly intelligent – and she breaks protocol from time to time. All characteristics I value highly.

I assured her that I had no Irish connections and we got down to formal business. I said the obligatory lines and then added a few of my own, referring to a theological article she had written a few years earlier. I could see she was interested in what I had to say, but of course there was no time for discussion. After the ceremony, we all had tea together. The president had a warm, relaxed chat with my children and Wilhelm. After some photographs, we said our goodbyes and headed back to the Conrad Hotel for another reception. And so my life as a diplomat formally began.

Since it had taken a few weeks for me to present my credentials, I had already met my staff. I was warned before I arrived that there were 'various challenges' in the Dublin embassy. It was immediately clear that this was the understatement of the year. Embassies are peculiar environments. There are of course the foreign diplomats, who are replaced every three or four years. They are assisted by locally recruited staff, who are usually appointed on a permanent basis. Given that they see the diplomats come and go and have not only the 'home advantage', but also the institutional memory, the locally recruited staff often have a very strong power base. Dublin was particularly difficult in this regard.

As I discovered when I had called months earlier, there had not been an ambassador for more than eighteen months, and there were only two other diplomats. The chargé d'affaires (the person in charge) was an inexperienced diplomat on his first posting abroad. This caused all kinds of difficulties for the smooth running of the embassy.

On my first day, before I had even met anyone, one of the staff greeted me in tears and said she felt bullied by another member of staff. This was to set the tone for the next few months. Some staff members reported that there had been physical fights, staff not talking to each other, pornography being watched on work computers and people not working at all. I never got to the bottom of whether any of this was true, but the place was clearly dysfunctional.

I made my position clear. Firstly, I wanted to be inclusive and more egalitarian. I did not care how they addressed me, either as 'ambassador' or by my name was fine. (Interestingly, as the months went by, the 'troublemakers' insisted on calling me 'ambassador', but as a mark of disrespect rather than respect.) Secondly, things had to change. No one was to touch or scream at one of their colleagues. If conflict could not be resolved, they would bring it to my attention before it escalated. People had to be at work on time. An internet policy was put in place, and I made it clear that I would monitor activity. If I discovered any form of pornography being viewed, disciplinary action would be taken. I also insisted on regular staff meetings and had a weekend of team-building.

After months of trying to resolve the problems with the second-in-charge, I eventually, and with great difficulty, arranged for him to be transferred to another, bigger embassy, where he would have fewer responsibilities and therefore be under less pressure. I felt this was the most sensitive way to handle the problem. To my relief, he consented. The only problem was that the position was not filled for more than a year, which meant that I was the only diplomat on the political side for almost half of my term. This was exhausting and ridiculous.

In the meantime, I was also getting used to the endless cocktail parties, courtesy visits by diplomats from one to the other, and formal dinners. I particularly hated the dinners and cocktail functions. I found them a complete waste of time and could not help wondering how much good the money spent on all these functions could do elsewhere. I became an expert at saying hello to the host at cocktail functions and then making an escape through the back or kitchen door. I later found out that the various embassy drivers who would be waiting outside would take bets on how long (or short) I would stay.

Diplomatic life in my view is mostly outdated. Before the arrival of the internet and the modern information era, diplomats exchanged information. Secret and coded telexes were sent to the embassies, which would then disseminate the information to the government of the host country. It is, in addition, the job of the ambassador and diplomatic staff to build and maintain relations with the country in order to foster strong political and economic ties. But in the modern era, this has become largely obsolete – especially with countries that are not at war. Information is now readily available on the internet, and officials in government departments will often form relations directly with their counterparts. In all my time, I think there was only one confidential telex sent, and the Irish Foreign Service was already aware of the issue before I received the information.

I realised this very quickly, and decided to put a different focus on my time in the embassy. I knew that political and cultural links between South Africa and Ireland were strong. What South Africa needed above all was economic assistance. Given that Ireland was at the height of the 'Celtic Tiger' boom, I decided to focus on tourism and economic ties. This would not only have a practical impact back in South Africa, but also suited my activist personality. I could not think of anything worse than going to one social function after another for four years only to maintain relations. I wanted to change and improve things, and this was the only way I could see to do it.

I started off with a focus on tourism. Since research showed that a majority of Irish people at that time were having three holidays a year, of which at least one was abroad, it seemed logical to try to position South Africa as the holiday destination of choice. After all, it is a beautiful country, has an enormous variety of attractions and was great value for money. 'A pint is only a euro' was usually my best selling point.

First, I had to send the tourism representative in the embassy to South Africa. It seemed ludicrous that she had been marketing South Africa for three years without ever having been there. Needless to say, she came back with the passion and energy of a new convert. Then we had to work on a strategy. There was no budget to do any marketing, so we had to think creatively. Eventually I decided that we would do a road show across Ireland, doing tastings of South African wines. People would buy tickets to cover the cost and then we would do some tourism marketing when we had a captive – and slightly drunk – audience.

We involved a brilliant wine expert, Jean Smullen, who has a passion for South Africa. I went to the wine importers, who donated the wine, and got the retail industry across the country to sell the tickets. The brilliant tourism representative, a young woman called Claire Corcoran, and the newly appointed and equally brilliant media and information officer, Elizabeth Mulville, joined me on the road show. To save money, we used the trains and would carry boxes of wine, brochures, banners, pop-up stands, spittoons (which were never used – apparently Irish people never spit out wine) and a big TV. I could see the amazement not only of my staff but also hotel staff when they discovered that the one with the TV on the trolley was the ambassador.

We went all over the country, sometimes staying in horrible places. It was exhausting but hugely rewarding, and did the trick. A buzz started to develop about South Africa. I then focused on the travel agents, sending Claire out to meet them in groups and then inviting them to the official residence for presentations, and to wine and dine them. I felt this was a far better way to spend my entertainment allowance than entertaining other diplomats. After a few months, the figures for Irish people travelling to South Africa started to go up, and South African Tourism took note. Research also showed that the average Irish tourist spent about three times what a tourist from the UK did, so even though the numbers were comparatively small – still well below 20 000 per year – it became a worthwhile and growing market.

As a result of this growth, South African Tourism invited a number of Irish journalists to the annual travel fair, called Indaba, and I arranged for an exclusive supplement in the *Irish Independent*. This meant taking a journalist, a photographer and a woman called Breda Justin to South Africa. It was an extremely successful trip, although I had to laugh when she described the

Bushveld as just like the Burren in County Clare, and insisted that our rural African guide must have Irish blood since he looked like Breda's family member from Donegal. Not knowing where Ireland was, the poor man looked completely bewildered. Luckily, the supplement was spectacular and caused a stir, not only in Ireland but back in South Africa as well.

On the back of the supplement and the growth in tourism numbers, South African Airways, together with South African Tourism, sponsored, on my request, 100 Irish travel agents to go on a week-long trip to South Africa. They were divided into groups, but we all came together at the end in Sun City for a massive banquet. I had taken a group of journalists with me – including Joan Scales from the *Irish Times*, Paul Hopkins from the *Irish Independent*, Michael Collins from *Abroad* magazine and Cleo Murphy, an award-winning freelance travel writer. After a wonderful few days in Cape Town, Johannesburg, and on safari, we arrived for the party of all parties, sponsored by Sun City. Before the black-tie banquet, we were entertained by a fireworks display to the music of 'Carmina Burana' by Carl Orff. Looking at the spectacular display in the African sky, I felt so proud of how much we had achieved in a relatively short period. Exhausted but happy, I went to bed around 1am. When I went down for breakfast the next morning, I realised that the party was still going strong. 'Please take them home,' groaned the exhausted hotel manager.

Back in Ireland, we continued to build on our presence by having exhibitions wherever there was an opportunity. We still had almost no budget from the Department of Foreign Affairs, so my brief was always: 'It must be the best stand, but there is no money.' This resulted in a lot of begging for favours, and some hilarious incidents. For example, we quickly realised that big golf tournaments would be an excellent opportunity to promote tourism. We brainstormed on how to make an attractive stand with almost no money. After much debate, we agreed on a fake putting green against a backdrop of a big banner reflecting animals standing on a golf course in South Africa. We managed to get the banner donated, but where would we get fake grass? It was far too expensive. Suddenly Elizabeth asked to be excused. An hour later, she returned with a roll of fake grass under her arm. When I asked her where she got it, she crossed herself and said, 'God forgive me, but I spun a story at a funeral undertaker and they gave it to me.' The stand was beautiful, and we reused it many times. The promotions worked well and I learned an enormous amount about marketing. I insisted on standing with my staff in the rain and cold, not only to show support to them and to give them a break, but also to understand what the public wanted and felt.

The National Ploughing Championship is a big agricultural fair, where livestock and machinery are exhibited and farmers compete to see who is the best at ploughing. After hearing that around 200 000 people attend the Ploughing Championship, I decided that this would be a wonderful opportunity to tap into a new market for tourism. A new trade representative, Elizabeth O'Herlihy, had joined my staff by then, after Claire left to live in Northern Ireland. The two Elizabeths were a bit apprehensive, but then agreed – as long as I got them good wellies for the mud.

That year the fair was held in a field close to Tullow, which made it quite difficult to find if you did not know the country roads. I had a new chauffeur called Gordon King, a kind, energetic and fiery young man who became a good friend to the family. Gordon became exasperated as we crisscrossed the countryside to find the event. We stopped to ask for directions numerous times, but that only made matters worse. One old man on a bicycle said that he would not start from where we were, and another said to turn left at a field with a white horse in it, but the horse had clearly galloped off to more peaceful pastures by the time we arrived. Others said to just follow the boards with 'Father Murphy's last way' on it, but we soon realised that – as is often the practice in the country – young ones had turned the boards around, so they would point in the opposite direction.

When we finally found the field, it was an eye-opener for me. Even though the event reminded me of the agricultural fairs back in South Africa, it was a side of Ireland I had not seen before. This was clearly the heart of agricultural Ireland, and it was impressive. There were hundreds of thousands of people and animals attending, and we had great fun over the few days. I am not sure that we convinced many people to go to South Africa, but at least the two Elizabeths got numerous marriage proposals.

Ploughing championships aside, we were making progress on numerous fronts. With Elizabeth O'Herlihy's help, we started to grow investment into South Africa as well as exports from South Africa. We originally focused on wine promotion, hosting huge wine fairs, among other events. This involved

South African wine farmers coming to Ireland to showcase their wine on a specific day to both consumers and importers. The first one was a few months after I arrived in Ireland. Out of courtesy, I hosted a cocktail function the evening before for everyone involved. It was a strange experience to entertain the farmers whom I had fought against for years. As I stood at the door welcoming them all, it was both humorous and uncomfortable. As one of them eventually remarked: 'Jeez, I never thought I'd see the day that I would be given a handshake and a drink by Melanie-f**king-Verwoerd!' But it worked, and with the help of the importers, through a Wine Advisory Board that I created, as well as getting members of the public to request restaurants to put South African wine on their wine lists, wine sales grew dramatically.

I knew that as tourism to South Africa increased, we would see trade and investment picking up as well. I never did any 'cold selling' of trade or investment opportunities. When I discovered a potential investor, I arranged for them to go and play golf or have a holiday in South Africa. I knew that if they were worth their salt as entrepreneurs, they would find opportunities, and our job was to help them make it happen. I would of course entertain the business community, and on two occasions arranged for exclusive dinners with South African golfers Retief Goosen and Ernie Els.

One of these meals took place during the Irish Open. A prominent Irish businessman arrived and asked someone where the ambassador was. She pointed in my direction. I saw him coming towards me, but before I could say anything, he shook the hand of the man I was talking to and said, 'Ambassador, welcome to the Irish Open.'

When told I was the ambassador, he looked me up and down and said: 'Oh? You look hopelessly too young to be an ambassador, and you're a woman!'

Not hearing that for the first time, I smiled coldly and responded: 'Well, yes. They tried the old men for the last few centuries. That didn't work out too well, so they decided to give us young women a try.'

Sexism aside, these events, as well as a trade mission to South Africa and a few business breakfasts, worked well, and investment and trade grew rapidly.

Although there were many successes to celebrate, all was still not well back in the office. I had appointed many new members of staff, but a few of the old guard were causing difficulties. The level of pettiness and dysfunction was mind-boggling. Almost daily, I had to deal with ridiculous complaints and conflicts. These included complaints that one of the new staff members was using too much toilet paper, that someone was cutting their nails in the kitchen basin, that one of the staff left her desk every day at 4.50 (exactly) to go and do her daily ablutions (the complainant's words) and then go home – therefore working ten minutes less per day than the others – and that one of the men always only put a penny into the birthday gift envelopes. One middle-aged woman requested a meeting with me to suggest that I keep a record of all the female staff members' monthly cycles in order to accommodate their moods better. I did not take kindly to that.

The most ridiculous complaint was made shortly after a female staff member came to me to discuss her return from maternity leave. She had brought the baby with her, but halfway through the meeting the baby clearly needed to be fed. I offered to postpone the meeting, but she was happy just to feed the little one under a blanket while we continued talking. I had no objections, but during the meeting one of the other staff members stuck his head in to ask me something. Word must have spread, and at the next staff meeting one of the men raised a concern about 'undiplomatic behaviour'. Knowing he was particularly difficult, I sighed inwardly, and cautiously asked what he was referring to. 'Well, ambassador, I'm referring to an exchange of bodily fluids between an adult and a minor in your office.' I had no idea what he was referring to and, having just listened to a report on the radio about clerical child abuse, I got the fright of my life. In a panic, I tried to think how something like that could have happened and how to handle the situation, but one of the women whispered: 'Ambassador, I think he's referring to breastfeeding.' I was annoyed at the nonsense and told him to put his complaint in writing if he felt that strongly. He never did. The woman got her own back, though. When she returned, she would express breast milk and leave it next to his milk in the fridge with 'My Bodily Fluids' written on the bottle.

I tried to resolve these issues during staff meetings, but this was clearly an alien concept for the staff. I would ask everyone at the end of the meeting if they were happy, and if there were any outstanding issues. They would assure me there were none, but immediately after the meeting they would break up into smaller groups, only to come back with new complaints.

Things took a more ominous turn towards the end of 2001. Before I had arrived, a decision was made by the South African Department of Foreign Affairs to bring all embassies in line with local legislation. This meant that locally recruited staff had to pay tax like all other citizens in their country. Even though it is expected of embassies to deduct income tax at source, many do not, leaving it to the staff to declare. Of course many do not declare it. South Africa felt strongly about this, and the embassy in Dublin was also brought into line. Apparently there was outrage, and this was still simmering when I arrived. I was lobbied to reverse the decision, but I could not, nor did I want to.

Towards the end of that year, 'bodily fluid man' arranged a meeting with me to tell me that he represented the staff. I had no problem with a staff committee, and had in fact suggested it. But they wanted more. He indicated that they had joined a union and now wanted formal recognition. I knew that I had to run this past Pretoria and phoned the director-general on his cell phone. He listened and then replied firmly: 'Absolutely not!' He explained that it would create enormous problems in terms of international law and diplomatic immunity. 'Since we are officially on South African soil and territory in the embassy, in terms of which country's laws would they operate?' he wanted to know.

As a rule, we applied the host country's laws when it came to working conditions, except where South Africa's laws were better, in which case we would apply South African standards. This was also true in Ireland, and the workers had a better deal than was required under Irish labour law. They were entitled to paid sick leave and had funds put into a pension fund (neither of which was obligatory under Irish law at that time). They also had more public holidays than Irish workers and were paid better than the average person at the same level. They got annual cost-of-living adjustments and – if you ignored the nail clippings and bodily fluids – a very pleasant working environment. Also, there was no legal requirement in Ireland to recognise a union. The director-general insisted that there would be no space for a union and that I should make this very clear to them. I argued against his position at first, but he had a legal opinion sent to me, stating clearly that it would pose almost impossible difficulties in terms of international law. I also consulted with the Irish Department of Foreign Affairs, who did not want to get involved formally, but told me quietly to stand firm, since they also felt it would set a dangerous precedent for their Foreign Service. I conveyed Pretoria's decision to the staff, insisting that, in the case of any disciplinary hearing, they could bring a representative, and that I would have no objection if that happened to be a representative of a union.

Most of the staff seemed happy enough, but from the body language and the small meeting afterwards I could see that a few were not going to accept it. A few days later, I was issued with a strike notice by Mandate trade union, which the staff had joined. Curiously, Mandate was not the most natural fit, being historically more focused on retail and bar staff, but the reason for choosing that particular union soon became obvious. In 1984, a number of women belonging to the union refused to check out South African oranges in Dunnes Stores. They were fired, and a long, highly visible strike ensued. The South African government's refusal to recognise the union in its embassy made for brilliant headlines. That no other embassy allowed any union representation made no difference, and Mandate indicated that they saw this as a test case.

It was clear that less than half the staff were joining the strike, but five members did go on strike. The former Dunnes strikers quickly joined the picket line outside, and of course the media were very interested. But the instructions from headquarters were that we must not speak to the media at all. This kind of strategy rarely works, since it just looks like you are hiding and it infuriates the press, who then give more and more column inches to the other side. We were heavily criticised in the press, but I was getting very little support from Pretoria. 'Just sit it out,' I was told day after day. This left even our Irish lawyer 'gobsmacked'.

In the meantime, the six remaining staff members were bravely crossing the picket line every day, being booed and insulted. The strikers even occupied the lobby of the office building for a while, courtesy of the sympathetic doorman, until the management company intervened. The strike and picket went on for seven very uncomfortable weeks. I hated it. I felt abandoned by Pretoria and frankly was not convinced of the position they had taken. I was concerned about the effect the harassment was having on the non-striking staff, and did not know how it would be possible to rebuild relationships.

At the end of February, the strikers indicated that they wanted to return. I felt that we should have negotiated some exit strategy with them, but in typical bureaucratic style, Pretoria instructed me to 'continue with business as usual'. How? The bitterness on both sides was tangible. The strikers had achieved nothing but losing almost two months' pay. Those who had stayed working would not forget the awful harassment, just as their colleagues would not forget what they perceived as 'betrayal'. How would we all continue to work together? These events marred the whole four years of my time as ambassador. The repercussions were felt for years, and would eventually lead to my departure from government service.

In the meantime, I tried to continue to work on getting positive results for South Africa. Together with the victories on the tourism and economic fronts, success was also achieved on the charity front. Towards the end of 2001, I was interviewed by Marian Finucane, one of the best Irish and, for that matter, international broadcasters I have ever met. I had done hundreds if not thousands of interviews in my life and the conversation, much of it about my past political involvements, was flowing easily with Marian. As I was relating the story of the long lines on the first day of the 1994 election, I saw Marian's eyes filling with tears. Having never seen this before in a journalist, I was slightly taken aback, but also touched. At the end of the interview, I asked if she had ever been to South Africa. She replied that she had not, and in the car back I spoke with South African Tourism to arrange a trip for her, as I did regularly for other journalists.

I insisted that she should see not only the 'pretty sites' but also the more challenging issues in South Africa. So I arranged for her to make a visit to Nazareth House, where they cared for AIDS orphans, and to spend a night in a township B&B. I also set up a meeting with Mandela's old friend and fellow Robben Island prisoner Ahmed Kathrada. Marian and her husband John bravely agreed to it all.

After their return, it was clear that the visit had had a profound effect on them, and they subsequently set up a charity called Friends in Ireland, which has done extraordinary work for AIDS orphans. Apart from feeding and giving thousands of orphans access to medical help, they built a hospice in a township outside Cape Town and have built numerous homes where foster mothers look after orphans in a family environment. All of this was as a result of their visit to South Africa, a fact they would grumpily remind me of every time they faced difficult times in the charity.

Of course, the interview with Marian was one of many I did as ambassador. There were very few radio or TV programmes that did not speak to me at some stage, and I built an excellent rapport with the Irish media. One of these interviews was on *The Gerry Ryan Show*. Gerry was the most listened-to broadcaster in Ireland. More than 300 000 people listened to his three-hour talk show every day. Even though I remember going into the RTÉ (the national broadcaster) studios and meeting the head of 2FM, John Clarke, afterwards, I have only the faintest recollection of the actual interview – which is strange, since I can remember most interviews I did in detail. Oddly, in retrospect, it made no impression on me.

One interview I remember clearly was with a less intelligent but equally charismatic presenter. Towards the end of my term of office, Elizabeth Mulville suggested that I accept a request from the children's TV programme *The Den* to go on air to announce the winner of a competition to name a new baby rhino at Dublin Zoo. It sounded like a fun thing to do, so I agreed. However, on our way to the studio it became clear that I would be interviewed by a rather grumpy turkey called Dustin. Apparently, Dustin did not like diplomats much and was in a bad mood that day. 'My life is getting really weird,' I thought. Thankfully, Dustin behaved reasonably well and even offered me some chocolates and insisted on a kiss. For the next few days, I was astonished to be stopped repeatedly by people in public who said that they had seen me with Dustin on TV. Years later I would appoint Dustin as a UNICEF ambassador, and he even travelled to Africa, where he performed for AIDS orphans – UNICEF being, of course, the United Nations Children's Fund.

Apart from media work, the embassy chaos and the economic promotions, I also had to play host to many delegations and guests. Usually the wife of the ambassador will share this burden, but understandably Wilhelm had no interest in this. In fact, we had agreed from the start that Wilhelm would only accompany me to the Presidential New Year's Party and South African National Day. For the rest, it was up to him. With a few exceptions, such as rugby matches or occasional concerts, I usually went on my own. This was tough and lonely, but knowing how he hated these functions I never put pressure on him to come with me.

My first visitor was, appropriately, Kader Asmal. While he was in exile in Ireland, Kader had been a law professor at Trinity College Dublin for almost three decades. Together with his wife Louise, he played a major role in the Irish anti-apartheid movement. In fact, according to Kader, the first draft of the South African Bill of Rights was drafted at his kitchen table in Dublin with Albie Sachs, who later became a judge in the Constitutional Court. After his return to South Africa, Kader became the Minister of Water Affairs in South Africa after the 1994 election – to the amusement of his friends back in rainy Ireland, who could not understand why such a portfolio was necessary. Kader kept his ties with Ireland and visited frequently.

Shortly after I arrived in Dublin, Kader's private secretary called to say that he would be visiting Ireland in a few weeks, but that it was a private visit and that he would not require any assistance. Knowing Kader from parliament days, I was not convinced. 'Are you sure he doesn't want me to arrange a social function for him with ex-colleagues and friends?' I asked. She assured me that he did not want anything. But two days before his scheduled arrival, Kader phoned me. After the usual pleasantries, he asked: 'Why aren't you arranging a cocktail party for me? I feel truly insulted.'

I sighed, and explained the earlier conversation with his assistant.

'No, no! That's all nonsense. I changed my mind,' he answered abruptly, and told me that a short invite list would be faxed to me. There were more than 100 people on the list and I only had two days to organise it all. It would be my first function, so I was not quite geared up yet. Still, I had no choice and, knowing Kader, it had to be perfect.

In the end it was a lovely evening, which ended after a late-night singing session. By then Kader had also decided that he wanted to meet a number of 'old friends' and instructed me to set it up. The problem was that the 'old friends' included President McAleese, the Irish prime minister (Taoiseach) Bertie Ahern, and the Minister for Foreign Affairs, Brian Cowen. I apprehensively called the protocol section to ask for help. In any other circumstances or country, this would have been impossible to set up so quickly, but the officials were good-humoured, and with an 'Ah, we all know Kader', they arranged the visits.

I accompanied Kader to the meetings, and even though I marvelled as always at his sharp intellect, I was also taken aback by how he would lecture everyone – including the president – on what he thought they were doing wrong. On a visit a few years later, we were at lunch with the then Minister of

Education, Noel Dempsey. During a long lecture by Kader on what he thought was wrong with the Irish education system, one of the senior officials whispered to me: 'Ambassador, it is not often that a minister from another country knows more about us than we do ourselves!' Despite his idiosyncrasies, I had great affection and respect for Kader.

13

During my four and a half years as ambassador, I hosted hundreds of visits. These ranged from the rugby and cricket teams' tours of Ireland to visits by important political office-holders. I also helped organise the summit between the EU and the African Union, which took place during the Irish presidency of the EU. Without a doubt, the highlight was Nelson Mandela's visit during the hosting of the Special Olympics by Ireland in June 2003. I had worked closely with Madiba's office as well as the organisers of the Special Olympics to make sure everything would run smoothly. I knew Madiba was not difficult or demanding personally, but the basics had to be in place, such as security, transport and a comfortable hotel room. As was the norm, two of his security personnel arrived a few days beforehand to ensure that everything was taken care of. We met with the Irish police and were assured that all was well. I double- and triple-checked everything.

The morning of Madiba's visit, I was at the VIP lounge at Dublin Airport early with his security. The VIP lounge was filled with arrivals – including the Kennedy-Shrivers, who are synonymous with the Special Olympics. Then the first crisis developed. The Irish police, the Gardaí, informed us that they had been instructed to accompany the Shrivers on motorbikes and that there would be no escort or security for Madiba. I thought that Madiba's security personnel were about to explode. There had been an agreement with the Irish police, confirmed the previous evening, on the basis that there was not enough South African protection with him and that, under Irish law, his South African security personnel could not be armed. I frantically made a few phone calls but was told that it was a direct instruction from someone senior, who felt that there was no threat to Madiba.

I was furious, but the plane had already landed, so I jumped into the car with the woman from the VIP lounge and raced to the runway. Madiba was waiting for me at the front row of the plane and gave me a big hug. He then took my arm and, leaning heavily on it, turned around and waved at the passengers behind him, who applauded him loudly. We slowly made our way down the ramp, from where we would take a lift down to the waiting car. Opposite the lift there was a glass panel separating us from departing passengers waiting at their gate. A little girl spotted us, and Madiba waved at her. She waved back, and even though we could not hear her, she must clearly have shouted: 'It's Mandela!' As one, all the waiting passengers turned to look, and again spontaneous applause broke out, with Madiba waving to them for a few minutes.

Back in the lounge, Madiba spent a while talking and posing for photographs with some of the young athletes before getting into the car to go to the hotel. The journey took about 45 minutes. Not only did we have no motorbike escort, but the chauffeur would not use the bus lanes because he did not have a taxi sign on and did not want the embarrassment of being stopped with Madiba in the car. I knew that Zelda la Grange, Madiba's personal assistant, and the security people were going to be furious. Luckily they were in another car and Madiba was taking it all in his stride. We were having an intense political conversation, but as we pulled up at traffic lights, people in cars next to us would recognise him. Time and again they rolled down their windows to say: 'How's it going, Mandela? Welcome to Ireland.' Madiba would politely reciprocate and, to his security's annoyance, roll down the window to say hello. 'The Irish are very friendly,' he would remark, before continuing our conversation.

Even though Madiba was, as always, gracious, I knew it could not continue like this; it was not only an insult to Madiba but also a real security risk. After getting Madiba settled, I made numerous phone calls, but got nowhere. Eventually I persuaded someone to get the Minister for Justice to leave the parliamentary chamber to take a call from me. I expressed my astonishment and said: 'Minister, with respect, if something does happen to Mandela while he's here – and you know it takes only one crazy person – I won't be the one who will have to explain to the world why the Irish government didn't put adequate security in place for the most recognisable and loved man in the world.' There was silence on the other side.

A few minutes after our conversation ended, I received a call to say we would get one armed, plain-clothes detective for the duration of the visit. It was not really good enough, but better than nothing. Weeks after the visit, a formal apology from the Department of Foreign Affairs was conveyed to me, to be passed on to Madiba. I never quite understood what was behind the drama, but thankfully all went well.

The rest of the visit was a huge success. We flew by helicopter to Galway, where Madiba received an honorary doctorate from the National University of Ireland. The ceremony was followed by a gala dinner in the Radisson Hotel, at which Marian Finucane was MC. The Corrs, the hugely successful Irish band that combines pop rock with traditional Celtic folk music, and the theatre group Macnas performed. Madiba loves The Corrs, and when they started singing he slowly got up and went to the dance floor to do his stiff but popular 'Madiba jive'. I stayed behind after Madiba returned to Dublin by helicopter. When I got up early the next morning to catch a flight to Dublin, the party was still going strong.

Back in Dublin we dealt with a string of visitors during the Special Olympics, including among others Sir Anthony O'Reilly, Mohammed Ali, the Shriver-Kennedys, Bono, the Edge, Arnold Schwarzenegger and Gerry Adams. One of the funniest meetings that took place was with the actor Pierce Brosnan.

He was staying in the Four Seasons Hotel, and after bumping into him in the lobby I offered to introduce him to Madiba. I knew Madiba was on his way down to the lobby and asked Pierce to wait a few minutes while I went over to the lift to warn Zelda. As the door opened, I quickly told Zelda in Afrikaans that Pierce Brosnan was around the corner. Zelda turned to Madiba and said: 'Madiba, Pierce Brosnan is out there to say a quick hello.'

Madiba frowned and looked puzzled.

'Who?' he asked.

'Pierce Brosnan, the actor. He played James Bond in the movies,' Zelda responded.

Madiba shook his head, clearly having no clue who she was talking about. It suddenly struck me that he had been in jail during the time all the Bond movies were made. Robben Island prisoners certainly did not have movie nights, and since Madiba's release there would have been no time to catch up on almost three decades of films.

Zelda looked exasperated and said: 'Madiba, we don't have time to explain, can you just greet him?'

Madiba nodded as he walked out of the lift. In the lobby I introduced Madiba to Pierce. Madiba looked at him, shook his hand and said warmly: 'Ah, Mr Brosnan. It is a real honour to meet you at last!' Pierce was of course overwhelmed to meet Madiba – and none the wiser.

Later that night in the stadium, while waiting in the Green Room for Madiba's turn to go on stage, we were all watching the opening ceremony on television. When Pierce came onstage to the accompanying Bond music, the crowds went mad. Madiba turned to Cyril Ramaphosa, who had arrived a few days earlier from South Africa. 'Hey, I met that fellow today! He must be famous with that amount of applause.' Cyril looked at Madiba in astonishment for a few seconds before bursting into uncontrollable laughter.

Madiba's security was also having a bit of fun with all the celebrities. At one point I heard one speaking into his sleeve to another: 'Makhathini, come in. Makhathini, come in.'

Makhathini responded.

'I just want to inform you that the Terminator has entered the room.' Across the room I could see Makhathini shaking with laughter. Even though they worked with Madiba every day, they were still starstruck by the Terminator.

During his few days in Ireland, Madiba won the hearts of the Irish, especially the children. On the day of his departure, he greeted some children outside the hotel. He picked up a little girl with Down syndrome and hugged her tightly. She gave him a big kiss and then said loudly: 'You are much nicer than Arnie [Schwarzenegger]!'

Madiba enjoyed this tremendously and as we said goodbye at the airport he chuckled, 'And to think I had to come to Ireland to realise that I'm nicer than Arnie!'

Apart from the goodwill, something else developed from Madiba's visit. On the opening night of the Special Olympics, Zelda asked me to invite The Corrs to Madiba's 85th birthday party in South Africa. It was a special request from Madiba, so naturally I would convey the message to their manager, John Hughes. I had met John and his wife Marie at a function at Sir Anthony O'Reilly's estate, Castlemartin in County Kildare, a year earlier. Over the dinner, John had told me about a recording he wanted Mandela to do, repeating words that he had said in Trafalgar Square a few months earlier about the importance of music. I agreed to try and arrange it – something that would take four years to get permission for – but it eventually gave birth to the spectacular 'Mandela Suite', composed by John.

In the meantime, John, Marie and I had become friends, so when I saw him in the passage outside the Green Room at the Special Olympics, I conveyed Madiba's invitation to him.

'Of course!' John said. 'When?'

'In seven weeks' time,' I responded.

John's face dropped. The band had just finished a long tour and the team were scattering across the world. All the equipment was in storage, so to get to South Africa in seven weeks was a massive and expensive undertaking. But, like most people, John could not even consider saying no to Madiba. Seven weeks later we all arrived in Johannesburg for the gala evening. It was spectacular and star-studded, with a strong Irish focus. Bono and the Edge performed, as did The Corrs. President Clinton read an Irish poem and Richard Branson jived to African singer Yvonne Chaka Chaka's singing on-stage. In between the speeches, birthday greetings from various heads of state and famous movie stars were flashed on screens in the room and read by the MC.

Wilmé had asked me earlier that day to fax a little birthday note to Madiba. It was covered with colourful hand-drawn balloons and in the note she wished Madiba a happy birthday, said how much she loved him and that she hoped he got loads of nice prezzies. That evening, to my surprise, a picture of Wilmé's note suddenly popped up on the TV screens across the big banqueting room. There was an audible gasp from the South Africans in the audience when the MC read out the note from 'young Wilmé Verwoerd' and then loud applause. Wilmé, watching the events on TV with my mum in Gordon's Bay, was equally surprised, but very pleased.

Shortly after this event, I was asked to involve The Corrs in the '46664' concert that was to take place in November that year. This was part of Madiba's ongoing attempts to force the South African government and the world to focus on the HIV/AIDS crisis. The South African government's position was becoming more and more troubling. The then Minister of Health, Dr Manto Tshabalala-Msimang, who was a medical doctor, bizarrely claimed that beetroot and garlic were natural antidotes to HIV, and as effective as anti-retroviral drugs, if not more so. She once tried to argue that point over dinner to the

Irish Minister of Health, Mary Harney, who kindly and quickly changed the subject.

In order to draw attention to the growing pandemic, Madiba agreed to lend his prison number (Prisoner 466 of 1964) to the campaign, arguing that as the apartheid government reduced them to mere numbers, we should not forget the human suffering behind the HIV/AIDS statistics. As part of the campaign, a big rock concert was to be held in Cape Town with a string of celebrities. The remaining members from Queen, Peter Gabriel, Annie Lennox, Phil Collins and U2 were among those scheduled to join the African stars on stage. I was delighted to be involved on the periphery, since the HIV/AIDS struggle continued to be close to my heart, and also followed me in Ireland.

A few weeks before the concert, a consultant in one of the intensive care units in Dublin phoned me. He explained that they had a woman on life-support who, they believed, was a South African asylum seeker. She had recently given birth to a little girl, who, like her mother, had tested positive for AIDS. Due to complications during the birth, the mother ended up on life-support with no hope of recovering. There had been no contact from friends or family, and the doctors needed permission to switch off the life-support machines. I promised to do whatever I could, and over the next few days the sad story unfolded. It turned out that, like many Africans, she and her Nigerian partner had decided to seek asylum in Ireland in order to get the right to remain, on the basis of having an Irish-born baby. (This provision was later repealed following a referendum.) However, the father of the baby decided at the last moment to seek asylum in England, so the heavily pregnant woman ended up alone in Ireland. Shortly after she arrived, she went into labour and disaster struck.

We traced her family to a township outside Pretoria and conveyed the sad news. They gave permission for the machines to be switched off, but immediately wanted the baby. However, the baby was now an Irish citizen in the care of the Irish state, and since South Africa was not providing anti-retroviral drugs, the Irish state questioned whether they should return the baby to the family. At the same time, they admitted that it was highly unlikely that a black, HIV-positive baby would be adopted in Ireland. In the end they agreed to return little baby Grace to her family. To make matters worse, the UK

165

authorities would not grant the father, who was desperate to see his child, permission to travel to Ireland. After the mother passed away, I paid for the cremation of her remains out of my own pocket, since her elderly parents in South Africa could not afford to, and arranged for the ashes to be returned to them. On the day of her cremation, there was no one present, just a lonely beaded South African flag that one of my staff arranged to put on her coffin. This terrible tragedy just made me more determined to do whatever I could to fight this pandemic, despite the South African government's position.

So in November 2003 I accompanied The Corrs to the event. It was a magical night. The weather was perfect and the sun was setting as the concert started. John and I sat behind Madiba and his wife Graça Machel. The concert was extremely emotional, especially when Peter Gabriel sang 'Biko'. I turned around to look at Steve Biko's son, who was standing behind me, and saw him crying openly while mouthing the words. When The Corrs came on stage, Madiba, who had started to get tired, sat up and asked Oprah Winfrey to stop talking to him so he could listen to them. He smiled broadly as he tapped his fingers: as I have said, he was a big fan. So was former Springbok captain, Francois Pienaar, who had led the team to victory in the 1995 World Cup. He recognised me and I introduced him to John Hughes, who is a huge rugby fan. I'm not sure who was more in awe, John or Francois.

After the concert, Zelda conveyed another invite from Madiba. He wanted me and The Corrs to join him and a few performers on his farm for the weekend, starting the next day. This of course meant a hasty change of flights, and the next day we flew to Johannesburg, before being flown by helicopter to a game farm where Madiba had a house. Brian May, Roger Taylor, Annie Lennox, Dave Stewart, Peter Gabriel and of course The Corrs were there, and we spent three days in the presence of Madiba. I had met Annie Lennox, who would later be named UNESCO Goodwill Ambassador for AIDS, in the hotel gym a few days earlier and I immediately liked this down-to-earth woman, who was such a passionate activist. We would stay in touch, and a few years later she would come to Ireland twice at my invitation to support UNICEF events.

One dinner session at Madiba's farm developed into an improv session with The Corrs on fiddle and whistle. Annie and the other artists sang along beautifully. In between we took elephant rides and went on game drives. One evening we all lay on our backs on the damp grass in the African veld while Brian May, who has a doctorate in astronomy, pointed out various constellations. It was somewhat surreal. I never get starstruck. I either like people or I do not, based on whether they are nice, caring and filled with integrity, irrespective of who they are. These were such people. There were no prima donnas, even though they have all been extraordinarily success-ful. It was an enormous privilege to spend time with them.

In 2004 South Africa celebrated ten years of democracy. I decided with my team to host celebrations culminating in a big garden party on the actual National Day. Among other events we held an art exhibition by two famous South African artists, Willie Bester and Abraham le Roux, in the Blue Leaf Gallery. A few days later we had a screening of *My Country*, a film by John Boorman based on the book by Antjie Krog about the Truth Commission. I also hosted a concert in the National Concert Hall.

The highlight was the garden party at the residence, representing a night in the African Bush. We built a big temporary structure representing an African lapa on the back lawn. Fires were lit everywhere and oil lamps lit up the pathways. For added impact we played a CD of African sounds on hid-den speakers. Not only did some guests jump when a lion suddenly roared behind them, but all the dogs in the neighbourhood went mad. Macnas, the theatre group from Galway, gave a spectacular performance together with a truly inspiring violin orchestra called Buskaid from Diepsloot township in South Africa. South African cuisine was served on tin plates and drinks in beaded tin cups. The night was splendid.

14

Although some events were great fun, a lot of my work was far less glam-
orous. For example, there were the prison visits to the many South
Africans in jail in Ireland, most of whom were in for being drug mules. We
quickly realised that many had been given huge amounts of money to carry
illegal drugs into Ireland. Desperate, they would agree on the assumption
that they would at worst be deported if they were caught. Many of them
were very naively caught in a web of greed and lies – there was even a pen-
sioner who was wheelchair-bound and had stuffed marijuana in the wheels
of the wheelchair. Among the many needing help was a young Afrikaner
who was in Maghaberry prison in Northern Ireland and could not speak a
word of English. After translating his story for the legal representative, I
was asked to attend the hearing the next day, in case they needed translation again. It turned out to be unnecessary, although the barrister did point
to the gallery and alerted the judge that the South African ambassador was
present. Gordon (my driver) and I were the only two people in the gallery,
and of course the judge looked at Gordon and nodded to him, saying:
'Welcome, ambassador.'

In an effort to stem the growing tide of drug trafficking, I decided to enlist
the help of the South African media. I alerted them to the story and asked
them to focus on the human tragedy of those getting caught and receiving
lengthy jail sentences. The print media responded, and eventually the top
current-affairs television programme, *Carte Blanche*, came to Ireland to make
a documentary about the issue. The number of arrests declined sharply after
these interventions and we were all very thankful, not least since I was not
looking forward to another visit – and body search – in Maghaberry Prison.

As the end of my four-year term approached, I had to make a difficult
decision. I was offered a posting to another country, but I knew in my heart
that I was not a career diplomat. I wanted to be part of changing things, not
just maintaining things. There was scope to do that in the relaxed diplomatic

environment of Ireland, but this would not be possible in most other countries. I also did not want to move my now-teenage children from one country to another. And I knew that my marriage was over.

I had hoped that being away from South Africa and in a more anonymous environment, Wilhelm and I would restore our marriage, but sadly this did not happen. We had increasingly grown apart. Despite finishing his doctorate and working at the Glencree Centre for Reconciliation, Wilhelm was hugely resentful of the demands of my work. I had, at a huge cost to my health and emotional well-being, done my best to be there as wife and mother, but our relationship did not improve.

The question then was what to do next, and whether to return to South Africa. I was not keen to go back to parliament. In my opinion it is seldom wise to go back to anything. I also hated being part of the bureaucracy. I despised the inefficiency of the paper-shuffling by mediocre people with too much power. My direct head in Pretoria once told me that he would not give written approval for something he had already approved verbally. Asked why not – especially since it would cause a huge legal issue for the embassy – he responded: 'Because I can and I feel like it.' In the end, I paid the huge bill out of my own pocket, despite the fact that it was the responsibility of one of the junior diplomats who had made the mistake of going ahead without written approval. But it was this kind of attitude that made it clear to me that unless I was at the top of the ladder, where I could instil a new work ethic, I would not be happy in the civil service.

In the end, it was a rather dramatic evening in Geneva that led to my decision to stay in Ireland. After the strike in 2001–2, the trade union made a complaint to the International Labour Organisation (ILO) in Geneva. In 2004, the relevant South African minister was informed about the case and clearly got a very limited (or non-existent) briefing from the Department of Foreign Affairs in Pretoria. He sent over some of his officials, who arrogantly came into the embassy with instructions to 'sort everything out'. They quickly realised that things were not that simple and reported this back to the minister. Shortly after that, my colleague who had been posted to the UN in Geneva called to ask if I would attend a dinner there with the same minister. I agreed, prepared well, and took two huge folders of all the correspondence with me. Having canvassed with him during the elections and worked with him in parliament, I knew the minister well, and since I had only followed instructions, I was not worried. At the dinner, he was accompanied by various officials from his department. The ambassador to Bern, a lovely woman called Nozipho January-Bardill, was also there.

The minister was in a strange mood and quickly launched into a tirade about HIV/AIDS. We all listened in horror as he defended and promoted the Mbeki position. Nozipho gently tried to debate the issue, but the minister just raised his voice and insisted, 'You will all still see . . . the president is always right.' I realised that his officials were terrified of him. Suddenly he stood up and said that he wanted to leave. His host reminded him that he wanted to talk to me about the ILO case. 'I have no interest in talking to her,' he said, looking away.

'But minister, I flew in specifically at your request,' I protested.

He glared at me. 'You embarrassed your country by your ludicrous decision,' he hissed.

'What?' I could not believe what I had heard.

'You know what I mean,' he hissed again.

'That's insane,' I said calmly. 'I have all the correspondence here. I have every instruction in writing. You can't blame me for only following direct instructions from the director-general.'

It looked as if the minister was about to explode, and behind his back his officials were wildly gesturing to me to keep quiet. He bent forward and put his face close to mine. 'I have no interest in your correspondence. You have embarrassed my country and I will now defend my country. You just stay away.'

'It's my country too!' I responded angrily. 'A country and its government that I have faithfully represented.'

The minister looked at me, said 'Ha!', then got up and left.

I was shocked. Despite his officials whispering to me as they left 'not to worry, he gets like this', I knew I had come to a crossroads. It was not so much his tirade, or that I was now blamed for something I did not agree with from the start, or even that after following the instructions from my superiors, they had hung me out to dry. What worried me most was how the ten years of power had fundamentally changed so many of the people I had respected as comrades. I did not want to be part of that process any more. I did not sleep at all that night and wept for two days before I accepted that my journey as part of the South African government had – at least for the time being – come to an end.

But what to do next? I was happy in Ireland and so were my children, so perhaps I could stay at least for a while so they could finish their school years. RTÉ had asked me a few months earlier to do a radio programme on multi-culturalism. Even though it paid very little, I could at least continue with that. I decided to make up my mind during a holiday in South Africa following my farewell as ambassador. Wilhelm decided to leave earlier with the children, since he did not want to be part of all the farewell functions. I had a great meal for some of my dearest friends in the Four Seasons Hotel. Even though I was in complete turmoil, it was a lovely evening.

On my final day, the diplomatic corps gave me a farewell cocktail party, and that was that. As I left the party, I realised that I did not have a lift back home any more, so I hailed a cab. Back home, I sat in the dark reflecting on the previous four and a half years. They had been very successful. Tourism had increased by 135 per cent, trade with Ireland was up 60 per cent, and investment had grown seven-fold. I had done many unconventional things, like visiting the seal sanctuary and feeding seals, inviting Traveller (Irish gypsy) women for tea at the ambassador's residence and going for lunch with homeless people at a shelter. There was so much to be proud of, and yet I suddenly found myself without a job, and with no real income. I also suspected that I would soon not have a marriage any more.

15

After the holiday back in South Africa, Wilhelm and I returned separately to Ireland. By the time I came back with the children, he had moved out of the family home, and the excruciatingly painful and treacherous journey of disentangling nineteen years of marriage began.

It was an unbelievably difficult process that I would never want to go through again. Apart from the awful negotiations around the material issues, such as property and maintenance, there was the emotional pain to deal with. Even though I felt a deep sense of freedom and never doubted that it was the right thing to do, feelings of failure, loneliness, disappointment and fear of the future left me reeling. For months I would wake up at around 4am and not be able to get back to sleep. I was desperately trying to minimise the pain and damage to the children, which left me with enormous guilt.

The next three years were to be a dark and lonely time in my life. Part of the difficulty was that as always the bulk of the financial burden to provide for the children fell on me. For a while, I did a bit of South African wine sales, but I knew that I would get bored quickly. I also did some work for the Mandela-Rhodes Foundation and, luckily, I did the weekly programme for RTÉ on multiculturalism.

Between 1995 and 2008 Ireland saw massive economic growth, transforming it from one of the poorest nations in the European Union into one of the wealthiest. With annual growth rates of between 6 and 9 per cent and almost no long-term unemployment, many people flocked to Ireland to seek work. This meant a rapid and dramatic change in population demographics. As this economic migration into the country grew, Ireland struggled with the demands of a new multicultural identity. A former South African, Lorelei Harris, who works at RTÉ, had asked if I would present a weekly programme on matters relating to multiculturalism, and I had agreed. I was paid very little, but jumped at the opportunity to engage with questions that were so close to my heart.

I am really proud of the issues we exposed, the matters we debated, and the programmes we produced. I worked with producers who patiently taught me how to present, interview, do voice-overs and write briefs. Aonghus McAnally was the first producer I worked with, followed by Ronan Kelly and Tom Donnelly. The first programme we did was an interview I had arranged with Archbishop Tutu, and it received a nomination for the best short interview at the annual PPI Awards, which recognise the art and skill of radio production and programming.

But the interviews I am most proud of were the ones dealing with female genital mutilation and the death of a little African boy following a botched home circumcision. These were gruelling but important interviews. Although I loved the work and enjoyed working with most of the people in RTÉ, I was shocked by how bureaucratic and incestuous it was. The culture inside was toxic and hierarchical, and it always surprised me how dysfunctional the relationships were between management and staff. Coming from the embassy, that said a lot! Even though I enjoyed the RTÉ work tremendously, and later also did a series on feminism called 'Whatever Happened to the F-word?', I knew it was not going anywhere career-wise and would at best be a hobby or sideline.

Fifteen months after my separation from Wilhelm, I got a call from my lawyer while recording a programme at the Educate Together school in Swords: an interim divorce had been granted. I felt really sad, and cried for a little while in the toilet, but then had to go back to the children to record the programme. Three months later, in December 2006, the final divorce order was granted. While it was happening in our absence in a courtroom in downtown Cape Town, I was part of an exclusive lunch with Madiba at the house of the head of the Mandela-Rhodes Foundation, Shaun Johnson. It was wonderful to see Madiba again and we had a good chat, but it was a sad day for me. Sitting on Shaun's veranda looking out over the Atlantic Ocean, I felt deeply alone and worried about the future.

Late in 2006, I bumped into Cathy Kelly at the hairdressers. Cathy is a best-selling author and a UNICEF ambassador. Strangely enough, after not seeing her for almost two years, I had spotted her in a restaurant the previous evening, but did not want to disturb her as she was with a group of friends. As we both paid for our haircuts, Cathy asked if I had heard that Maura

Quinn, the head of UNICEF Ireland, had resigned. Since this had not been formally announced yet, I had not. 'Hey, you should apply,' Cathy said. 'You would be perfect.'

Afterwards, I took a long walk on the pier in Dun Laoghaire. I had met Maura a few times before and had always thought that being the head of UNICEF Ireland would be my dream job. Even though I was worried about the fundraising responsibilities, I knew I would apply. After all, I had eighteen months earlier written in my 'five-year dream plan' that I wanted to work for UNICEF. So I applied. I had heard that the second-in-charge was the candidate to beat, but also that there had been a huge number of outside applications.

The recruitment agency called me to a pre-interview. This was a bizarre experience. Before I even sat down, the agent said: 'I don't understand why you applied for this job.' I was surprised, and turned the tables by interviewing him on why he thought I should not have applied. I eventually figured out that he had very strong preconceived ideas about former ambassadors, when he asked me: 'Who buys your newspapers and milk for you?' I assured him that I had always done that myself. 'So you would not object to, for example, ordering stationery?' he asked.

I went through two more rounds of interviews before being offered the position by the chair of the board, Chris Horn. Chris is a highly successful man who founded, among others, a global computer company called Iona Technologies. He has a really big heart and cares passionately about the children in the developing world. I was delighted to be offered the job, even though I knew that the relationship with my number two would be challenging. Chris presented me with a contract and a salary offer. I accepted it, but insisted that the base salary be lowered slightly, since I felt that it should stay below €100 000. Chris laughed that I must have been the first CEO in history to negotiate a salary downwards.

I started at UNICEF in April 2007. As expected, the transition was difficult for many of the staff, especially for the number two. There were a lot of things I wanted to change in order to grow the organisation, but I also wanted to give the staff time to adjust to me. In any case, nothing could faze me after the embassy. At the time of my appointment, I had asked Chris what my brief was. I was told that they wanted me to keep the income at least stable and to grow it if possible, but the main task was to raise the profile of UNICEF in Ireland. This would be a challenge, since research showed that spontaneous awareness of the organisation was around 11 per cent. There was also an outstanding case in the Employment and Arbitration Tribunal, and dealing with this matter was one of my first tasks. We won the case, but much of the detail of the testimony I heard confirmed for me that there were many serious shortcomings in the organisation.

So in the first few months, I tightened financial controls and, with the help of the second in charge, who later resigned for personal reasons, brought working conditions in line with good practice, as well as ensuring that staff would be protected in the case of whistle-blowing. For me, transparency, good governance and tight financial controls were the first priority. When I declared that I was a R100 donation for a day and wanted my staff to take me through the process from arrival to being banked, I gained a lot of insight into how the organisation worked.

After tackling these issues, I worked with the staff and the Geneva regional office on our long-term vision. I surprised everyone by declaring that I wanted us to be a R100 million organisation by 2010. (It was at R30 million in 2007.) I also said that by then we would have an awareness rating of over 60 per cent. A few staff members resigned, but the rest enthusiastically became part of this new vision and dream.

I changed the organogram and appointed a few new people to focus on events and corporate fundraising. I scaled down sections that were not making money and diversified the income – a step that would turn out to be crucial when the recession hit. Most importantly, I insisted on a new approach to working with the media. As far as I could see, UNICEF Ireland had a very defensive, reactive approach to the media. I had encountered this same attitude in politicians and government, and always felt it was the wrong way to go about matters. The media is an uncontrollable beast, but fundamentally it is made up of people who are mostly good individuals trying to do their job of writing stories. If you treat them with respect, openness and honesty, they will usually respond positively, and when you have a story that is newsworthy they will write it. It was a long, difficult struggle to change the culture, but gradually it changed and we started to get more – and more positive – media coverage of our work.

One of the most challenging but rewarding parts of my job was travelling to the field to see UNICEF's work on the ground. My first UNICEF trip to Africa was to Rwanda in July 2007. Rwanda has a special significance to South Africans. As we were celebrating our new democracy and the election of President Mandela in 1994, the TV images of the horrendous massacres in Rwanda started to filter through. We watched in horror as almost a million people were slaughtered over a period of 100 days, while the rest of the world did nothing. It was now thirteen years later, and the country was relatively stable under the leadership of Paul Kagame, yet I was nervous about the emotional impact that this tiny country of less than 8.6 million people would have on me and the rest of our delegation.

Our group, which included Cathy Kelly, flew to Amsterdam and then to Nairobi, Kenya. From there we took a smaller plane, which landed first in Bujumbura in Burundi before flying to Kigali in Rwanda. As soon as you get off the main routes in Africa, on land, sea or air, the fun starts. In this case, the plane was like a taxi plane, which flew on a circular route a number of times each day. There were no assigned seats, so people got on and off with all kinds of agricultural produce, while chatting loudly. It was brilliant.

In Kigali, it was a strange and unsettling feeling to recognise the airport building from the TV images thirteen years before. After a friendly welcome by passport control, and after Customs officials had confiscated any plastic bags on us – for environmental reasons, they are banned in Rwanda – we were met by our UNICEF drivers, Cedric and Josef, both Rwandan. On the drive into Kigali, I tried to distract myself by talking to Josef.

The thought that thousands of people had been slaughtered on these roads was really upsetting. In the rest of Africa, it is regarded as an important courtesy to ask about a person's family. So I asked Josef about his wife and children. His answer broke my heart.

'My second family,' he said quietly. 'My first wife and all my children were killed in the genocide. I was away on work and when I came back a few days later they were all dead. I now have a new family.' This conversation would be repeated time and again during our visit and was to be the introduction to a very intense few days.

Wherever you go in Rwanda, the legacy of the genocide seems to follow you. Signs and memorials are everywhere. Even in the UNICEF office there is a memorial to the thirteen staff members who died there. Unlike in the rest of Africa, people do not greet you with boisterous waving and with beaming, white smiles. People are far more reserved and suspicious. The children are different, though, as we discovered on the three-hour journey to Lake Kivu on the first day. As soon as they spotted the Land Rovers, they would run alongside shouting, 'Welcome, welcome' and 'Mzungu, bachuka, bachuka' (white people, bottles, bottles). They were desperate for empty plastic drinks bottles, which they sold for a few cents.

The journey down to Lake Kivu on the border with Congo is spectacular. It is truly a country of a thousand hills. Once you get into the volcanic region, the scenery is breathtaking, as is the site around Lake Kivu.

Over the next five days we visited schools, maternity hospitals, government officials and HIV centres. There was a sense of purpose and a determination to rebuild this country that was easy to get excited about. There were many hopeful statistics, such as that between 1970 and 1995 only 3 500 university students had graduated in Rwanda, but by this time the same number graduated every year. The crime rate had become extremely low (I felt completely safe even at night) and tourism was growing – mainly linked to the gorilla viewings.

On the last day we visited the Genocide Memorial. I recalled how Archbishop Tutu had broken down years before on a visit there, and I quickly understood why. It was harrowing, in particular the section dedicated to children who had died. There was poster after poster of victims, with their name, age, favourite food and activity. And then, their last words and how they died. Anane Umutoni loved cake and milk and to sing and dance. She was stabbed in the eyes and head. She was only four. David Mugiraneza was ten years old. He was good at football and loved to make people laugh. He wanted to become a doctor. His last words were, 'Don't worry, the UN will come and rescue us.' He was tortured to death.

For me the most heart-breaking story was that of Fabrice Minega, who was eight years old. He loved swimming, and chocolate was his favourite food. He always said that his best friend was his mum. And it was to her, his best friend, that he called in a panic as he was chased by an angry mob: 'Mummy, please tell me where to run to. Please tell me what to do.' He was bludgeoned to death.

It all became too much. Like Tutu I went outside in tears. As I stood weeping in the memorial rose garden, Josef came up to me. 'I am sorry,' he said. I looked at him, puzzled. 'I am sorry my country has made you sad.' And as happens so many times in Africa, the one who should have been crying was comforting me.

I always feel that I leave a piece of my heart in places and with the people I have visited. Rwanda will always have a big part of my heart and as we boarded the plane I vowed to return soon. As it turns out, I returned there seven months later, as my personal life took a dramatic turn.

At the end of my first year in UNICEF, it was clear that we were making progress and I felt challenged and stimulated on the work front. My personal life was a different story. I had thrown myself into work and, with the exception of a few girlfriends, had become fairly reclusive. Although I have never minded my own company, I knew that I was lonely. My friends had encouraged me to have coffee with a few men, but I found them boring and had no interest in anyone.

But this was all about to change.

16

In late December 2007, post-election violence broke out in Kenya, creating a massive humanitarian crisis. In the following weeks, many agencies withdrew their European staff out of fear for their safety. I wanted to go and help, and towards the end of January 2008 I flew out and landed in Nairobi. After the necessary security briefings, local UNICEF staff and I travelled to the north-eastern part of the country, where the violence was at its most intense. We went to refugee camps and started the harrowing process of visiting homesteads across the rural areas.

At the first house, there was an ominous silence. Even the cows seemed nervous. I glanced over at the UNICEF driver, who looked around anxiously.

'This is not good,' he mumbled.

A young man suddenly came out of the mud hut and rushed us around a corner. 'They killed my mother,' he wept. 'They said they were coming back.'

I listened to him recalling the horrible events of the night before. The story was all too familiar. The violence had resulted in atrocities being committed in an otherwise stable country. For the previous four days, I had been listening to endless distressing stories. Neighbours had turned on one another. Old feudal disputes between clans who had lived in peace for decades had, for no apparent reason, suddenly reignited. Houses were indiscriminately being burned down, livestock slaughtered, women raped, and thousands killed – mostly hacked to death with machetes.

'Come with us,' I said. 'We can take you and the two small boys to a refugee camp, where you will be safe.'

'No,' the young man answered. 'If we leave, they will take everything and we will have nothing. How will we live?'

I tried to convince him, but none of my arguments could move him. This was all he had, and it was the only way he could provide for his little brothers, who were staring at us around the door frame of the hut with the wide, tired eyes I have seen all over Africa in children who have seen too much, too young.

The young man suddenly looked up at the trees on the hill behind us. A look of horror came over him. 'You have to go! They are coming back! They will kill us if you are here.' The UNICEF team followed his gaze and started running, pulling me along with them. I shouted back at the young man, hoping that he would come with us, but he was already back in his hut with his two small brothers.

As we sped away in the Land Rover, I struggled to get to grips with leaving the children. As we drove through the apocalyptic-looking landscape, I raged about the chaos that can develop so quickly due to politics and about the suffering of those who are too young to vote, who are innocent but always seem to carry the brunt of pain caused by decisions and actions made by others far away.

While I fought back tears of anger, my phone rang. It was my office in Dublin, where my staff were trying to keep the media interested in what was going on in Kenya. My press officer, Julianne Savage, said that *The Gerry Ryan Show*, with which I had done an interview when I was ambassador, wanted a live interview. Could I do it in an hour or so? I said that I would of course, but that there was no way we could stop for too long; it was just too dangerous. I said I hoped we would have cell phone reception. The interview was to take place just before 11am in Dublin – noon in Kenya.

A few minutes later, we stopped in what was left of a tiny village. People stood in shock next to the dusty road in the remains of what had been a little spaza shop. Some were scratching with sticks among the smouldering ashes to see if there was anything metal that could be salvaged. We got out of the Land Rover, and the familiar smell of violent chaos – smoke, blood, sweat and fear – hit my nostrils. I started to speak to people, listening to their stories and asking whether any medical help was needed, when suddenly the tension in the group rose. I turned around, to be confronted by a group of young men with bloody machetes hanging from their hands.

In Africa, machetes are usually used as farming implements, to cut maize or sugar cane, and are sold in supermarkets. As the violence escalated, the machetes sold out fast, and the government, realising that people were buying them in bulk, finally banned the sale of more than one at a time. These young men had clearly used them to kill people and, from the blood dripping off their machetes, I knew they had done so recently.

'Mzungu [white person], what are you doing here?' asked one young man with bloodshot eyes, his breath smelling of alcohol. 'You should not be here. Go back to Europe.'

I looked at the group of angry men and then over to my UNICEF colleagues, who were quite a distance away and had their backs turned to me, talking to people. I was on my own, and had to think fast. 'Well, I am not European, I am African; I am from South Africa,' I answered. I knew that this could go either way – badly, if they thought I was a racist white South African. I hoped that, being young, they were not too conscious of South Africa's past. I hoped they would only think about Mandela and soccer. 'I am also part of UNICEF,' I added quickly, pointing to the logo on my T-shirt. The young men stared at me, breathing heavily. Holding their gaze, I wondered if they were on drugs, which would make them completely unpredictable.

Suddenly my phone rang again. 'Sorry, I have to take this,' I said, walking backwards for a few steps before turning around and answering it.

'Hi, Melanie!' said a very chirpy voice. It was one of the researchers from *The Gerry Ryan Show*. 'Just wondered if we can have a quick pre-interview chat so I can brief Gerry and check the line?'

'No, it's chaotic here. Gerry will just have to wing it. I'm sure he will be okay. He's interviewed me before about development issues,' I responded.

The researcher hung up, promising to call back in 30 minutes if I could be in a place where I could talk. The situation was becoming increasingly tense, with more young men arriving. After assisting people as best we could, we made a hasty retreat to the Land Rovers and got back on the road.

Just outside a little town called Molo, my phone rang. 'Melanie, it's *The Gerry Ryan Show* again. We will be with you in a few minutes. I'll put you on hold, but you can listen to the programme in the meantime.'

The driver pulled in next to the road and I jumped out. There was no way I could do an interview in the boiling-hot Land Rover squeezed in among various UNICEF staff. I walked a few metres away, with the driver begging me to be quick. From thousands of miles away, I could hear Gerry Ryan's familiar deep voice talking to a listener. It struck me how mundane and sur-real it all sounded. I was standing next to a busy road in the middle of Africa, with trucks loaded with people and all their possessions moving past in a slow, funereal procession. Military vehicles with machine-guns sticking out of the window were speeding wildly in the other direction. And next to the road there was a tired, antlike procession of people walking as if in a trance to anywhere they could find safety.

With the sun beetles screeching their high-pitched song in the midday sun, I looked around in vain for a tree to get some shade. Children started to surround me, looking at me and touching me, saying over and over again: 'Mzungu, Mzungu.' This was not going to be an easy interview.

During the interview, Gerry asked me about the conditions in Kenya, and I spoke at length about everything we had seen. After about ten minutes, I thought we were winding down the interview, but Gerry said: 'Listen, I want to talk to you a bit more. Can you stay with us a few minutes longer, while we do the 11 o'clock news?'

The guys in the Land Rover were by now beeping and gesturing wildly to me to get back in. We needed to move. 'Gerry, it's actually a bit . . . ' but the signature tune for the news was already on and I knew that Gerry was not listening to me any more. 'Shit!' I exclaimed.

'Sheeet!' the kids around me repeated, mocking me. I smiled at them and shouted back at the team to give me five more minutes. Looking down at the kids, I thought of the previous time Gerry had interviewed me.

A few months earlier, I had been in Mozambique examining the devastating effect of the HIV pandemic. Squeezed into the tiny, airless office of a centre for orphaned children, I tried desperately to focus on the interview. It was over 45 °C in the office, sweat was running into my eyes, kids were screaming outside, and yet the story had to be told: one out of every eight children born were HIV-positive, and there were fewer doctors in the whole of Mozambique than qualified in a year in Ireland. It irritated me that so few in the media wanted to hear the story – except Gerry.

A few days before I had flown to Mozambique, we had still not been able to line up any interviews. I had bumped into Gerry the week before in RTÉ. He was on his way to lunch with the newly appointed head of radio and I was just coming in to do a recording for *Spectrum*, the radio programme I was presenting at RTÉ. Since my time as ambassador we had never said more than a quick hello. This time he wanted to know how I was, how the programme was doing and how things were going at UNICEF. 'Let me know if I can help,' he said. He gave me his cell phone number and rushed off.

With no interviews lined up, I sent him a short text the night before I departed: 'Did not think I would have to ask so soon, but can you help?'

'Yes of course,' his text came back immediately. 'Tell your people to speak to Siobhan in my office. Mind yourself.'

Back in Kenya two months later, I was listening to the weather report in Ireland: it was rainy and windy with a few sunny patches. I smiled. *Why do they even bother changing the weather report daily?* I wondered.

Suddenly Gerry was on the line again. 'Melanie, we are still off air, but are you okay?' Not prepared for the personal question, I momentarily could not speak as the realisation hit me of how much stress I had been under in the last few days, and how tired I was. But before I could answer, we were back on air. At the end of the interview, Gerry thanked me and told me to 'tread carefully and be very, very safe'. I listened for a while longer as Gerry encouraged people to donate money to UNICEF. As the programme went into an ad break, I waited for the usual mutual thank-you with the producer, but it was Gerry who spoke to me again. 'Melanie, it sounds mad out there. Can you please text me later to tell me that you are okay? Please be careful.'

The rest of the day became a blur of ever-increasing stress and chaos. Roads were blocked, more and more reports of killings were coming in, more and more people next to the roads needed help, as we tried to find a safe road back to the hotel before it got dark. In the early evening, we finally stumbled back into the hotel. On the veranda the locals were sitting watching the news, exclaiming loudly as it showed a policeman shooting, at close range, a young man who was lying on the ground.

Sitting with them was Paul Hopkins, a journalist with the *Irish Independent* who had come along with me to report on the unrest. Paul had stayed behind in the hotel that day, since he needed to meet a deadline. I suspected that he had also seen a bit too much. I was desperate for a shower, but needed to get some stories and photos back to Ireland, so I headed for the internet centre. The name was far more grandiose than the reality. The tiny room, without air conditioning, had three computers and a few broken chairs. I sat down next to a man who was reporting for Save the Children. He looked over at me, swatted a mosquito, nodded and said, frustrated: 'It takes twenty minutes to send one photograph in this godforsaken hell-hole. No f**king broadband anywhere.' I knew this meant spending the rest of the evening there and I was not feeling well. I put it down to stress and exhaustion, and ordered drinks for the Save the Children guy and me. While the photographs were loading, my phone beeped. It was Gerry texting.

'Hi, are you safe?'

'Yes, just back in the hotel. Thank you for the interview. Sorry if I sounded a bit frazzled. I was a bit under pressure.'

'My pleasure and you were great. R u OK? Things look very crazy from here.'

'It's pretty out of control – was a pretty scary day.'

'Pls look after yourself. There are people here that care about you.'

Too tired to text further, I went up to my room and fell into bed – without the shower I was longing for earlier. Around midnight, a call from Marian Finucane woke me. She did not know I was in Kenya and wanted to talk about a problem she had with her charity in South Africa. I cannot remember much of the call, but it registered that I was feverish and not feeling well. This was never good in the middle of Africa, especially since I never take malaria prophylaxis. 'Please Lord, let it not be malaria,' I prayed quietly.

The next morning, with a very unwell stomach and a pounding headache, I watched CNN news and spotted Aoife Kavanagh in the middle of a teargas attack by the police in Nairobi. Aoife, an exceptionally brave journalist who loves Africa, was there for RTÉ. We had spoken a few times since I had arrived and made plans to meet up the next day in Nairobi. I texted to check if she was okay and to give her some advice on how to make the effects of teargas less uncomfortable. 'Just one of those useful things you pick up when you are part of the anti-apartheid movement in South Africa,' I joked.

Back in Nairobi, I tried to rest in the comfortable rooms of the colonial-style Holiday Inn. I was really sick, no doubt about it. I was pretty sure it was not malaria, but rather some stomach bug, which is so easy to catch when you spend time in refugee camps. That evening my phone beeped. It was Gerry texting again: 'How are things today?'

I explained that I was back in Nairobi, where things were a bit calmer. We texted for a while about the political and humanitarian crisis that was developing. Gerry again wanted to know how I was. I said I was fine, although I was very tired and not feeling well. Gerry asked if he could help with anything. I smiled and responded: 'Like what? Sending in the army to evacuate me?'

'No, although I could organise that if you want,' he texted back. 'Just wish I was there.'

I started to wonder what he was up to. 'Why? Would you bring the programme here?'

'2 things! I like being in bizarre situations especially if there is a message to take out! 2 I want to see it with you. PS men are stupid, remember that!'

Confused, I stared at the message for a while. What to text now? Before I could do anything, the phone beeped again.

'I hope I don't annoy you by saying these things?'

'Annoy no – just confused,' I texted back.

'Please know that I am free to say these things to you and have been for a while,' he replied.

This confused me even more. I did not read tabloids or *Hello!* magazine nor listen much to *The Gerry Ryan Show*, but I was pretty sure Gerry was still married. I grabbed my computer and Googled his name. There was no story anywhere about him being separated.

My phone beeped again. 'Are you still there?'

'Excuse me, but are you not a happily married man?' I texted back.

And with that my phone went silent for the rest of the night. In between getting violently sick, I agonised about the texts of the previous two days. From the little interaction I had had with him on a professional level, I knew I liked Gerry, but what was he up to? I would never be part of something that would break up a marriage or a family – I knew that for sure. But what if he was separated? Would I be interested? Having not heard anything from Gerry by the next morning, I left for Nairobi Airport.

I had decided to de-stress in Rwanda for a few days, before taking a group of potential funders around the country and going up into the mountains on the border of Congo to see the gorillas. So, shaking with fever, I got onto a plane and flew to Kigali. In Rwanda, I became increasingly ill, and eventually my PA in Dublin, Niamh, who knew from speaking to me that I was becoming delirious, arranged for the UNICEF staff to take me to a doctor who spoke only French (I speak none) at the Belgian embassy in Kigali. He told my doctor in Dublin – who did speak French – about my blood results. I was seriously ill. She spoke to me again, warning me to stay flat on my back and close to a hospital. But I had no intention of doing that. There was work to be done.

185

For four days, I weakly showed the Irish businessmen around. It was tough going, but there was one happy surprise. On our second day, the group travelled down to Lake Kivu, on the border between Rwanda and Congo. I was still very sick, and the moment we arrived at the hotel I went straight to bed. A few minutes later, there was a knock on my door. It was one of the UNICEF staff, who excitedly told me that George Clooney was outside. At first, I thought that it was a silly joke, but they insisted that I put some clothes on and go and meet him. George was there for another UN mission, and after greeting him we spent some time with his entourage discussing the refugee crisis. It was of course lovely to meet George, as it was also to see the equally impressive – although less handsome – wild gorillas high up in the mountains a few days later.

After an eventful week, I boarded a plane to return to Dublin, via Belgium. As I landed in Brussels, my phone showed 30 new messages. There are no roaming agreements with Rwanda, so my phone had stayed off. There were numerous texts from Gerry, who was increasingly concerned about my safety. I later heard that he had eventually phoned Niamh, who was slightly surprised to get a call from Gerry Ryan inquiring about 'your boss's health'. Only much later did she realise the significance of the call. Back in Brussels Airport, I sent a quick text back to Gerry, but made up my mind that there would be no social texting. Over the next few weeks, Gerry kept texting, but I kept it strictly professional. Nonetheless, he was now on my radar. I was listening to his radio programme regularly, and secretly getting more and more intrigued by this man.

17

Back in Dublin, I settled into my old routines of work and children. I was never one for partying, and since I was a non-drinker I did not enjoy going to pubs. But it was not much fun staying in at the weekends either. Since my separation almost three years earlier, this had become a pattern. At my girlfriends' insistence, I had gone out with two or three guys for dinner or lunch, but these dates all ended in disaster. Watching TV with my cat was definitely the safer option, albeit, as my teenagers would say, 'a bit sad'.

On a Friday night early in February, I was folding laundry, thinking that I might end up a spinster hidden away in her house, a Miss Havisham, when my phone rang. 'Gerry Ryan' flashed on the screen. He explained that he was on his way to a charity event, where he had to deliver a keynote address. But he had just realised that he did not know much about the charity and wanted to know if I had any useful information. He listed a few questions. I did not know a lot, but as luck would have it, I had had lunch with someone earlier that day who worked for the charity from time to time, and I offered to phone him to get more information. 'But I'm only phoning once,' I said firmly. 'So is this all you want?' I asked, referring to information relating to the charity.

There was a short pause on Gerry's side. 'No, actually, I also want you, but you are clearly not interested, so I guess I'll just have to be satisfied with the information.' For a moment I was stunned, but then I felt anger rising in me. 'Jesus, Gerry! I'm not the one that's married here. I've been separated for years and divorced for more than a year. You're the married man. What on earth gives you the idea I'd have an affair with you? How can you insult me like this?'

There was a long pause on the other end of the line as I considered whether to put the phone down. 'Melanie, can I trust you?' Gerry's usual confident, upbeat tone of voice had changed. I froze.

'Of course,' I said apprehensively.

'Look, about three people know this, but I've been separated for a while.

I don't live at home. In fact, I've been living in my childhood bedroom in my late mum's house.'

I suddenly felt dizzy and sat down on my son's bed, the laundry dropping to the ground.

'Are you there?' Gerry asked anxiously.

'Yes, sorry, I'm sorry to hear it, I'm . . .' I mumbled. 'Why didn't you tell me earlier?'

'I'm sorry,' Gerry said in a strained tone. 'I was hoping to keep it out of the media for as long as possible. I wasn't sure who I could trust, but I really like you and I think I have messed up my chances by not telling you.'

'How long? How long have you been separated?'

'I've been out of the house for a while . . . But almost nobody knows. I couldn't bear . . .' – his voice trailed off – 'the kids . . .'

I needed time to think. 'Gerry, we need to talk some more, but if you really need the information about the charity, I have to call my friend now.'

'Will you please call me back?' he asked. I promised and rang off.

My head was spinning. What now?

I remembered how, on New Year's Eve a few months earlier, I had sat on a rock in the Italian countryside, where my two kids and I had met my sister and her family for Christmas. After more than three horrible years during which I had gone through a separation and divorce, I was weeping with loneliness. In between the tears, I prayed that I would find someone to share my life with, or, as my good friend Abraham often said, 'someone who could witness my life and I his'. Looking over the hills of Italy, I had an intense feeling of calm and a deep awareness that something big was about to change in my life. I have only had such strong feelings a few times in my life, and every time it resulted in dramatic changes. Could this be the answer to my prayers of a few months earlier?

But there was one big problem. Gerry was well known and had a high public profile. After the breakup of my nineteen-year marriage almost three years earlier, I had made myself only one promise: I would never get into a relationship with anyone who had a high public profile again.

How could I even consider going out with Gerry Ryan? He was an institution in Ireland, everyone knew who he was and had an opinion about him. His daily three-hour radio show was the most popular radio show in the country with between 300 000 and 400 000 people listening every day. For almost a quarter of a century, he had been a familiar voice and face on radio and television for Irish people. Yet the more I thought about it, I knew that, apart from the public side of things, the fit was good. But – and it was a very big but – he was famous. (To be honest, I did not fully understand how famous he was until months later.)

Deep in thought, I jumped as my phone beeped. It was Gerry. 'Any information? In a cab, about to arrive at the venue,' the text read.

I quickly phoned my friend and got the background information. Knowing that Gerry was in a taxi and would not have time for a personal discussion, I phoned him back and relayed the information.

'Can I call you later tonight?' he asked.

'I might be asleep,' I lied. I knew full well I would not sleep much that night.

'I'll try and not make it too late,' he said, leaving me in a state of turmoil.

It was not long before my phone beeped again. Having finished his speech, Gerry was clearly bored, and a string of hilarious text messages describing the event and the attendees followed. At around 11:30pm he texted that he had finally made his escape.

'Would you meet me somewhere for a drink?'

'No', I replied firmly. 'That will not be a good idea.'

'OK, I'll call you as soon as I am home. Don't fall asleep.'

Twenty minutes later, he called. We talked and talked and talked. It was as if we had known each other all our lives. Conversation was easy, perhaps because we had so many shared experiences and, as we quickly discovered, many similar interests. There was no use denying it, we both realised that the bond was instant and intense. It was after 3am when we finally said goodnight. A few minutes later he sent a goodnight text: 'You are gonna be my girl! I know it! PS I will not hurt you, I promise. Goodnight.' At that moment I knew that I was in real danger of falling in love with him.

Over the next few weeks we spoke and texted frequently, often deep into the night when he was back in his single bed in his mum's house in the Dublin suburb of Clontarf. Gerry's mum, Maureen, had left the house to him and his two brothers after her death in 2006. After his separation from his wife about a year later, Gerry moved in with his youngest brother Michael who was living there. It was just around the corner from his own house, where his children still lived with their mother, and which he always referred to simply as 'Clontarf'.

He repeatedly asked me to meet up, but his public profile bothered me. I knew that seeing him anywhere in public would likely be noticed. Knowing how quickly gossip spreads in Ireland, I was determined not to give in to his charm. I declined every time, but, as I was to learn, Gerry was very persistent and persuasive if he really wanted something. He gradually wore me down, and one Monday afternoon he sent me a text: 'Look, I have just moved into a lovely penthouse. Please just have one drink with me. It is private and safe, and if you hate me after that, I will stop bugging you.'

So I decided to go. If nothing else, it would give me some clarity on how I felt about him. After work I hailed a cab and headed off to Ardoyne House on Pembroke Park Road in the upmarket area of Ballsbridge in Dublin. As we pulled up outside the apartment block, I started to panic. Gerry had warned me to keep an eye out for journalists outside the apartment and to go past the doorman to the top floor without saying where I was going. This was already getting weird, but I knew I could not pull out now. So, as instructed, I headed straight past the doorman, avoiding eye contact, and stepped into the lift. 'Sorry, ma'am, where you going?' shouted the Malaysian doorman, whom I later came to know as Anwar.

I mumbled something, and thankfully, before he could say or ask anything more, the lift doors closed behind me. On the eleventh floor, there was a penthouse on each side of the lift, but no numbers on either. I phoned Gerry, who promptly opened the door on the right.

For a moment he said nothing, just gave me his very broad smile, opened his arms, gave me a big hug and said, with a mixture of joy and surprise: 'You came!' Dressed in cream slacks and a white jumper, his hair clearly wet from a shower, he apologised for the 'gaff' not being 'a hundred per cent' yet. 'I just moved in,' he explained. We walked past a table covered in lit candles to the sitting room, where a gas fire was roaring and in the background Neil Young was singing 'It's a dream, only a dream . . . .'

'So how are you?' Gerry asked.

'Nervous. No, shit scared, to be honest.'

'I am too,' he answered, to my surprise. 'I'm getting a whiskey. What can I get you?'

'Just a sparkling water if you have it.'

Gerry lifted his eyebrows. 'Look, call me ignorant, but as far as I know, sparkling water is not much good for calming nerves.'

'No, but I don't really drink,' I responded. He looked surprised.

'Nothing at all? How the hell have you survived in Ireland?' He paused, then laughed. 'Great! Cheap date and a designated driver, fantastic.'

I followed him to the kitchen, which he had clearly never used. But the oven doors were open and the oven was on, as were all the rings on the stove. 'Eh, Gerry? Why?' I asked, pointing at it.

'Oh yes, sorry. The heating isn't working, so I could not think how else to warm up the place.'

Life with this man would clearly be strange and surprising, I thought, feeling amused and attracted at the same time. Whiskey in hand, he pulled me out onto the balcony to show me the view of Herbert Park, the city and the coastline in the distance. It was breathtaking. 'Wow! This must work wonders on women,' I teased him.

He put his arm around me and, in a deep voice, said: 'You are the first person that I have invited here socially. But I tell you, it has given me some sense of dignity again.'

And that was that. We spoke for hours about politics, our lives, our respective broken marriages, our children. Gerry's recalling of some of the painful experiences of the previous few years, even at this early stage, moved me to tears – which in turn touched him deeply.

By the end of the evening, there was no question that we would be together. As soon as I was back in my bed in Dalkey, about twenty minutes from where Gerry lived, he phoned again. The conversation continued till 3am – as it would every night after that for months to come.

18

A few weeks after our first night in the apartment, I was lying awake one night, unable to sleep. I was listening to the bells of the nearby church in Clyde Road ringing every fifteen minutes. I looked over at Gerry, who was asleep, propped up on one arm next to me. He was snoring lightly and I watched his chest rise up and down. *How is it possible to love someone so deeply so quickly?* I wondered. I stretched out and gently stroked his hair.

He stirred from my touch and mumbled: 'You okay?'

'Yes, sleep my love,' I whispered back.

He pulled me close and whispered: 'I love you, I love you.'

The early days of our new relationship were full of intense excitement and happiness. As time went by, the excitement and happiness did not become less, as is usually the case. In fact, in the years to come, the love and intensity of our feelings deepened. We both knew this was our second and perhaps last chance at happiness, and spoke of it often. We also knew that, given our personalities and past lives, finding a partner who would be able to deal with either of us would be tricky.

Gerry often said, with pride and a sense of achievement: 'I spotted you, I wanted you, I made a plan and I got you.' When I asked him how he could have been so certain I was the right one, he had a long list of reasons. I used to joke that it sounded calculated and not very romantic, but he just laughed: 'Don't worry. I'm still deeply romantic, you will still see.'

And he was. Often I would arrive back at his place after a difficult day at work and find Gerry cooking a meal. He would run me a bath and I would soak away the stresses of the day among the candles and the bubbles, while he finished preparing the meal. It felt as if my whole life had led me to be with Gerry. The decision to come to Ireland, my divorce, even his interviews with me. All had led me to this place of happiness, joy and intense love.

Of course, life with Gerry was not quite the normal, run-of-the-mill experience. Two days after our first night in the apartment, he called me. 'I wish you could see what I see . . . It is fantastic!' Gerry was down in County Wexford, about an hour south of Dublin, with his good friend, businessman Harry Crosbie, who was busy building a new house close to the sea. Gerry described at length every detail of the view, the house and the weather. He then asked if he could see me that evening.

'Sure,' I said, 'but I will be finished at work in about an hour. I don't fancy hanging around in town for hours.'

'Don't worry, I'll fly down,' he responded.

'Be careful,' I said, 'don't have an accident.' After I put the phone down, it suddenly dawned on me that he might mean it literally. 'You didn't mean flying as in really flying, did you?' I asked him two hours later.

'Oh yes, I have a pilot's licence,' he responded suavely.

'Show-off,' I laughed.

The most challenging part was to keep the relationship private. We wanted as much time as we could get away from the public eye to make sure this was what we both wanted, and that it would work for both of us. We knew it would be a big story once the media found out. Gerry spoke to me a few times about this, worried that I did not quite understand how big a fuss would be made of it. I assured him that I understood and that it would be fine, even though privately I was panicking. This was exactly why I did not want another public relationship. Yet I knew I wanted to be with Gerry and this was the price I had to pay for it. But I wanted to get as much time with him on my own as I could.

Having both lived in the public eye, we knew the rules: if we wanted to keep it quiet, we could not go anywhere together, nor could we talk about it to anyone. As long as we kept to these two rules, we might get a few weeks – or perhaps, if we were really lucky, a few months – of privacy.

That is what we did. For months, we only saw each other in Gerry's apartment. This sounds simple, but it posed a few difficulties. The entrance and exit strategies caused the greatest anxieties. I was always worried that a journalist might be hiding somewhere outside the apartment block, so I would drive through the car park a few times to survey the area. I would wear hoodies, hats and glasses. Once, for fun, I bought a long, blonde Abba-like wig. This had Gerry in stitches. Thankfully he did not like me as a blonde!

The doormen remained a problem. When asked, I would give them a different apartment number. To confuse things, I would get off on the floor of the apartment number I had given them – in case they were keeping an eye on the lift. I would then run up the fire escape the rest of the way. Of course the whole process had to be reversed when I left. Years of dodging the security police in South Africa came in handy as I kept an eye on my rear-view mirror to check if someone was following me when I drove away. Eventually we compromised on the rules and decided that we could each confide in one close friend. In fact, Gerry had already told his trusted friend and producer, David Blake Knox, and I had told my best friend, Brid Walls.

Although all the hiding made things challenging, it was also an extraordinary time, and a huge gift. We spent night after night cooking, watching DVDs and listening to music. Having grown up during the cultural boycott in South Africa, I had many gaps in my knowledge when it came to music and movies. Gerry took pleasure in teaching me. Watching a DVD would often take four hours, as he constantly paused the film to share some important cultural or historical reference with me. I could not help but marvel at his enormous knowledge of such a huge variety of subjects. I had grown up in a university environment and had always mixed with exceptionally intelligent people, but I can say, without any doubt, that in addition to being gentle, sensitive, kind, funny and charismatic, Gerry was one of the most intelligent people I have ever met.

The months we had together away from the public eye were like a hothouse for our relationship. We got to know each other really well in a very short time, and I quickly realised that we were in this for the long haul. David Blake Knox told me later that it was clear from the early conversations he had with Gerry that he felt the same way.

There was another reason why this was an important time. Gerry said that in order for the relationship to work, there could not be any secrets – that he wanted me to know everything about him and his past. He never wanted anybody to tell me something that I did not already know. 'Believe me,' he said, 'there will be many people who would want to do that, to hurt you, to hurt me, or just to claim a stake in me.' So over a period of weeks, he systematically took me through his life journey. He told me all the things he was proud of, but also the things he regretted and was ashamed of. He was brutally honest about everything that had happened to him in his youth, and about his marriage and why it had finally ended. We talked about the few people he called his close friends and those he was disillusioned with.

During these discussions, drugs were also mentioned. He admitted he had used cocaine recreationally in the past – as, he said, had many of those in the circles in which he moved, both professionally and socially. But he was adamant that he was never addicted to it and had stopped using it some time before he met me.

It was important to me to make my position clear. Because of my dad's addiction issues, I would absolutely not tolerate any drug use. For years I put up with lies, erratic behaviour and mood swings, and I was and remain – perhaps unfairly – intolerant of all forms of addiction. For this reason, I have never even tried a cigarette and have never drunk more than half a glass of wine. I have never been drunk – not even tipsy. I hate drunken behaviour with a passion and get quite scared when I am around anyone who gets drunk – too many bad childhood memories. I have never been in a place where anyone used drugs that I was aware of, and I hope I never will be. I made it clear to Gerry that I did not want to be associated with anyone who was using drugs. He promised I would never have to worry about this. 'My heart would never cope with it,' he said. 'I decided ages ago never to touch the stuff again.'

Of course I asked what he needed from me – whether he had any ground rules. He answered: 'Please don't ever humiliate or put me down in public. If I do or say something you don't like, please just keep the criticism for afterwards, when we are alone.' That was all he wanted – for me to love and respect him privately and publicly. That was a promise I could easily make, and had no difficulty keeping for all our time together. I was immensely proud of Gerry, and loving him was the easiest and most pleasurable thing I have ever done.

In retrospect, I think that these discussions were like therapy for Gerry, or a type of catharsis. I was deeply touched by many of the things he had gone through, and his experiences frequently moved me to tears. This was not the public Gerry Ryan; here was a man who was deeply sensitive, emotional and hurt. I felt so honoured that he trusted me with all his stories so early in our relationship. As time went by, I was extremely thankful that he had had the foresight to tell me all the stories. The knowledge he entrusted me with not only protected me, it also meant that when times became difficult, I could contextualise his struggles and, to some extent, protect him and his legacy.

But in the meantime, we were just happy to spend time with each other. I gradually started to help him recreate a life 'with dignity', as he put it – which was so important to him. Gerry loved to cook and was good at it. His chicken stuffed with lemon and his potatoes in goose fat are legendary. However, his kitchen had only a few old, rusted pots, and horrible china with green and red flowers. Gerry hated this, but somehow having to go and buy domestic equipment was just too much for him – even though he would usually not be fazed by anything like that. So I went out and bought everything he needed for the kitchen, as well as more linen for the beds. Otherwise, Gerry was well and truly domesticated. He was extremely tidy and would clean the kitchen meticulously every night before going to bed. He ironed very well, and could do basic needlework: he would fix buttons or do hemming.

One thing he did not like was grocery shopping, which he usually did in Tesco's on Merrion Road before the weekend visit from his children. It was not the actual shopping – which he tackled with military precision – that bothered him, but the women talking to him in the shop. He often phoned me while he was shopping: the idea was that he would have a better chance of being left alone if the women saw that he was on the phone. This did not always work. I would often hear women interrupting our conversation and sympathising with his separation, and then offering to come over to his apartment to help with his domestic arrangements. Even though he was very touched by the empathy and support of his fans and listeners, things sometimes went a bit too far.

For example, we both always found it strange that women he did not know thought it was acceptable to touch him, especially his hair. One woman – while I was on the phone to him – actually licked him. According to her, he looked like he would taste nice. Naturally, he was freaked out (but also amused), and I sent him to have a shower as soon as he got home. I set up internet shopping for him and offered to order the groceries for us every week. But the first time a delivery came to his apartment, someone else opened the door and the delivery man ended up in Gerry's bedroom. He said he wanted to see how Gerry Ryan lived. So that was the end of that.

During this period, we gradually introduced our children to the new relationship. This was a challenge, not only because there were seven of them – of whom five were teenagers – but also because of the huge age differences. Gerry's youngest, Babette, was eight years old and the eldest, Lottie, was 22. In between were Rex, Bonnie and Elliott. And of course there was my Wilmé, who was eighteen, and Wian, who was sixteen. It was extremely important for both Gerry and me to get the introductions right by doing things gradually, gently and in a child-centred way.

I thought it would be easier to tell my children than Gerry's about our relationship, as my marriage had ended almost three years before. Even though I wanted them to know that I was seeing someone, the need to keep it confidential made the situation complex. I decided to tell the children that I had met and fallen in love with someone who was famous, but that we wanted to keep it quiet for as long as possible. I told them I did not want to burden them with having to keep such a big secret. Of course, then the pestering and guessing games started in earnest, but for weeks they never got close to guessing correctly.

For some reason, though, Gerry started to come up in conversations. After a few weeks, Wilmé, over dinner, related a story from the Meteor Music Awards, which she had attended. She went on to tell me how mad the crowd had gone when Gerry came on stage and how one of her friends adored Gerry. 'Is he *really* famous?' she asked.

'Yes, pretty much,' I answered.

Suddenly I saw her having a 'lightbulb' moment as she put two and two together. Her brother, who was engrossed in his food, did not see this, so I signalled to her to keep quiet. But as soon as dinner was finished, she pushed me into another room and said: 'Oh my God! It's him, isn't it?' And so Wilmé knew, and was pleased. One down, six to go.

Wian decided that it was his 'manly' duty to find out who was dating his mum and was determined to trick me into revealing his identity. In the end, it was Gerry who gave it away. One evening, unable to reach me on my cell phone, he rang the house and Wian answered the phone. From the next room, I heard Wian say, in an over-polite voice: 'Yes, she is home. Who may I say is calling?' A few seconds later he stuck his head round the door, gave me the phone and said: 'Gerry Ryan for you.' I waited for a reaction, but there was none. However, a few seconds later the penny dropped and I heard him shout in the next room: 'That's it! It's him! It's Gerry Ryan!' To which his sister responded: 'Idiot! It took you long enough.'

I will always remain extremely thankful to my children for accepting Gerry so generously. They did not care about his fame. In fact, having hardly ever listened to him on the radio, they did not know much about him – hence Wilmé's questions after the Meteor Awards. To them he was a lovely, kind man who made their mum happy, and as far as they were concerned that was all that mattered. He was great with them from the start and would spend hours entertaining them over dinner with the most outrageous stories. They loved it, and quickly came to love him. In the months to come he became an important part of their lives and was there for all of the important events in their lives. Even though he was cautious not to overstep boundaries with their dad, he quickly became someone they saw as a father figure they could trust and rely on.

The situation with Gerry's children was more complicated. There were more of them, they differed greatly in age, and it was not long after their parents' separation. Gerry wanted things to flow as naturally as possible. I gradually met them one by one; thankfully, these meetings went well. I quickly built up close relationships with them, especially the youngest two, whom I saw almost every weekend.

Finally, all the children and our former partners knew about our relationship. The only question that remained was when it would become public knowledge.

19

It was astonishing that it took the press so long to find out about us. Yes, we were extraordinarily careful, and *very* few people knew about our relationship, although Gerry did eventually tell Harry Crosbie and his friend Des McEvaddy as well. I think it was also because the press and the public just did not see me: I was not really in the public eye as a 'celebrity' and they clearly did not put two and two together.

In early 2008, when Gerry was the MC for the screening of the movie *Sex in the City* for UNICEF, we arrived and left together, and even posed on the red carpet together, but not a single photographer took a photo of us. It was obvious that people and the press were expecting Gerry to hook up with a different type of woman – and there were many rumours, mostly involving leggy blondes.

Of course, we went out separately too. After all, we both still had work to do. On one such occasion, Gerry had to go down to Kinsale to host a casino night. He was not looking forward to the evening. Still, he had committed to do it, and, professional that he was, he went. He texted me frequently from the car, and once he was at the venue he called me every fifteen minutes. He *really* was not enjoying the evening. 'It's all the women,' he complained. 'They all want to talk to me and find out how I'm doing. Then they offer their help in whatever way I might need it. It's freaking me out.'

'You poor innocent puppy,' I giggled. 'Well, just keep phoning me.'

Our public lives inadvertently nearly exposed our relationship a few times. I had been invited, in my UNICEF capacity, to the Variety Club Ball, where Michael Flatley was to be honoured for his work in *Riverdance* and *Lord of the Dance*. During the preceding week, Gerry and I discussed the fact that we were both going to an event on the Friday evening, but for some reason we never even considered that it might be the same one, and neither of us mentioned what the event was. It was only when I saw Gerry's invitation the night before that I realised that we were going to the same event. So we got ready at the apartment, took two different cars, at different times – and sat at separate tables across the room from each other. Gerry kept texting me and pulling faces at me across the room, and it all became very funny. He dared me by text to come and say hello – thinking that I would not. Of course I did – pretending that I was just saying hello to a colleague from RTÉ. That was the first time I met Harry and Rita Crosbie, as well as David Blake Knox – or 'DBK', as Gerry called him.

Another night ended with a lot more laughter. Shortly after we started seeing each other, Bruce Springsteen was performing at the Royal Dublin Society outdoor arena. I was dying to go, and mentioned it to Gerry the day before. He was going, of course, but knowing that I could not go with him, I asked if he could get me standing tickets. He phoned me the day of the concert and said he had got a few tickets. My friend Brid, who knew about our relationship, came with me, along with another friend of Brid's. Gerry went off to a VIP area and we happily found a standing place towards the back, on the grass. I got a few texts from Gerry, saying how bad he felt that I was not with him, but I texted back that I was really happy and would see him after the gig.

A few songs into the concert, someone tapped me on the shoulder. It was a security guard from Aiken Promotions, the promoters of the concert. 'Sorry love, are you Melanie Furwood?' he asked, struggling with the pronunciation of my name.

'Yes?' I responded nervously.

'Will you please follow me?' he said, in a serious tone.

'Why?' I asked, confused.

'Mr Gerry Ryan needs you to come and meet him,' responded the security guard, while firmly steering me through the crowd. Clearly I had no choice in the matter. We went outside the stadium, and then he pushed open some barriers. We were at the back of the wheelchair section, right next to the stage. Gerry was waiting for me with a big grin on his face. He thanked the security guard, then whispered in my ear: 'No girl of mine will ever be in the standing places while I am in the VIP section.'

I am still not sure how the security guard found me in the crowd. Gerry always had good relationships with the backstage and security people. Apparently he described me to the guy, who went off and found me among the thousands of fans. Gerry knew that the wheelchair section was the best place to be, as it was so close to the stage. From the banter he was having with the ticket holders, this was a regular hangout place of his during concerts. He was clearly not the only one. A short while later, Paul McGuinness (the manager of U2 and a great friend of Gerry's), some of the members of U2 and a few other people joined us. My friends had also joined us, and I was trying hard not to make it too obvious that the reason I was there was Gerry. He, on the other hand, could not keep his hands off me, and constantly came over to whisper something in my ear or give me a little touch. I kept shooing him away. Paul McGuiness told us afterwards that he realised something was up when he saw Gerry touching me when he thought no one was watching.

To make matters worse, not knowing until a few hours before that I was going to the concert, I had not had time to go home to change after work. It was an outdoor concert, so I had grabbed a hoodie that belonged to my daughter out of the boot of the car. It was only at the end of the evening that I realised that it was her hockey jumper and that it had her (and my) surname embroidered on the back. So much for keeping a low profile.

At the end of the evening, I asked Gerry how he was getting home. Uncharacteristically, he had not made arrangements for a car or taxi to pick him up. He asked if I could give him a lift in my car, which was parked in a near-by car park. I asked how he intended for us to do that without anyone seeing us together. He had a plan (or what he thought was a plan). He would walk ahead and get into my little Mini. I would follow him, jump in and drive him home. I agreed to do this. I kept a few steps behind him as he put his head down and walked briskly through the crowd. Since I was a bit behind him, I could see and hear the reaction of people who were going in the opposite direction. It struck me just how well known he was, and that everyone had an opinion of him.

When I got to the car, Gerry was sitting in the front passenger seat with his jacket over his head! 'Eh, Gerry, that looks very weird!' I said, laughing. Of course neither of us had thought about how I was going to drive slowly through the crowd on the road without us – or rather, him – being seen. Gerry's solution was to put the jacket over his head. I insisted that he put the seat back and pretend to be sleeping. This was not easy either, because, as Gerry was a big man, the Mini did not easily accommodate him in a stretched-out position. Apart from complaining bitterly about being squeezed in like that, he also kept doing a hilarious running commentary on what was going on outside – from under the jacket – all the way home.

Another incident resulted in physical discomfort for me. I was having Sunday lunch with John and Marie Hughes, whom I had met at the function hosted by Sir Anthony O'Reilly shortly after I arrived in Ireland. After the supper, I had facilitated a few meetings for John with Nelson Mandela and of course accompanied him and The Corrs to the '46664' concert in Cape Town a few years earlier. On this Sunday, they had invited me with a few friends and family members – including John's sister Mary, whom I adore. It was a great day, with lots of laughter and chat, and Marie outdid herself with the cooking. After the main courses, she presented us with eight different desserts. Already full, I asked for only one helping, but got all eight – and was told to eat only what I could.

Suddenly John's sister Mary said: 'So who knows the story with Gerry Ryan and his breakup?' A lot of discussion followed, with various suggestions as to the reasons for the split, and whether he would find someone else. Somebody wondered aloud who would be brave – or mad – enough to hook up with him, and whether he would talk about her on the radio. Knowing that if I caught anyone's eye I would never be able to keep a straight face, I kept my head down and just kept on eating. Not only did I eat all eight helpings of dessert on my plate, but two more platefuls, before the conversation moved on. Of course, I felt incredibly sick afterwards – to the amusement of Gerry, and – when I finally confided in them – John and Marie.

Although we were very careful, rumours started to surface. I got a call from Paul Hopkins, the journalist who had been with me in Kenya. He asked if I knew anything about Gerry Ryan having a relationship with the South African ambassador. 'The current ambassador?' I said with shock in my voice, trying to mask my anxiety. 'Gosh, Paul, have you seen the new ambassador? I really don't think she is Gerry Ryan's cup of tea.' (My successor was of Indian decent and was a very big woman who always wore elaborate saris.)

'Yes, that's what I thought,' responded Paul. 'It's just that there's this rumour about town. Could it be someone else in the embassy?'

'Paul, I really don't know what is going on in the embassy anymore,' I responded honestly.

Paul gave a deep belly laugh. 'It's not you, is it?'

'Now you're just fishing, Paul. Gosh, where do you guys hear these rumours?' I did not want to lie outright to Paul.

Luckily, he did not pursue the issue. 'Yes, I thought that would be ridiculous. You wouldn't be his cup of tea either.'

Around the same time, another journalist, Sam Smyth, told Gerry he had heard that Gerry had become very interested in foreign affairs. Gerry just laughed, and thankfully Sam did not persist.

Although in this case there was some truth to the rumours, it still amazes me how gossip becomes fact in a small place like Dublin. There is definitely a cultural difference in the level of gossip between South Africa and Ireland. When I grew up, gossip was regarded as a very bad thing and we would get into real trouble at school if we were caught gossiping. Culturally, South Africans, and particularly Afrikaners, are very upfront people. We deal with issues head-on and would sort out a worry or annoyance with someone directly. I found out quickly that this was not the Irish way, and I was often told that I was too direct. Talking about others seems to be a national pastime in Ireland, and when I first arrived I found it very difficult when people would spend a whole evening over dinner talking about other people I did not know. I still find it interesting to sit in restaurants and listen to the various conversations around me – inevitably about what so-and-so did or said. This became less entertaining, however, when either Gerry or I, or our relationship, became the topic of conversation. The problem is that what is pure rumour quickly becomes the truth in the public's perception. So someone makes up a story or shares a suspicion that they concocted on a bit of false information, and within a matter of hours it spreads, and soon becomes an accepted fact.

During the early days of our relationship, I went to the hairdresser. Although I hate gossip and would always try to avoid it, this day the hairdresser just *had* to tell me the most *fantastic* story. Did I know that Gerry Ryan was living in the Four Seasons Hotel? In the top penthouse, living the life of Reilly. *And* he was having an affair with X! (I will spare the woman the embarrassment of mentioning her name.) It is important to note that, contrary to what has been written a thousand times in the press, Gerry *never* lived in the Four Seasons Hotel after his separation. He often went there for lunch or a drink –

the staff ensured that he got a quiet, private space during that very distressing time – but he never lived there. After initially staying in his mum's house with his brother, Mick, he moved into Ardoyne House, where his friend Des McEvaddy kindly lent him his apartment for free for a year.

'Are you sure about this?' I asked the hairdresser, knowing of course that it was all nonsense.

'I swear on my life,' she responded. 'Sure, everyone knows about him living there, and the affair. I'm surprised you don't know.'

An hour later, when I got back to Gerry in Ardoyne House, I had fun entertaining him with the 'facts' of his love life and living arrangements.

As the months went by, we started to get cabin fever, and needed to get out. We knew this would increase the risk of people finding out about our relationship, but the apartment was getting too small for us. We were still desperate to have time on our own, and we sometimes fantasized about how great it would be if we were just able to go out like any normal couple, ignored by the press and the public. We knew that this was never going to be the case, but we needed to do a few normal things – like have a coffee somewhere.

Our first meal out was in September 2008 in a small Malaysian restaurant called Langkawi. We were having a great night, with Gerry pulling out all the stops to impress me on our first dinner date, until a woman at an adjacent table choked on her food and started vomiting. It was a rather unpleasant sight, but after watching in disbelief, Gerry burst out laughing. 'It is just like Mr Creosote in *Monty Python's The Meaning of Life*!' he roared.

Gradually, we went out more frequently. We started to go regularly to Harry and Rita Crosbie's house. We would arrive and leave separately, but once we were inside we knew we were safe – or so we thought. One day we visited Harry while Rita was away. Just as we sat down, there was a knock on the door. It was someone working with Bono, who said: 'Bono says Gerry should come and say hello, and bring the girl.' Unbeknownst to us, U2 were rehearsing next door in their studio, which is attached to Harry and Rita's house. They must have seen us coming on the security cameras.

We also started to take drives together. We felt safe in the car as long as I made sure to turn my head away from cars next to us when we were at traffic lights. Late one afternoon, Gerry picked me up from my house in Dalkey. Alfa Romeo had just given him a loan of a Spider Cabriolet to test-drive for a while. He loved the car, even though it was a bit small for him inside. 'Bring something for your head, like a scarf,' he said on the phone. Before I could ask why, he had hung up. He arrived in real movie style – roof down, classical music playing. Although I was thrilled with the romantic nature of it all, I knew it would draw attention to us, and asked him whether he minded this. Gerry responded: 'This is Dalkey. Nobody will pay any attention. Now if we were on the northside, it would be a different story. Come on, get in.' A few seconds later, barely at the end of Sorrento Road where I lived, some builders drove past us in a van. One hung out of the window and shouted: 'How's it goin', Gerry? What you doin' on the southside, and who's the bird?' Gerry grunted, clearly feeling a bit foolish, and I burst out laughing. We laughed all the way to town. Only in Ireland.

Gerry suggested that we go on holiday to France after he had spent the first part of the annual holidays with his children in New York and Disney World. There would be a switchover with their mother half way, after which he would fly back and we would have a break. To save money, he arranged for us to stay with his old friends Paul McGuinness and Kathy Gilfillan in their house in Eze. Having only met Paul briefly in a work capacity years before, I was a bit nervous. I also knew that once we travelled together, word would most probably get out. But we needed to do something 'normal', and I was fairly comfortable with the thought of people starting to know about us.

During Gerry's time with the children in America, we spoke constantly on the phone. It struck me how good he was with all the children. It was clear that he was an old hand at it. In America, he dealt with the needs of all five children with his usual flair and efficiency. He hated leaving them and when the time came to fly back to Dublin, he became very distressed, and phoned me in tears on his way to the airport.

We flew to Nice the next day for our first holiday together. It was a magical ten days. Paul and Kathy have a lovely house on the mountainside in Eze, overlooking the sea. We stayed in a separate apartment on the property. The days were filled with lovely meals, lying next to the pool and occasionally going out. U2 were just a few blocks down the road, finishing the *No Line on the Horizon* album. To my confusion and Gerry's great amusement, Paul insisted that he (and therefore us as well) was only to listen to Gregorian chants or other very heavy classical music – absolutely no rock and roll. Gerry teased

Paul endlessly about it, but nothing could sway him: there would be only classical music until the album was finished.

Paul and Gerry were good friends for many years, even though their personalities are quite different. Gerry could tell the funniest stories about things he and Paul got up to, and it was obvious that they were very comfortable in each other's company. Gerry could relax with him. It was extremely hot during our time in Eze, and Paul and Gerry would bob in the swimming pool for hours, like two lazy hippos, chatting away. The second day we were there, Paul suggested we go on his little motorboat and have lunch somewhere on the coast – all very exotic. We piled into Paul's open-top Bentley, but there were too many of us, so I sat cramped up on Gerry's lap, keeping an eye out for the police. Feeling like students on holiday – apart from the Gregorian chants blaring over the radio – we laughed all the way to the harbour.

Once on the boat, Paul said we were making a quick stop on the way. A few minutes later, we 'pulled in' next to an enormous luxury yacht. Jimmy Iovine, the legendary music producer and chairman of InterscopeGeffen-A&M, was staying on the yacht to keep an eye – literally – on the progress of the U2 album. Gerry told me that Jimmy apparently had binoculars focused on the studio door at Bono's house across the bay. I am not sure if this was true, but if it was, some pressure!

The rest of the day was like a movie. We went for a leisurely lunch at an outdoor restaurant in a little bay and then gradually made our way back home, stopping every now and then when it got too hot, to dive into the crystal-clear water for a swim. As the sun started to set, I sat in Gerry's arms at the back of the boat, looking over the Mediterranean, feeling like a princess. Back in Eze, we stopped at Bono and Ali's house to say hello. Ali entertained us and other people who had stopped in, until Bono took a break from the recording.

Bono and Ali had been friends with Gerry for decades and they were happy to see him. I had met Bono and Ali a few times when I was ambassador. A few years before, they had come to my house to see Archbishop Tutu, who was staying there during a visit to Ireland. The archbishop offered to say a prayer and to do a blessing for the soon-to-be-released 'How to Dismantle an Atomic Bomb'. We stood in a circle as he prayed in Xhosa first. When it sounded like he was winding down, Bono, in a real rock-and-roll gesture, lifted his fist into the air and said 'Amen!' Tutu opened one eye and said: 'I am not finished, man!' He then continued in Afrikaans. Once more, it sounded like he was winding down, but before Bono could do anything, Tutu, again with one eye closed, said: 'Not yet!' He continued in English and then gave Bono a little nudge: 'Now!' he said, and we all laughed as Bono threw his fist into the air as the archbishop did a dramatic 'Amen!'

Back in France, Bono and I had a quick catch-up on international-aid strategies. As always, I could only marvel at how informed and strategically shrewd he is when it comes to these issues. Earlier, when Bono had left the studio, he was followed by someone he introduced to Gerry and me, but somehow, in the noise, neither of us heard his name. The guy looked vaguely familiar to me, with his braided hair, big sunglasses and different-coloured shoes and socks. He kept pretty much to himself, but was clearly influential. After we left, I asked Gerry who he was. Gerry had no clue. It was only a few weeks after we got home, when I saw a YouTube video my children were watching, that I thought that the guy had looked just like Will-i-am of the Black Eyed Peas. My children nearly fainted with exasperation about the fact that neither Gerry nor I could say for sure whether we had been in this amazing musician's company.

Back in Eze one day, Paul and Kathy told us they had invited two people over for dinner. People had been coming and going, but I am not sure how many realised that Gerry and I were there as a couple. Being very discreet, Kathy and Paul never said anything, and I think it was just assumed that we were both guests of Paul and Kathy, but not together. I was dozing next to the pool in Gerry's arms – who was reading *The Looming Tower* by Lawrence Wright – when Paul came over to give us the background of the guests. They had invited a friend, who is in PR. 'The thing is, we just realised that his girlfriend works in RTÉ,' he said.

My ears pricked up. 'Who is it?' asked Gerry.

Paul did not know her surname, but told Gerry her first name. I immediately suspected that it was someone both Gerry and I knew from RTÉ. I knew that if she realised we were together, the story might spread fast. I told Gerry what I thought. In typical Gerry style, he immediately called someone in Dublin to ask him if this person was in France. I was right.

While Gerry was on the phone, Paul had gone back to bopping in the pool. When the phone rang, he was out of the pool in a flash; he grabbed a towel and headed for the car. 'What's happening?' Gerry shouted after him.

'There is white smoke, my friend,' Paul shouted back, before speeding away in the Bentley.

It turned out that the call was from Bono. A few hours later, Paul was back, beaming, with a track of 'I'll Go Crazy If I Don't Go Crazy Tonight'. Miraculously, he also had a few T-shirts with that line printed on them. That night we listened to rock and roll music again.

In the meantime, the dinner guests had arrived. They were clearly very surprised to see both Gerry and me. We settled down with some drinks, with Kathy keeping a watchful and protective eye over us. 'So when did you arrive?' they asked Gerry, who answered.

'And you, Melanie?' I answered that it had been the same day.

'Where are you staying, Gerry?'

He answered, and then they repeated the question to me.

I started to see the humour in the situation. As Gerry looked over at me, I could see that he was about to explode with laughter. I could not keep a straight face and fled to the kitchen, where I laughed so much that Kathy thought I was going to hyperventilate.

After the week with Kathy and Paul, we stayed for a few nights in a small hotel in Nice before heading home. As I would do in future, I insisted on paying my half of the holiday. We spent lazy afternoons next to the rooftop swimming pool overlooking the sea and took long walks on the beach. I was always surprised by how much fun it was to be with Gerry. He loved life with such intensity. Whether it was the view from the balcony, the food, the weather, the hotel or even the Arabic Channel on the TV – everything was just so 'fantastic', and he kept saying how delighted he was to be there, alive and happy.

One of the best things about being with Gerry was how much we laughed. We shared a similar sense of humour and would see the same ridiculous and funny things in everyday situations. If we were out, I would often spot something, catch his eye and know that he was also highly amused by the same thing, while trying to keep a straight face.

During our few days in Nice, he was particularly amused by the effect the French attitude to marriage and relationships had on me. I, on the other hand, did not think it was funny. When we checked in at the hotel, the French manager came over. 'Welcome, Mr Ri-aaan. Welcome, Mrs Ri-aaan,' he greeted us. Feeling strongly about these anti-feminist assumptions, I immediately corrected him. I was not Mrs Ryan. But the manager just dismissed it. 'We don't see, we don't hear, we don't care. We are French!' he said, while winking at me. I heard Gerry snorting with suppressed laughter behind me. To Gerry's amusement, I made things worse by trying to explain, but of course the manager had no interest in what I was saying. Every time I had to sign for something, the same conversation took place. Exhausted by it all, I eventually accepted defeat and for the rest of the stay I indignantly signed as 'M. Ryan' – to Gerry's delight.

On our last day, we went for coffee in the old historic part of Nice, close to the hotel. As we walked past the Louis Vuitton store, Gerry said he wanted to buy me a handbag as a gift. I strolled through the store, but having never before been in a Louis Vuitton store, it came as a shock that most of the bags were priced at over €1000. My Calvinist upbringing made it hard for me to believe the price. Gerry, on the other hand, could not believe that I would not let him buy me one. 'Man, you are a different type of woman,' he laughed. I insisted that it was ridiculously expensive, and eventually agreed that he would buy me a beautiful red leather notebook which was on sale for less than €80. I treasure the little notebook, together with my memories of the lovely holiday.

Between all the laughter and fun, there was a dark cloud on the horizon. During this time I understood for the first time the difficulty Gerry was in financially. I had known from what he had told me that there had been issues with his finances, and (as I would testify two and a half years later) that these had been exacerbated by the separation. As a result, he was very worried about money. But it was only during that trip that I realised the full extent of the problem. I questioned him about it over the few days, and he gradually told me the details. Since I had always managed my own finances and been the main bread-winner for my family since my mid-twenties, I realised that it was a big problem that would develop into a huge crisis if it was not tackled.

But Gerry was reluctant to discuss any possible solution. He was adamant that he wanted to keep his family in the lifestyle that they were accustomed to, 'even if it kills me', as he put it. He wanted to ensure that nothing would impact negatively on the children and also that his public image would not be tainted in any way. 'Even if I have to live in a shack, people will *never* say I don't look after my family,' he said. Gerry acknowledged that the sums were never going to add up, but he had an absolute belief that he could earn more money by doing extra work outside RTÉ.

20

B ack in Dublin, we settled into a gentle routine. Even though we kept two houses for our children's benefit, we stayed together most nights, either at Gerry's apartment or at my house in Dalkey. I also tried to spend at least one evening with Gerry at the weekend, to see his children. When we were not together, he would almost always go to Rita and Harry. Harry phoned every day to check where Gerry was having his 'tea', and when I was not around Rita would give him dinner. After dinner, Gerry often fell asleep on their couch, dreading the idea of going home on his own.

We still rarely went out, which did not bother me at all. Since my early twenties, I had juggled a very demanding career with raising children. Attending social functions has always been part of my job, and when I do not have work obligations, I have always been happy just to stay at home. But I was worried that Gerry was becoming lonely. I quizzed him about this. 'Why don't we go out with your friends?' I asked him one night.

'Well, as it turns out, I don't have that many friends after all,' Gerry said quietly.

'How do you mean?'

Gerry explained that almost all of their joint friends had taken sides after the separation. With few exceptions, he did not hear from or see any of them. Gerry was confused and upset about it all, and in the beginning spoke about it often. He could not understand why this had happened. I told him to give it time and that I believed that people would come around. But I was wrong. Things did not change. In fact, the situation would get worse over the next two years.

Gerry's loneliness was not my only concern. Even in the early days, I was worried about his health. He was clearly constantly under stress and did not eat well. He slept badly; I would often lie awake at night watching him while he slept fitfully. He liked rich foods and got no exercise. Even though he had given up smoking years before, and I only saw him twice smoking half a

211

cigar, he did drink frequently. Given my dad's history with drinking, I was very sensitive to drunken behaviour and heavy drinking. Gerry had a large capacity for alcohol and could consume a lot before it had any effect on him. He liked drinking whiskey. Twelve-year-old Jameson was his favourite, although he was an expert on all good whiskeys. When he went out, he would have a Martini before dinner and occasionally a brandy after a meal. He had a few favourite wines, but did not really like champagne. He would open a bottle only on special occasions and every time the remainder would go off in the fridge.

Even though he liked to drink, Gerry did not *have* to drink. This made a big difference to me. He acknowledged that he often drank more than was healthy for him, and quite frequently, to give his liver a break, would not take any alcohol for a few weeks. During all the time I was with Gerry, I only saw him really drunk about five times – each time after something really dramatic had happened, personally or professionally. I did not like it at all, and he knew it, but all the other times he would only become funnier and more sociable. At worst he would get very tired and just want to go to sleep – which would cut an evening short.

Of course, he himself was partly to blame for the image of him 'guzzling copious amounts of wine and spirits', to quote a newspaper article. I often heard him say on the radio that he was hung over, and he would make a point of dissolving a painkiller on air for the headache, when I knew that he had not had any alcohol the previous night. When I asked him about it, he would always answer that he had a few minutes to fill and that it made for good radio. In the time I knew Gerry, he was always conscious of having to go to work the next day, and he *never* missed a day's work because of being hung over: in fact, he almost never had a hangover.

Did I want him to drink less? Of course I did, because I was worried about his health. Did my presence, and the fact that I don't drink, influence him to drink less? Perhaps, but I also know that it is a fatal mistake for anyone in a relationship to try to change the other person. From day one, I knew that I had to be comfortable with all of Gerry, the way he was – warts and all – as I hoped he could be with me. And it was part of Gerry's character to enjoy good wine and whiskey.

One of the rare occasions we went out during this time was a visit to the residence of the British ambassador. David Reddaway and his wife Roshan had met Gerry and me at the Crosbies' one night. He then invited us to Glencairn for a party on the occasion of 'Her Majesty's birthday'. We debated whether to go, but given my diplomatic background we felt that we could perhaps get away with it, without it being too obvious that we were a couple. I had asked Gerry (who was due to pick me up in Dalkey) to come a bit earlier so that he could meet my parents, who were visiting from South Africa.

'Oh God!' he complained. 'This is going to be hard.'

'You're not nervous, are you?' I teased.

'No, of course not,' Gerry replied. 'It's just important to make a good impression with the folks.'

When he arrived, he was clearly very nervous. I opened the front door and he stood there all dressed up, looking very formal. He kissed me, then whispered in my ear: 'Please tell me you have whiskey somewhere.' Slightly amused, I introduced him to my parents, who were also very formal. While they interrogated him, I went to the kitchen and looked through the cupboards. I thought I still had a bottle of Jameson from my embassy days a few years before. I found it, and went back with the half-full bottle and a glass. I poured the whiskey, but thought it looked a bit strange, and saw my dad looking over at it with an equally puzzled look. I wondered whether whiskey could go off, but Gerry did not say anything, so I assumed it was all in order.

In the car on the way to the British residence, Gerry wanted to know what was up with the whiskey. It turned out that the whiskey had been diluted with water. Both my children denied any knowledge of this age-old teenage trick of drinking from the bottle and then refilling the missing space with water. 'If there was ever a night that I needed a strong whiskey, it was tonight,' Gerry laughed. 'I didn't think I would get so nervous at my age.'

There was no need for nerves, however: my parents adored Gerry. Two years later, my mum showed me a beautiful text Gerry had sent her about me, and she confessed that Gerry had occasionally sent her a text to tell her how much he cared about me, and to check how they were.

The evening at the British residence was the first public event we had gone to together, but people did not seem to realise that we were there as a couple. After years of attending diplomatic functions on my own, I loved being there with Gerry. He was very entertained by my 'brashness' when I

213

slipped my hand into his while he was speaking with some high-ranking army officials. Nobody noticed.

Still, it was getting more and more difficult to keep things under wraps. Shortly before our relationship became public, I had an operation in Holles Street Maternity Hospital. I insisted on a spinal block and not a general anaesthetic, since I was not keen on staying overnight. However, I was last on the list and was only back in the ward in the early evening. I was told that I could only leave once the epidural had worn off and I could walk on my own. I was determined to go back to Gerry's apartment that evening, where I was going to stay for a few days to recover. Originally the plan was that my daughter would pick me up – after all, it would be a bit strange for Gerry to stroll into Holles Street Hospital – but eventually it had got very late and my daughter, who was in her final school year, went to bed. Just before midnight, when I was finally able to walk a short distance, I got the green light to go home. I had to assure the nurses that someone would pick me up and take care of me for the next week to ten days. But how would I get home? I was not really stable on my legs yet, and was in a lot of pain, so a taxi was not an option. Gerry said that he would come and get me. 'This is going to be interesting, but I'll be there in a few minutes,' he insisted. I described exactly where I was, hoping that since it was in the middle of the night, and with mostly foreign nurses on duty, no one would notice.

Of course, this was never going to happen. The man at reception greeted him with, 'Jaysus, Gerry, is it a naughty one, or a grandchild?' The pregnant women who were waiting to be admitted all wanted autographs, and promised Gerry they would name their babies after him. After about an hour, I heard footsteps in the passage and, as luck would have it, the only Irish nurse on duty bumped into Gerry. I could hear her greeting him with surprise and asking why he was there. The next moment, she stuck her very puzzled face through the curtain around my bed and said: 'Your lift is here!' She stood watching us for a few minutes, while Gerry helped me get out of bed. Then she shook her head and got her professionalism back. She gave Gerry strict instructions on how to care for me and, with a frown, waved us off. Hanging on to Gerry, hoping my legs would not give way, I felt her eyes on us all the way down the corridor.

Gerry looked after me with great care for ten days while I was recovering.

He rushed back every day after the programme to make me lunch, and then stayed with me in bed, reading and watching DVDs. At night, when I was walking around in agonising pain, he would make me hot chocolate and sit with me until I fell asleep. Being Gerry, he studied pain management with great enthusiasm on the web and discussed it with some medics he knew. I always thought that with his interest in medicine, he could have easily been a doctor or, perhaps even better, a psychologist.

It was, of course, just a question of time before the press printed the story of our relationship. We had had many months of anonymity, and I would have loved for it to have stayed that way. But when you hook up with one of the most recognisable people in Ireland, that simply is not possible.

In early October 2008, UNICEF Ireland hosted an international youth summit on HIV/AIDS in conjunction with Irish Aid. It was a very busy three days, with the global head of UNICEF, Taoiseach (Prime Minister) Brian Cowen, various other Cabinet ministers, international delegates, and special guest Annie Lennox attending. We took care of them all, as well as the general arrangements – quite a challenge for my small staff. In addition, Vanessa Redgrave was performing in the Dublin Theatre Festival. As a UNICEF ambassador, she had agreed to speak at a special women's lunch I had organised for some of our regular donors, and invited me as her guest for the Saturday matinee of her one-woman show *The Year of Magical Thinking*. I was still not well after the operation, so it was going to be a challenging few days.

The conference delegates arrived on Friday in advance of a workshop on Sunday and the opening ceremony on Monday. The lunch with Vanessa, who is an inspirational and charismatic person, was also on Friday and it went well. On Saturday, in between conference meetings, and late for the performance in the Gaiety Theatre, I rushed into Gerry's apartment to drop off a few things. I ran in the door, threw the bags into the bedroom and shouted at Gerry that I would see him later. When I turned around, he was behind me, looking worried.

'What's wrong?' I asked.

'The story is going to break tomorrow,' he said. He had heard from a newspaper contact that the *Sunday World* was running with the story on the front page the next day. His information was that it was fairly neutral, but that it was going to be big. Apparently, journalists had been following us for a while, trying to get a photo, but of course we were too careful. In the end, they had decided to run with the story without the photo.

No matter how many times we discussed this inevitable day, and our feelings and approach to it, when it actually happened it was still frightening. It is hard to describe the sense of vulnerability you feel when the media print even the smallest story about you, especially about your personal life. I have dealt with this since I went into politics over twenty years ago, but I do not think I will ever get used to it, or be comfortable with it. Luckily, I did not know at that stage what lay ahead.

Gerry and I spoke briefly, but I had to go to the performance. I promised to come back immediately afterwards. Gerry was nervous, as I was, and needed company. I sat in a daze at the performance and struggled to concentrate on the sad story of a woman who lost both her husband and daughter in one year. (The story took on special significance for Vanessa, who a year later lost her daughter, brother and sister in one year.) I was conscious of all the people in the theatre and wondered whether, by the next day, they would all be looking at me if I were there again. I tried to stay calm, but my heart was pounding.

The rest of the afternoon and evening was a flurry of phone calls and discussions between Gerry and me. By the time I got back, he had warned everyone he needed to – most importantly his children. I phoned my children, Wilhelm, the chair of UNICEF's board, and then all my staff members. Gerry and I had decided months before that we would not discuss our relationship in public. We thought that if we persisted with this approach, there was a chance that the press might eventually leave us alone – but we could not waver or make any exceptions. Gerry was not convinced that we would be able to sustain this in the long run, but I was adamant about it, a decision I came to regret later. We reaffirmed our approach, then waited for the bomb to explode the next day.

On 5 October 2008, the *Sunday World* led with 'Gerry's African Queen'. It was a huge spread, but mostly neutral. I went to the conference, determined just to continue with my life as before – and that meant my work. Of course, this is not easy when every newsstand has your face on the front page of a newspaper. I went to meet the head of UNICEF, who made no reference to it. A meeting later that day with Irish Aid produced a few winks and nods – all very mild. But of course the word was out. Both our phones were hopping with text messages and phone calls from friends and the media. We ignored all the calls from the media. I succeeded in avoiding all photographers, who clearly did not know I was at the conference that day. By the next day, almost all the newspapers were covering the story.

To complicate matters, this was the big opening day of the summit, with Annie Lennox and the Taoiseach as the main speakers. This would always have brought a big media contingent, but it seemed to have doubled. Even the celebrity photographer Mark Doyle appeared. I had to introduce Annie Lennox to the Taoiseach, who had been Minister for Foreign Affairs during my term as ambassador. The government press officer, Eoghan O'Neachtain (an old and good friend of Gerry's, who has a great sense of irony and humour), said with special emphasis:'Taoiseach, of course you remember the former South African ambassador, Melanie Verwoerd? She is quite well known these days.'

Brian Cowen shook my hand and said: 'Yes, indeed, indeed.' And then, nodding towards the media, he said softly: 'Do you think they are here for me or you?' Throughout the day, journalists tried to get a comment from me about the relationship with Gerry, but I was determined to focus on the conference and insisted that I would only talk about the HIV/AIDS crisis.

The next day, I had arranged for Gerry to interview Annie Lennox about her work in the field of HIV. It had been arranged weeks before. I would always accompany guests to media interviews, but now I had to go into Gerry's studio in RTÉ and, even though I was not going to go on air, it would be a strange experience. At first I was not sure what to do, but in the end I stuck to my rule: I was going to do what I would have done before. In the control room, the papers were strewn around as usual, except on that day almost every paper had the story of our relationship on the front page. The *Ryan Show* team were all very happy to see me – and of course Annie Lennox – and Gerry blew me a kiss through the glass window. That Gerry and Annie got on so well ensured it was a brilliant and moving interview.

After two days of wall-to-wall coverage, and with the summit behind us, I thought the story would die down and that would be it. After all, how many times can you print that Gerry Ryan is seeing Melanie Verwoerd? I was to learn quickly, however, that stories about Gerry sell papers, and so the stories

217

about us just kept appearing. The coverage was across-the-board neutral or even positive, which was a relief. Gerry was a bit indignant about the surprise everyone expressed about the 'unlikely match'. One paper published a big article under the headline: 'Could Gerry really be dating the ambassador?' Gerry was annoyed: 'What the f**k is that all about?'

Of course, now the press wanted a photograph of us together. Soon after the story broke, Gerry got a call offering him €60 000 for an exclusive photo. We debated whether to accept the offer and donate the money to UNICEF, but both of us were wary of this kind of collusion with the press, so we declined.

During this time, another problem developed from an unexpected quarter. A few months into our relationship, I had taken the then-chair of the UNICEF Ireland board, Chris Horn, into my confidence. I wanted him to be forewarned should any stories leak out, and most importantly I wanted him to know that the relationship had started after Gerry's separation, and that it had never been an affair. Chris was delighted for me and insisted that it was a personal matter. The night before the story broke, I phoned him and asked him to warn all the board members. He maintained that it was a personal matter and that there was no need to inform board members. I did not agree and told him so, but he was the chair, and it was his call to make.

As it turned out, a few board members were really annoyed that they had not been warned. Even though they did not say it to me directly at first, tensions arose quickly and a few uncomfortable months followed. Some board members insisted that Gerry could not do anything again for UNICEF – he was to MC the business luncheon a few weeks later, as well as the première of the new Harry Potter movie – or even accompany me to events. Even though he had been a big supporter of UNICEF for years before I had become the executive director, these few board members now felt that he 'did not fit the corporate image of UNICEF'.

Naturally, Gerry was hurt by all of this, and it added to the stress and vulnerability both of us felt during that time. Luckily some board members supported Chris's opinion that this was a private matter, and eventually things calmed down. In fact, the board seemed happy with all the coverage that UNICEF was getting on the back of our story.

The first public event we attended after the story broke was the première of the new Harry Potter movie in aid of UNICEF at the Savoy Cinema. In light of the unhappiness of some board members, Gerry had withdrawn from doing an introduction beforehand and it was agreed that one of my staff, Mar Healy, would introduce me and that I would say a few words. The press was speculating for days about whether we would go together, but I did not want this to be a distraction from UNICEF, so we left from Gerry's apartment in different cars. He arrived first, joking with and posing for the press on the red carpet, as always. I waited around the corner until he texted me from inside. Then I arrived, and even though all the photographers shouted at me and took photos, I just wanted to get inside as soon as possible.

After drinks with some of the guests, we went inside the theatre. Gerry went to his seat and I waited for the introduction from Mar, who was ready with the microphone. I saw Gerry waving at her, and she went over to him. She later told me that he just said: 'Right, where's the mic? I'm doing the introduction.' I had a bit of a fright, but what could I do? So Mar introduced Gerry, who gave a brilliant speech and then introduced me. I walked over to him, and as he handed me the microphone he took my hand and kissed it. There was an audible gasp from the audience, but my children and their friends were now cheering loudly, so the moment passed. At the end of the evening, we left separately, so even though there was extensive coverage of the event the next day, they had to settle for a photo of Gerry's colleague Ryan Tubridy and a model called Laura Toogood together instead.

The next day, I flew to South Africa for my sister's wedding. Arriving at the airport, I could not believe how much media coverage there was of the event of the night before.

During this time, Gerry was also busy writing his book, *Will the Real Gerry Ryan Please Stand Up*. I found it amazing that, with all the stresses and changes in his life, he could still find the energy and head-space to do this. I asked him why he continued to do it, and he said he needed the money. Gerry received one of the highest advances ever paid in Ireland for a book. He was delighted about this, since he was already having a hard time managing additional obligations following his separation. So two to three times a week he sat for three to four hours in the afternoon and dictated the book to someone, who then transcribed and edited it. Gerry found this regime gruelling, but the book had to be out before Christmas, so he persevered. He was excited when it was finally finished, and he gave me and DBK rough drafts to read. I thought the book was a great read, but it struck me that it did not quite sound like the Gerry I knew. I asked him about this, and he said that it was all show business and that he would never let anyone publicly know who he really was. He was thrilled with the cover when he saw the mock-up and was looking forward slightly apprehensively to publication. There were a few legal issues beforehand, and the threat of an injunction. Many lawyers got involved, and the fees consumed much of the advance. Gerry was very bitter about it, since he desperately needed the money to deal with the debts.

Meanwhile, Gerry and I were happily settling into a routine, building our relationship and trying to merge two families. At least life was easier now in Ardoyne House. The three doormen – Anwar, Brendan, and a kind elderly gentleman we all just knew as 'Mr Ryan' – and I were now friends and there were no more interrogations when I arrived. Many of the residents knew who I was and greeted me in a friendly way, but there was one lady who insisted on speaking to me in Irish. Each time I apologised and explained that I was from South Africa and did not understand Irish. I then had to endure a lecture from her about the fact that I was in Ireland now and should learn Irish.

I bumped into her one day when Gerry was having a very busy week and did not have time to take some of his clothes and linens to the laundry. He needed something urgently cleaned for work the next day, so I offered to drop it off on my way to work. It was only after he left that I realised what a big load it was. I was running late and did not want to walk to the car twice. So I carried the huge load down, stumbling under the weight. When I stepped out of the lift into the lobby, the 'Irish' lady opened the door for me. 'Where are you taking all of this?' she asked (thankfully in English).

'To the laundromat,' I said, slightly out of breath.

'Why?' she said, tipping her head sideways and looking at me disapprovingly.

I was getting a bit irritable. 'Because it is dirty,' I said, trying to get past her.

'Why don't you just wash it? Don't you have a washing machine?'

'Look,' I said firmly, 'it is not mine, I'm doing someone a favour.'

To which she responded: 'This is the problem with you young, foreign women. You're lazy and incompetent, wasting your man's money. Gerry could have done so much better.'

Even at this point, the press still did not have a photograph of us together, although it was not through lack of trying. I did not want the first photograph to be at a UNICEF event, so when Cathy Gilfillan invited us to the annual Ice Ball in aid of the Rotunda Hospital, Gerry immediately accepted. I bought a dress on sale for €97 in Monsoon and got home an hour before the event. Through years of practice, I knew I would only need an hour to get ready, so I was relaxed. Gerry, on the other hand, was panicking and repeatedly complained that we must not be late. I assured him we would not, and eventually kicked him out of the room because he was making me nervous. He was amazed when I joined him right on time in the sitting room. When we arrived together at the Shelbourne Hotel, celebrity photographer Mark Doyle spotted us immediately.

'Please tell me I'm getting this picture tonight,' Mark said.

When we nodded, Mark beamed from ear to ear. 'Oh great, this is my money for the month.'

Mark took the photos and then left. The next day, with our photograph on the front page of the *Daily Mail*, Gerry got an e-mail from Mark with a copy of the photo. 'On my way to a holiday in Miami,' he joked. 'Thanks a million.'

21

Festive days, in particular Christmas, are difficult to navigate after a separation. The more traditions and children (especially younger ones) you have, the trickier it gets. I used to love Christmas, but after my separation I started to hate the day and its memories, trying to keep things as normal as possible when everything had changed, and trying to do the complicated juggling act of ensuring that the children spent enough time with both parents and both sides of the family. 2008 was Gerry's first Christmas after his separation. Even though he dreaded the festive period, he spent an enormous amount of time getting the presents sorted out. Christmas Day was additionally hard for him, as his mum had passed away on Christmas Day two years earlier.

I knew he wanted to keep as many traditions as possible, which would mean going over on Christmas Eve for a party at Clontarf, being there with his kids early on Christmas morning for the opening of Santa's presents, and then cooking the lunch. In the build-up to Christmas, Gerry got more and more stressed and frazzled. In between working, trying to sort out Christmas presents and calming everyone down, he was also trying to sort out all the food for Christmas lunch. I was surprised and impressed when he told me that he had done the Christmas lunch for years. I think every woman in the world would love a man to take that burden off her hands, and I told him so.

Gerry went very quiet and then said, with an angry and bitter tone: 'The one on the day of my mum's death was the worst. I hated it after that.'

I asked him what had happened and he got so upset that he had to sit down. He related how, after seeing his mum off the previous evening, he got a phone call from his youngest brother, Michael, early on Christmas morning simply saying: 'She's gone.' Gerry went down to his mum's house to say goodbye one last time and to deal with the undertakers. He wept as he told me how he had carried his beloved mum's body to the gurney downstairs, since he did not want anyone else to do it. Amazingly, as he was to describe in his book later, on his return home he still had to make the Christmas lunch.

Knowing that I would see very little of Gerry over those next few days, and not wanting to add to the stress, my kids and I decided to spend Christmas in New York. Gerry had arranged for us to stay at the Fitzpatrick Hotel on Lexington Avenue, where his friend John Fitzpatrick very kindly put us (and later Gerry) up for two weeks. I was worried about how to get the Christmas spirit going in a hotel room, but when we arrived we found that Gerry had arranged with the hotel to put a Christmas tree in our room.

The day after Christmas, my kids flew back to Ireland to spend time with their dad. Gerry had taken his children to Dromoland Castle in the west of Ireland, as had been the practice for years. He stayed with them for a few nights until just before New Year's, when he flew over to meet me in New York.

I could not wait for him to arrive, and he was delighted when I surprised him at the airport. As soon as we got back to the hotel, he gave me my Christmas gift. It was two identical packages. Both had a little heart necklace – one with a black heart, the other with a silver heart. The card explained: 'For my African girl . . . I know that a part of your heart will always be in Africa, but I hope the other will be with me. Thank you for saving my life.'

We spent a week together in New York. Gerry was exhausted and it was freezing outside, so we took it easy. Every morning he would wake up and start working his way through the Zagat restaurant guide. He spent hours every day researching, deciding on a place, and then looking forward to where we would eat that night. This was a new world for me. On all our previous trips, my kids and I ate as cheaply as possible, mostly in diners or by having takeaways in the room. For Gerry, the ritual of eating out was part of the great joy of holidays. On our first night, we went to Maloney and Porcelli, where we ate steak and butternut purée. The next night we went to Trattoria dell'Arte, where I ate a pasta called *strozzapreti* (strangled priests) and Gerry had an enormous pizza. Later in the week we went to a special Indian restaurant called Devi. The curry was delicious and Gerry spoke lyrically about Leipziger Gose beer for months afterwards.

I convinced him that we would always eat a main course only and share a dessert, to save money, but also to control the amount of food we ate. Gerry happily agreed to this, although I heard that he jokingly complained afterwards to Fiona Looney about his Calvinist girlfriend. We tried to walk as much as we could; Gerry drank very little, and even lost some weight. He started to feel a lot more rested. We loved the performance we saw of Liza Minnelli at the Palace in Times Square, and when I was freezing on our way home, he gave me his jacket and waved away my protests. 'That's what real men do,' he said firmly.

We were like two lovesick teenagers. We went for long walks in Central Park and threw snowballs at each other. We wanted to go to Staten Island, but nearly froze to death waiting at the pier for the ferry, so we went to Grand Central Station instead and had drinks while watching the light show projected on the roof and walls. We were deeply in love and nothing – not even the daily 'How's it goin', Gerry?' from Irish people in New York who would recognise him and wanted to have a chat – could dampen our spirits.

On New Year's Eve, we went early to Smith and Wollensky restaurant, where we ate the most delicious steak. Soon after we sat down, the waiter brought a note from the manager, who had seen our booking but was not on duty that evening. It read: 'Hi Gerry, the Ryan Line is open. My family back in Tyrone are big fans of your morning show. Thanks for coming to s&w. Sorry I missed you this time and happy New Year.'

Back at the hotel after dinner, and keen to miss the crowd of Irish people who were already congregating in the bar of Fitzpatrick Hotel, we went to our room and watched DVDs in bed. Just before midnight, we heard helicopters hovering low over Manhattan. Gerry muted the TV, listened for a few seconds and then identified the type of helicopter. He realised they were there for Hillary and Bill Clinton, who were scheduled to 'drop' the famous ball at midnight. Gerry started laughing. 'Christ, here we are, just ten minutes from Times Square, and we are in bed watching it on TV! We better never tell anyone about this, we'l sound like some boring aul' ones!' Of course he dined out on the story for many months.

Before we went to New York, Gerry had decided that he wanted a new coat. It needed to be a long black coat, he explained – a Jewish coat, he called it. So we looked and looked. We went into shop after shop, but nothing was exactly right. I do not really like shopping and thought that many of the coats he tried on looked fine, but Gerry was not happy. None was the right one.

Exhausted from hours of trying on coats, we headed back to the hotel, but on our way Gerry spotted one last shop. He went in, to be greeted by an enthusiastic Italian-American salesman. While he tried on a few coats, I spotted a beautiful one. I knew Gerry would love it. A few minutes later the salesman showed it to Gerry. 'Very exclusive, only three made, I give you 50 per cent discount,' he said.

Gerry's eyes lit up, 'What do you think?'

'You should get it. After all, you have bought only gifts for the children and nothing for yourself,' I replied.

Gerry was delighted, but just as he went to the counter to pay, I noticed it had a fur lining. 'Excuse me,' I said to the salesman, 'what type of fur is this?' I could see the salesman's face drop and an irritated there-goes-my-sale look crossed his face for a few seconds before he put on a big smile.

'Fur? Ah, not important fur,' he said, dismissing it with a hand gesture.

Gerry was smiling, knowing I would not let it go that easily. 'No, what fur?' I insisted.

'It's vermin, just vermin, like chicken,' the salesman said.

'Chicken?'

'Yes, like underwater chicken!' The salesman had suddenly lost his command of English.

'What is underwater chicken?' I insisted, looking over at Gerry, who just shrugged his shoulders.

'It's vermin,' he said, imitating the salesman's accent.

The salesman did not seem to notice; he was hastily swiping Gerry's credit card.

As we left the store, Gerry burst out laughing and hugged me. 'You were never going to win that one, my darling.' I never found out what fur it was, but Gerry loved his coat. He called it 'Gerry Ryan's big coat'. He wore it throughout the winter and in summer he would take out the removable lining. After Gerry covered me with it a few times when I fell asleep on the couch in front of the TV, I made my peace with the 'underwater chicken' coat.

Apart from an emergency call from my daughter on New Year's Eve, after one of her friends needed stitches in her foot, there was thankfully no crisis back in Ireland, and we had a peaceful time. In the taxi on our way back to JFK Airport, Gerry took my hand. 'Would it not be nice to live here?' he asked.

I loved the idea and told him that for years I had wanted to do some work in New York with the UN or some other philanthropic organisation. 'What about work for you? Will you get some here?'

'Of course,' Gerry responded. 'Perhaps not at the same level, but God only knows what is going to happen at RTÉ over the next year or two.' He squeezed my hand and said: 'Well, that settles it then. We'll get married as soon as I'm free, and we'll start working on this plan. Perhaps a few months here, a few in Dublin and then the summer in South Africa?'

'Shouldn't you first ask me if I *want* to marry you?' I said, trying to hide a smile.

'Don't you?' Gerry asked, looking worried.

'Of course I do, but I want a proper proposal, okay?'

'If I get you a ring, will you wear it?' he asked.

I thought about this for a few minutes. 'No, you have to get legally separated first. Ask me again then, and of course I will wear your ring.'

'Okay, I will. It's a promise,' Gerry replied.

22

Gerry dreaded going back to Dublin. His friend, Des McEvaddy, needed his apartment back for family reasons. Gerry loved the apartment and felt safe there. Surrounded by all the other tenants, he did not get too lonely when I, or the children, were not there, and most importantly, he kept repeating that it gave him some dignity. The idea of having to find another place made him feel depressed. I scoured the internet, made him a shortlist and then arranged for the agents to show us around. Gerry hated everything we saw and became deflated.

Then one of the agents said she had a house on Leeson Street she thought Gerry would like. He was not too keen about the idea of living on Leeson Street, but she convinced us to have a look. The moment we walked into the three-storey Georgian house, he seemed a lot happier. The rent was quite high, but Gerry phoned Harry Crosbie to ask him to come over and have a look. Harry agreed that it was a good property, but that the rent was high. As luck would have it, he knew the owner and gave him a ring on Gerry's behalf. The owner agreed to reduce the rent significantly and the deal was signed. But he wanted the first year's rent up front, and Gerry could not afford it, so Harry lent it to him.

Over the next few weeks, I made arrangements with a removal company to move the few belongings Gerry had from the apartment to the new house. I also moved some of my possessions over. It took Gerry a while to get used to our new house. It was pretty and spacious, ideal for when the kids were there. But when he was on his own, the house was too quiet and too big. He also felt a bit unsafe living on such a busy road and had various additional locks installed on the doors. Every night before he went to bed, he would set the alarm and meticulously lock all the locks.

All the children, mine and his, liked the house. The small ones liked the space, both inside and out. The older ones could drop in at any time. My children in particular loved its proximity to town and would stay over after nights out. Gradually we started to build a new family life together.

- 1 line please

On Sundays, Gerry took all his children for lunch. He often asked me to join them, but I felt strongly that the children needed time with him on their own and, with a few exceptions, I declined. Gerry hated it when the kids left after the weekend. I tried to be there just before the children left or shortly after, but the few times I was late, I would find him sitting in the dark, deeply distressed.

I tried to convince him to get a pet to help with the loneliness – thinking of a cat or a dog – but shortly after he moved in, Gerry got a fishbowl with Siamese fighting fish as a gift. He had had a huge fishpond in Clontarf, where he had bred koi. Fighting fish were not quite koi, but he looked after them with the same passion. The fishbowl was upgraded to a tank, and he added a few more fish, including a little lobster he named Norman. When he originally sent me a photo of Norman on my phone under the heading 'Our new baby', I texted back: 'Eew, he definitely looks more like you than me.' I was not too sure whether I cared much for the little creature. But gradually I grew fond of him and was equally intrigued and amused by Gerry's attention to Norman. Norman amused him endlessly, and video clips of the lobster appeared on the *Ryan Show* website. He even spoke to it over the radio, pretending that he had left the radio on next to the tank.

Gerry loved his job and the listeners with a passion. It was one of the things that defined him. Even when he felt really sick and struggled to get out of bed, as the time came closer for him to leave for work, I could see and feel the energy building up. By the time he went out to the car, he would be energised and excited, adrenalin pumping. He was fascinated by the sharing of ideas, the possibility of making a difference, of giving people an ear to share their stories with him, or as a vehicle to try and change things. And he was brilliant at it. I do not think many people knew, but on a daily basis after he had gone off air, he would sort things out for people who had phoned or e-mailed the programme. Places in a pre-school, operations that were urgently needed, tickets for someone who was sick, psychologists for those who were distressed – the list went on and on.

Unsurprisingly, he became the person thousands turned to when they needed help or advice, no matter how big or small the problem. One day, a listener called him after getting a flat tyre on a national road somewhere down the country. She did not know how to change the tyre, so she decided to call Gerry, who put her on air. 'Why don't you call your husband?' Gerry asked.

'Oh no!' the caller replied anxiously. 'I don't want him to know I can't change a tyre!'

Gerry laughed, and reminded her that hundreds of thousands of people had just heard her say it, so there was a good chance that her husband would find out. He then asked exactly where she was, and if there was anyone close by who could help. Within seconds, you could hear horns beeping as people listening in their cars passed her. After a few moments, she announced that someone had just pulled up. The 'rescuer' took the phone and (after giving his own business a quick plug) told Gerry not to worry, that he would take over and sort it all out.

Some calls for help were far more serious and emotional. One such call was from Cian O'Daly. Cian and his wife, who was 28 weeks pregnant, were told during a routine scan that their unborn baby boy had been diagnosed with hypoplastic left heart syndrome, where the left side of the heart is severely underdeveloped. This meant that he had a very small chance of surviving after birth, and if he did, he would require numerous painful operations. Cian and his wife were told by the medical profession that they could travel to another jurisdiction to end the pregnancy, but this was not what they wanted. Cian told me later how he and his wife had got up the morning after the diagnosis in 'utter despair', not knowing what to do. He said he sat on the edge of the bed and the only thing he could think was to phone Gerry. 'I just felt, if someone can fix this, or at least give us hope, Gerry can,' he told me later. So he called *The Gerry Ryan Show*.

It was one of the most painful and moving radio conversations I have ever listened to. Cian poured his heart out and begged for information on the condition, and for help. Gerry spoke quietly and gently to him, man to man, father to father. Gerry also asked people who could help to phone in. Women who had had babies with similar conditions responded and spoke of the challenges, but also the successes: you could hear their babies gurgling in the background. Cian told me that by the end of the conversation with Gerry, he and his wife knew for certain that they would do anything they could for little baby Henry. In the following months, Cian kept the country spellbound with updates on Henry's progress via the radio show.

After the initial broadcast, Gerry came straight home. He was exhausted.

'That was the hardest programme I ever did,' he said, with tears in his eyes. 'What if I did the wrong thing by giving them hope? What if that little baby will just suffer after his birth?' As it turned out, baby Henry has made remarkable progress, even though he has had many surgeries. Gerry did what he always did – gave people hope and advice.

Of course not all the stories played out on air, and we would frequently meet people who would talk about the effect Gerry had on their lives. One day when Gerry and I were grocery shopping, two elderly women came up to us. They were sisters, and the elder of the two stood quietly, watching Gerry with tears streaming down her cheeks, unable to talk. The younger woman explained that her sister had been in one of the harsh, church-run Magdalene laundries for years after falling pregnant as a teenager. After she left, she suffered badly with depression. She said that for years the only thing that had kept her sister from committing suicide was the fact that she could look forward to listening to Gerry in the morning. 'You became her only friend,' she said emotionally. At this point, Gerry took the weeping woman in his arms and just held her. She kept whispering through the tears: 'Thank you. Thank you.'

Gerry also really enjoyed meeting listeners outside of work and would often tell people on air that he would be at a certain public event. This would exasperate me because even though he loved meeting people, he also got really anxious when a crowd built up or women got too excited. He hid it well, though, and few people were aware of it. I quickly learnt to read his body language and knew when to step in and get him out. An 'Excuse me, ladies, can I please get my boyfriend back?' would usually suffice, but not always. Sometimes, they would not let him go and I had to physically detach women from him.

It never ceased to amaze me how forward women could be, even in front of their husbands or partners. Gerry would often be asked: 'Won't you marry me?' or: 'Why don't you dump the South African bird and hook up with me, I'm great in the sack.' I was frequently elbowed away and a few times pushed off a couch, nearly ending up on the floor, when someone tried to sit next to Gerry to get a photo. I learned that it was easier and quicker just to take the photos, preferably of everyone in the group at once. Otherwise everyone wanted a turn and it could take forever. I am now an expert on every camera-phone in existence.

Luckily it was not only my photographic skills that Gerry found attractive. Something that formed a very strong bond between us were our intellectual debates. Gerry and I shared a passion for similar topics. Politics, law, human rights and sociology all fascinated us. We would debate and discuss issues till late in the night. Often we would wake up early morning, around 4am, and pick up where we had left off – whether it was about the death penalty or local politics. Gerry (more than me) loved history, especially political history. He had a phenomenal memory and would recite long political speeches off by heart. One night he got so excited during a discussion about Charles Haughey that he jumped up and stood at the foot of the bed, reciting a lengthy speech Haughey had made in the Dáil (the Irish parliament) decades ago. Looking at him standing at the end of the bed, I started laughing and urged him to get back into bed. 'What? Don't you find this a turn-on?' he said, with a slightly foolish grin.

To my surprise it took him a while to get used to having intellectual debates with me. As soon as the debate got a bit heated, he would stop it and just bail out of the discussion. This annoyed me, since I thought he was patronising me. Eventually he confessed that he was worried it would escalate to a full-scale argument and then I would not talk to him for days. I had to explain that as far as I was concerned, a debate is a debate and as long as it does not become personal, it is all fair game and an essential part of a healthy relationship. Once he understood this, he went for it with a passion, and the sharing of ideas became a central part of our relationship. We would often debate through the night with him arguing passionately against me, but when he went on air the next day he would bring up the issue and almost always put forward my point of view. When I pointed this out to him, he answered that he loved testing his (!) ideas on me. He would never admit that I had won an argument!

Early in our relationship, and before I knew this pattern, we had a big row that nearly ended it. We were getting ready for work one morning when I spotted the heading on a brief for an interview he was going to do that day. The interview was with an author, Elizabeth Pisani, about her new book on AIDS, called *The Wisdom of Whores*. Gerry had been reading the brief in bed, before the show. I was intrigued and started to read the information while he was in the shower. But the more I read, the more upset I got. The RTÉ researcher was falling into all the old European stereotypes and was clearly not sufficiently familiar with the field, or the deep feelings in Africa surrounding AIDS. When Gerry got out of the shower, I told him so. I told him that he could not go down the route the researcher was suggesting. Gerry argued against every point I was making, and the discussion got more and more heated. Gerry even suggested that perhaps I should not read his briefs in future. After Gerry left for work, I was in tears, seriously questioning whether I could continue with the relationship if this was Gerry's attitude not only to an issue such as AIDS, but also to my opinions on matters that are close to my heart and on which I am fairly knowledgeable. At work, I apprehensively tuned in to the programme and listened to the interview. Within minutes it was clear that Gerry had completely deviated from the brief (as he almost always did) and was doing an interview based on the issues I had raised. I could not believe it. Apparently the author commented afterwards that he was the best-informed interviewer she had ever met. When I phoned him after the programme, he just said: 'They were good points. Keep arguing with me, but then trust me.' I did from then on.

At my insistence, Gerry never mentioned me on air, but he would often warn me in the morning that he would play me a song at a specific time. The first song he played for me, shortly after our relationship started, was 'The Ship Song' by Nick Cave and the Bad Seeds. It is a beautiful love song with poignant lyrics, in particular the chorus, which goes: 'Come sail your ship around me, and burn your bridges down. We'll make a little history, baby, every time you come around.' Gerry loved this song and played it a few times. When I was in bed with a bad episode of vertigo, he predictably played me 'Vertigo' by U2. He would also frequently text me during an ad or a news break on the programme, sometimes just to say hello or to warn me if he thought something was coming up that I might enjoy. The moment he got off air, he would phone again to ask how much I had heard and what I thought of it.

By this time, the relationship was easy and relaxed. We rarely argued, and even when we did it was over in minutes. Neither of us sulked, and we spoke often about how grateful we both were to have found a happy, calm and loving relationship.

But all was not well for Gerry. Money was becoming a bigger and bigger issue. As well as me, his accountant, his lawyers, Harry Crosbie and a few other friends were trying to convince him to take steps to control the expenditure. But Gerry just kept repeating that he could not do anything and he would elaborate at length about all his fears as to what would happen if he did. In the beginning I thought he was exaggerating, and spoke to DBK and the Crosbies about the issue; they all thought that Gerry's fears were valid.

To make matters worse, a drama around the top presenters' salaries erupted at RTÉ early in 2009. Expecting a massive reduction in advertising revenue due to the recession, the director-general of RTÉ at the time, Cathal Goan, had predicted a loss of €68 million that year. At the same time, he announced that the top presenters would be expected to take a 10 per cent pay cut. Some presenters immediately accepted it, but Gerry panicked. Given his already bad financial situation, he could not see how he could manage such a cut. He discussed it with some of the other presenters and felt confident that at least some of his colleagues would stand firm with him on the issue. When he told me this, I was dubious. I told Gerry that even though I understood his personal dilemma and would support him, I did not think that he would survive the bad publicity it would generate. I strongly urged him to take the cut, but Gerry just could not see a way to survive it financially.

I was right about his colleagues, and Gerry ended up being the only one resisting the cuts. I urged him to explain to RTÉ management and the public that it was because of the financial pressure of his personal circumstances, but Gerry was too proud, and would not. Over the weeks that followed, Gerry felt RTÉ did nothing to protect the senior presenters from the horrendous media onslaughts. In fact, it seemed to Gerry that they were adding to it by, for example, door-stepping their own presenters. One morning when Gerry arrived at the steps of the radio station for work, he was confronted by one of RTÉ News' own reporters, who challenged him, with a tape recorder running, about the salary cuts. Fellow presenter Ryan Tubridy had a similar experience, when he was challenged by the same journalist with a tape recorder, at his desk. Gerry was shaken by it all and felt deeply betrayed by RTÉ. He could not understand how RTÉ could do this to them. For weeks he could not sleep or eat properly because of the stress.

During this time he had a very bad night, during which his sleep was further interrupted by a stream of text messages. These nightly text messages were happening with increasing frequency and would usually start around midnight and continue until the morning, whether Gerry responded to them or not. Afraid to miss any text from his children, Gerry would never put his phone on silent. However, by this stage his financial concerns, the pressure at RTÉ and the unpleasant text messages were starting to take a toll.

After this particular night, he was completely exhausted by morning time, but got up to shower. I went down to the kitchen to make some breakfast and his usual cup of tea. When I got back to the room, I could hear the shower running, but also some other strange noises coming from the bathroom. I put the tray on the end of the bed and pushed the bathroom door open. Gerry was on the floor of the tiny en-suite bathroom, crouched on his knees, bent over, with his forehead on the floor tiles. He was sobbing.

'Oh my God, Gerry, what's wrong?' I asked in a panic.

'I just can't do this anymore. I can't deal with all this pressure. I'm trying so hard. I won't survive this!' he said, while bashing his fist on the floor.

I was shaking with shock and anger, but tried to get him up and back to the bed. He could not get up. He asked me to sit with him, so we sat on the bathroom floor and I held him while he gradually calmed down. I begged him to take the day off and see a doctor, but he would not, and eventually went to work still pale and shaky.

In early March, he publicly announced that he would take the pay cut. He hoped that it would be the end of everything, but the fallout was not over yet.

After his collapse in the bathroom, I had been increasingly worried about Gerry's stress levels, so in early April I convinced him we should go away for a weekend to celebrate my birthday. After much discussion, we agreed on Venice. The plane tickets were cheap, and as always I would pay for my portion of the holiday.

Gerry enjoyed Venice with childlike wonder. He could not contain his excitement on the water taxi from the airport and immediately texted all the children. He had spent hours on the internet to find us a really good deal in a lovely hotel, for which I paid half. Shortly after we arrived the first night, we had dinner in the hotel dining room. As soon as we sat down to eat, there was a call for Gerry and he went outside to take it. There was a lengthy conversation and when he came back he looked worried. He explained that the call was from someone at RTÉ, who had told him that Pat Kenny, present-er of *The Late Late Show*, a hugely popular three-hour long show on Friday nights, was stepping down and that the show that night would be Pat's last. I asked why he looked worried, and he responded: 'Now it all starts.' I asked whether he thought he would stand a chance of being offered the position after Pat.

'Of course I should. I'm the only one that has done the "audition", but after the salary drama, I don't think I stand a chance. Too many people in manage-ment hate me,' he said tiredly.

'Then take yourself out of the race, Gerry. Don't let them humiliate you by not giving it to you,' I urged.

For the rest of the evening, we discussed the various scenarios that might unfold. I felt strongly, given what had happened in the previous months, that he did not stand a chance and that he should make it clear he was not interested in the position. But of course he was. This was the ultimate in broadcasting in Ireland and Gerry had always wanted it. More importantly, he felt he deserved a chance at presenting the show. He knew who the other candidates would be: Miriam O'Callaghan, who presented a current affairs programme on TV, and Ryan Tubridy. He thought Miriam would have the edge because a woman had never fronted *The Late Late Show*, but he had his doubts as to whether she would be able to carry the 'monster of a show' for more than two hours. He felt Ryan would be better suited for the job in a few years, but that he was still too young and needed a bit more time. He was concerned that Ryan was too intellectual and perhaps not close enough to the ordinary people, and that his interests and knowledge base were possibly not broad enough. From personal experience, he also worried about what that kind of fame would do to Ryan at such a young age.

After dinner, still debating the issue, we moved into the bar, where a pianist was playing. He was dressed in a tuxedo and black tie, but strangely enough had Wellington boots on. We realised that this was true of all the hotel staff, as they started to wrap the piano legs with plastic. They put the empty chairs onto counters and moved the tables out. Carpets were rolled up. We asked what was going on. They explained that there was a high tide coming and that it would flood the ground floor of the hotel. But they insisted that there was no need to be concerned – that it was a regular occurrence in Venice (as we found out the next night) – and they continued to serve customers. As the water started to flow in through the doors, the pianist kept playing. 'This is starting to feel a bit too much like the *Titanic!*' Gerry laughed. 'Isn't it fantastic?'

The next morning we went out to discover Venice. Just as we left the hotel, we bumped into some Irish tourists who wanted to talk and take photos. Gerry wanted to buy my son his first shaving kit, so we went into endless stores to find the shaver with the right balance and a shaving brush with the right type of bristles. 'Every young man needs this,' he said. Needless to say, my son was delighted and treasures the shaving kit.

We eventually found the right one in a tiny shop on the Rialto Bridge. Afterwards we stood on the bridge, overlooking the Grand Canal. Gerry, who was slightly absent-minded, drew me close and said: 'Man, there's a lot of water activity in this place.'

'Eh yes, it is Venice after all,' I smiled. Gerry looked foolish and then we both laughed.

On our way back late that afternoon, we shared a gelato. We were tired, so Gerry asked a gondolier how much it would cost to take us back to the hotel. He said something close to a €100. Gerry just walked away. 'They really take the piss in this place,' he said, annoyed. He repeated the comment later that night, when they sent us a bottle of an expensive white wine with room service, and Gerry was so annoyed when he saw the bill that he sent it back. We flew back to Dublin on the Monday, after three romantic days.

Back in Ireland, one of the tabloids ran a story on the Tuesday morning talking about us being away on a romantic weekend. The problem was that the way the story was written, it sounded as if we were throwing around huge amounts of money on an extravagant, luxurious weekend in Venice, when nothing could have been further from the truth. They even superimposed a photo of us onto a photo of a gondola, which made it look as if they had been there to take the photo, when we had in fact not been in a gondola at all. This was not good, given the salary drama and Gerry's attempts to control his outgoings.

Gerry rarely remarked on the radio on stories about himself, but this time he could not resist. He told the story of the gondola and how we had not gone on one at all. He also mentioned that we had only shared one ice cream and complained about how he felt that tourists get ripped off in Venice. That afternoon, another newspaper published a story under the headline: 'Gerry grabs cheap deal for romantic weekend in Venice'. 'Now I sound like some cheapskate who won't treat my partner. You can never win!' Gerry groaned after he saw it.

Two months after our trip to Venice, RTÉ announced that Ryan Tubridy would be the new host of *The Late Late Show*. As Gerry had predicted, Ryan, Miriam O'Callaghan and Gerry himself had been the three candidates for the job. After the announcement was made, Gerry phoned Ryan to congratulate him. Publicly he was gracious, but privately he was bitterly hurt. He knew he could do the job and do it well. After all, he had done the 'audition' the previous year and had passed with flying colours. Given that Ryan was so young, Gerry also knew he would probably be too old to take over when Ryan retired from the job. It really upset him that he would, in all likelihood, never get the 'gig' he had always wanted.

23

Shortly after *The Late Late Show* announcement in late July 2009, Gerry got wind of a big 50th birthday party being organised in Killiney, where many of his friends were going to be. He did not want to go, but what really distressed him was the triumphant way the press, clearly briefed by PR people, was writing that all his friends and a who's-who of Dublin were going to be there, but Gerry was not invited.

His sense of having been betrayed by most of his friends – some of whom had been friends with him for decades – had grown since his separation. Despite my earlier beliefs that things would settle down and improve, they only got worse, and almost no one got in touch unless they needed something from Gerry, like a mention on air. This added to Gerry's sense of bitterness and made him extremely unhappy.

More than once Gerry arrived at his house in Clontarf to pick up the children and find some of their mutual friends and colleagues from RTÉ having a dinner party. He could not handle that at all. Every time it happened, he would come back home raging: 'My friends that cannot bother their arses to call me, in my house, eating food, drinking wine . . . and they barely greet me. They look at me as if I'm the servant coming to take care of the children and then I'm asked to leave!'

The week of the 50th birthday party, Gerry was told to pick the younger children up on the night at around 9pm from the house in Killiney where the party was being held. However, it was made clear that he would not be allowed to go inside and would have to wait at the door. He was distressed about being humiliated like that. I was adamant that this was not going to happen, and insisted that he got a driver to do it. 'If not,' I said, 'I'll do it.' In the end, we thought it safer to get the driver.

Gerry had been to the big horse-racing event in the west of Ireland, the Galway races, with the radio programme for a few days that week and arrived back late on Friday afternoon. I knew he would be upset about everything that was happening, so I cooked him a special meal with all his favourite dishes as a surprise. He was delighted and very moved, but so tired and up-set that he could not finish the meal and went to bed while I waited up for the children.

That Sunday, after reading the extensive coverage of the party in the pa-pers, Gerry became very quiet for a few hours. In bed that evening I tried to speak to him about it. Gerry said he had thought about it long and hard.

'F**k them!' he said. 'F**k the lot of them. I don't care any more. I have you and I have DBK and the Crosbies. I have my children and I have the lis-teners. That will do!'

Despite all of this, Gerry was getting ready for the usual Disney trip. As all the listeners to Gerry's show know, the family had gone to Disney World every summer for many years. Despite the financial difficulties, he wanted to keep the tradition in place for the sake of the children. Like the previous year, he was going for the first few days with the children, after which there would be a handover of the children and he would join me for a few weeks in South Africa. I had pulled in many favours for the South Africa trip and insisted that I would pay for everything there. I knew that Gerry was increas-ingly concerned about his financial situation, and he had reason to be.

The afternoon before Gerry and the children were due to leave, there was a crisis. There was another huge credit card bill Gerry did not expect. The bank had had enough. Over a period of months, they had called Gerry or his accountant in for meetings, insisting that he get the overall spending under control. Gerry found all of this very humiliating. This time, though, the bank took action and decided not to honour any further cheques until a substantial amount had been paid into the account. Gerry did not know what to do.

I offered to lend him some money, even though I knew it would mean we would have to cancel the South Africa trip. But I also knew that it would be devastating to him if he had to let the children down. His accountant, who was at the house with us, drew me to one side and strongly advised me against lending Gerry money. She knew how carefully I managed my money, and that I would need it later in the year to cover some of my living expenses. In the end, Gerry would not take the money. He borrowed it from a good friend of his, who was generous and kind, and really saved him.

After his week in Disney World, we left for South Africa. Gerry loved flying.

He loved the whole occasion and did it with gusto. There were no last-minute arrivals at the airport. He insisted on being there at least three hours beforehand. Then we would have a leisurely wait. He would look forward to the aeroplane food with childlike excitement. I know of no other person who would wake up in the morning and actually get excited about the Aer Lingus full Irish breakfast. Imagine, then, the excitement about a long-haul flight. He always went on the plane armed with at least five heavy books, his iPhone for music, big noise-reduction earphones, and a medical kit for all eventualities. And he *loved* it. Without exception, every flight would involve a flow of information about the type of plane, the flying techniques, the weather conditions – until he (thankfully) got distracted by the food and the movies.

We had been planning the South African trip for months and were both really excited about it. I wanted it to be a special trip – after all, this was Gerry's introduction to my world, and I wanted to show him where I came from. I wanted him to understand the deep love-hate relationship I have with this extraordinary country. He was also going to meet the rest of my family. Ultimately, I was hoping that we could spend some time there every year, so it was important that the trip went well.

It was not Gerry's first visit to South Africa. His radio show had been broadcast from there for a week a few years earlier. I was South African ambassador at that stage, and my team and I had helped with some of the arrangements for him and his team, including a visit to the townships. On the night of the arranged visit, I got a message that some of Gerry's team were there, but not him. I was annoyed about this, and not knowing him well enough to have his cell phone number, I called the hotel and asked them to track him down. Years later, Gerry told me that he was sitting in the cigar lounge, dressed up for a fancy dinner he was planning to have later on, when the hotel staff brought him a phone and said that the ambassador wished to speak to him. He answered the phone with an exaggerated posh accent, which just annoyed me even more.

'Mr Ryan, this is Melanie Verwoerd, the South African ambassador, speaking.'

'Good evening, Your Excellency,' Gerry said over-politely.

I was biting my lip. 'Mr Ryan, I gather you are not in the townships. Where are you exactly, and can I ask why you are not there?'

'Well, Your Excellency, I am at the Table Bay Hotel looking over the bay towards the townships. I can assure you I can see the townships from here. I thought that would do.'

Now I was seeing red. 'Mr Ryan, I'm going to say this as diplomatically as I can manage. You better get your arse out of the hotel and into the townships, or else I'll tell the whole Irish media about this.'

There was a pause on Gerry's side, and then he said: 'Right, I better get a move on then. And may I add, very well put, ambassador.'

I have to admit that I'm more of an activist than a diplomat at times like these, but it usually has the right effect.

This time round, the trip would be more harmonious. When we arrived in Johannesburg, we split up as I went through the South African passport queue and Gerry joined the 'other passport' holders. For once the roles were reversed. 'Shout if you have any difficulty,' I joked as Gerry walked off, pretending to be indignant. I handed my passport to the African official, and as would often happen, she stared at my surname, raising her eyebrows.

'Verwoerd?' she said, with a coldness in her voice.

Nothing new here, so I gave my standard answer: 'Yes, but I'm one of the good Verwoerds.'

Usually this either triggered their memory of my political involvement or they would ask what I meant. Not this time, though. 'There's no such thing,' she growled and furiously stamped my passport. As I walked past her, she started to hum an old anti-apartheid song, 'Pantsi Verwoerd' ('Down with Verwoerd').

'Great, so much for the new South Africa,' I sighed under my breath, knowing well that you should never argue with a passport official.

From behind the glass partitions, I could see Gerry was at the front of the queue and, slightly concerned, I hung around to make sure he did not also encounter some difficulty. But within seconds I heard the passport official laughing uncontrollably. A few minutes later, Gerry strolled through with a huge grin on his face.

'What was that all about?' I asked.

'Ah, you know the black birds, they just adore me!' Gerry replied.

'Gerry,' I said anxiously, 'please promise me you won't say anything like that publicly here.'

That was the worst thing I could have said, because he saw it as a challenge. When I told him what had happened to me, he roared with laughter, loving the irony of it all. I had got grilled in my own country and he was waved through.

We took another short flight up north, where we were met by a driver from the camp we were staying in. He was a disgruntled former army pilot. All too delighted to meet a Verwoerd and of course assuming that I had very conservative views, he insisted on speaking about his political grievances to me on the two-hour journey to the camp. I could see that Gerry was amused, although he said afterwards that he thought I was going to hit the man. We stayed at the Jock of the Bushveld camp in the Kruger National Park. It is named after the famous Staffordshire bull terrier who lived in the 1880s and whose story was written by Sir Percy Fitzpatrick. Most South Africans are familiar with Jock of the Bushveld and I assumed that Gerry was too. It was only when he asked one of the African guides what clothes Jock used to wear that I realised that he thought Jock was a man and not a dog.

The camp was idyllic. Our rondavel looked out on a dry riverbed and had an outside shower. We spent hours in the lapa high up on stilts overlooking the riverbed, while rhino, buck, giraffe and other wild animals leisurely strolled past. One afternoon I spotted a snake next to us on some wooden slats. I knew it was a tree snake. Although they rarely bite people, they are extremely venomous, and I decided that it would be better to get one of the game wardens to chase the snake away. I asked Gerry to keep an eye on it. On our return, the warden was taken aback when he saw Gerry crouching very close to the snake, the two keeping a wary eye on each other while Gerry took endless photographs 'for the folks in Ireland'. The guide and I followed the snake as it slithered away among the shrubs and trees.

When I came back, Gerry had fallen asleep in the chair. Framed by the river and the African landscape behind him, he looked so beautiful and peaceful with his book *The Gamble*, about the war in Iraq, folded open on his lap. Wanting to capture the moment forever, I quietly took out my camera and took a photo of him. Sensing my presence, he woke up and slowly turned his head to me. Like a child waking up, he lifted his arm up behind his head and smiled at me, almost shyly, as I took another photograph. 'I love you,' he whispered. It is my favourite photo of Gerry. Every time I look at it, I smile and then I cry. It is so unlike any other photo I have ever seen of him: unguarded, relaxed, unposed and gentle.

The Lions rugby team was touring South Africa at the time, and on the Saturday we decided to be brave and watch the game with a group of South Africans in the TV room in the camp. It was great fun and Gerry defused any potential tension with his usual charm. By the end of the match, the men seemed to be best mates – helped by the fact that South Africa won – and agreed to watch a big soccer match together the next night.

On the game drive the next afternoon, it was clear that the soccer-mad African guides were dying to get back to watch the match. I asked whether they had satellite TV in their 'compound'. They did not. They told me that a small child would stand outside the window with the aerial to get the best reception. Of course the guests had satellite TV with perfect reception in the camp, or so we thought. As it turned out, monkeys had played on the satellite dish earlier that day and broken it. It could not be fixed, so we could not watch the match. The drivers were kind enough to phone Gerry every now and then with the score. I am sure they loved the irony.

At night, after a meal around the campfire, we would go to bed, where Gerry constantly got entangled in the mosquito nets. He could not figure out how to get in and out of bed without getting caught in the net. We would lie in bed talking and reading, with the lions roaring outside. Gerry had bought a book on Eamon de Valera, the famous political figure and former head of state, just before we left Ireland. It was the only thing of interest he could find at an organic market I had dragged him to a week earlier. I love the weekly market, but the virtues of the raw-food movement did not interest Gerry. So de Valera went everywhere with us on the trip, and despite my best efforts to get Gerry to read something more African, or even light-hearted, he remained enthralled by this book and read me long extracts from it at night, trying to convince me of similarities between Ireland and South Africa.

After we had spent the night with one of my sisters and her husband in Johannesburg, we departed from Pretoria by train to Cape Town. It is a lovely train journey that takes about a day and a half. Gerry was in his element, although he was amused and slightly puzzled that I was frequently recognised while, of course, no one knew who he was. This was new to him. At Pretoria station, the food and beverage manager greeted us. I had met

243

Fanie twice before, when I had been on the train to promote tourism. Fanie looked over at Gerry and pulled me aside. In Afrikaans, he whispered, 'That does not look like Mr Verwoerd?' I explained that I was divorced, but he did not seem pleased. Although he was polite to Gerry on the journey, he treated me far better. Gerry was amused.

In Cape Town, I showed him around my hometown. I love Cape Town and loved showing it to Gerry. We looked at some property, dreaming of a time in the future when we would buy a place there. The only dark cloud during this time was the death of Michael Jackson. Gerry was upset about it, commenting about how young he was and what a tragedy it was. Little did we know what was lying ahead a few months later.

We then spent some time with my parents, and after doing some whale-spotting we flew back to Ireland. It was a trip I will remember forever.

24

Towards the end of 2009, I developed severe vertigo. At first I thought it was just stress, but increasingly I found it hard to function. The dizziness, nausea and exhaustion made even the most basic tasks difficult. Once it was diagnosed, I started a long and gruelling course of physiotherapy and was advised to take a few months off work. My children and I had planned to spend Christmas in Cape Town, but I was advised against long-haul flying, and in the end I decided to stay in Ireland with Gerry while the children were in Africa.

I moved into Leeson Street with him, and for the next two months we spent every possible minute together. Although the vertigo made things very uncomfortable and we almost never went out, we really enjoyed having so much time on our own, especially since Gerry took a break as well.

Like the previous year, Christmas was stressful for Gerry. On Christmas Eve he went to the annual party for the children's sake, but came home early to have dinner with me. The next morning he went over very early in the heavy snow for the opening of the presents. There was one difference compared with the previous year. Gerry was not making the Christmas lunch, which meant that he had some free time after the children had opened their presents. He came to pick me up so we could visit his parents' grave.

He had once before taken me to the grave, in Dardistown Cemetery, close to Dublin airport, to 'introduce' me to his mother. On this Christmas Day, he was particularly sad. I knew he was very tired, but he had really missed his mum recently. We lit a few candles I had brought, and stood in silence for a little while. 'It's a great site to be buried in,' Gerry remarked. 'I like that all the planes landing at the airport come in so low.' But there was not much time to reflect; he had to take me back to Leeson Street to get back in time for lunch in Clontarf. That evening we spent time with Harry and Rita. On the way home, Gerry said, 'Thank God, another Christmas over.'

Gerry could not afford Dromoland Castle again for New Year's. Harry and Rita Crosbie, sharing my concern about Gerry's health, insisted that we come with them for New Year's to their apartment in the south of France. It was a lovely, peaceful few days. Gerry read and slept a lot. He took long walks with Harry and they talked for hours.

On New Year's Eve, we went to Monte Carlo, where we had a fantastic meal in Café de Paris. It was a great evening filled with laughter, good food and great wine. Gerry was relaxed and in top form, as he always was when he was with his best friend. During the meal, he and Harry wanted to know from Rita and me which of them could make the best fake loving face. Even though this was a silly game they often played, we all laughed so much that I thought we were going to be thrown out by the French waiters, who were looking at us disapprovingly, as only French waiters can.

We left at around 9pm just as a big crowd, in tuxedos and evening gowns, arrived. We realised that the menu had just tripled in price. Harry, never one to miss a bargain despite his enormous business success, was delighted that we got the 'early bird'. Chuckling about the 'idiots' paying so much, he went across the square, which was lit in beautiful blue lights, to collect the car.

While Gerry went to get our coats, I watched a string quartet that had set up outside the restaurant. I thought for a moment of my family back in South Africa who were all together just outside Cape Town, about my sister who was scheduled to have her first baby the next day, and about how different my life was now, so far from the most southern point of Africa. Lost in thought, I did not realise Gerry was standing behind me until he put his hands on my shoulders and turned me around. 'Dance with me, my darling,' he said as he gently pulled me close.

I snuggled in under his chin and rested against his broad chest, smelling his aftershave and the slightly damp smell of his big, long black coat.

'I love you so much,' he said into my ear.

'I love you too,' I answered. 'Please never let go, Gerry.'

'Never,' he responded, and tightened his grip. 'Happy New Year, my love. This will be a good year for us.'

'Yes, it will.' I looked up at him and we laughed. At that moment, Rita took a photo, capturing us beaming with joy and hope.

As the days went on, however, Gerry became increasingly withdrawn. I knew he was concerned about money, and eventually challenged him about it. It became more and more incomprehensible to me why he could not get on top of it, when it was causing him so much stress. Rita Crosbie was part of the conversation and, having been a friend of the family for many years, she backed Gerry up when he tried to explain to me again why he was so fearful.

'But Gerry, it can't go on like this,' I pleaded with him. Rita agreed with me on that point – and for that matter, so did Gerry. He promised both of us that it was a New Year's resolution of his to get everything under control by February. But as he said it, I caught his eye. I knew Gerry so well, and he could never lie to me – not even the smallest white lie. And in that moment, I knew that his many fears about the repercussions of doing something, and of the stories that would follow, would make it almost impossible for him to honour this undertaking. An awful sense of dread came over me.

I could not shake the feeling, and later stood in a scalding-hot shower for a long time, weeping. As I had suspected when I had first become aware of the situation a year and a half before during our holiday in France, the situation could not be sustained: unless something drastic was done, I knew there was every chance Gerry would go bankrupt in the coming year. In the previous few months, I had started to carry more and more of his financial obligations, and he had had to borrow a substantial amount of money from me so he could meet his outgoings. I did not mind doing this over the short term, trusting that he would pay me back at some point. Nor was I concerned for my own sake. I earned my own money and would not take any money from Gerry. I honestly did not care whether he had money or not, but I knew what it was doing to him.

For Gerry, making money to provide for others defined him as a man. Gerry took care of others. He was the most generous person I have ever met – with his time, energy and money. There are endless people around Ireland to whom he had given money over the years – sometimes large amounts – never expecting any repayment. I can count on one hand the times anyone else paid for a meal when we went out with others, and contrary to what is often said, he almost never got anything for free. People knew they could count on him for a sympathetic ear and that, if someone needed help, he would stop at nothing to provide it. If he could not provide for others – and in particular for his children – I knew it would be absolutely devastating for

247

him. Of course, given that his going bankrupt would inevitably end up in the media, it would also be humiliating for him. I was not sure he would be able to survive it.

Back in Ireland, I became increasingly worried about his health and his stress levels. He was exhausted most of the time, vomited frequently, and suffered terrible indigestion and stomach aches from irritable bowel syndrome, or IBS. I begged him to go for a proper physical; he said he would as soon as he had the time.

In early February, on my mother's birthday, we went for a meal and Gerry started feeling unwell. He was running a high fever and we left quickly. When we got home, I phoned his GP and friend, Tony Crosby, who came over immediately. Gerry was diagnosed with swine flu and was under strict instructions to stay in bed for the week. Gerry was very worried, though; a drama relating to sick leave had been unfolding at RTÉ.

As part of the financial cutbacks, the top presenters at RTÉ were informed that there would be a reinterpretation of the sick leave provisions in their contracts and they would no longer be entitled to paid sick leave. Gerry was upset by this. He was rarely sick and never abused the sick-leave provision. If anything, he would push himself too hard and go in even when he was really unwell. This time round, he could barely move, so he had to take time off.

However, they were midway through the recording of a series of *Operation Transformation*. Gerry had been presenting this hugely popular weight-loss show for a few years. It involved a selected group of people whose struggle with weight loss would be followed for a few weeks on radio, TV and the internet. The latest episode was usually filmed early in the week, and Gerry then had to do a voiceover on the Wednesday, in time for the Thursday broadcast. The production team knew he was very ill, and reluctantly started looking for someone else to do the voiceover. But this was not ideal, and Gerry decided to do it. Knowing how ill he was, I drove him to the sound studio in Upper Mount Street so I could keep an eye on him. Just before we left the house, he fainted twice, but insisted on going. The professional that he was, he did the voiceover, even though it took quite a long time. After saying goodbye to the very relieved production team, I took him home, where he collapsed. A few weeks later, he was furious when RTÉ said that they would not pay him for that day.

The situation with some of the senior management in RTÉ would increasingly become a source of distress, and stress, for Gerry. He still loved doing the work – particularly the radio programme. He really enjoyed working with his new team and felt they were getting better and better as the weeks went by. Every day, without exception, he would call me after the programme and say: 'Man, we were rocking!' In particular, he loved working with his new series producer, Alice O'Sullivan. She was clever and strong, and understood Gerry's mind well. Most importantly, she was kind and caring. He also greatly enjoyed his weekly on-air chats with the journalist and long-standing friend, Fiona Looney. These chats usually ended up being far from politically correct, but extremely funny and entertaining.

Yet increasingly he felt 'under siege', as he put it, from some people in management. First it was the salary issue and then *The Late Late Show*. Then *The Saturday Night Show* became an issue. Originally, RTÉ had asked Gerry to do an eight-week 'audition' for the proposed new show, after which well-known journalist Brendan O'Connor would do the same, followed by TV presenter Craig Doyle. RTÉ would then decide, on the basis of their performances and the ratings, how and with whom to proceed. Gerry felt insulted by this. He could not believe that this was even suggested to him. He felt it was an insult to be put on the same level as the other two guys, who had very limited experience compared to him, and he also felt he had done the ultimate audition a year before, by stepping in at the last minute to present *The Late Late Show* when Pat Kenny's mum died. All the reviews had been positive, and the ratings were extremely high. Many people assumed he would be the next presenter when Pat Kenny retired. Not only did that not happen, but by handling *The Saturday Night Show* in this manner, he felt that RTÉ was adding insult to injury. He insisted he would not do the eight-week audition.

It was only months later, after Brendan and Craig had done their stints, and after a few lunches with some members of the senior management in RTÉ, that Gerry was offered the show. But they insisted that there would be no additional payment. According to Gerry, he was told to 'wear the green jersey for Ireland'. Yet he wanted to do the gig, and it was agreed that he would present the show between September and Christmas. Between the following January and March, he would, apart from his daily radio show, do

Operation Transformation (the weight-loss show), from April to May *Ryan Confidential* (in-depth, one-on-one interviews with celebrities), and then again *The Saturday Night Show* (an entertainment show with music and interviews) for the rest of the year.

But ultimately it was a relatively small thing in relation to sick leave that was the final straw. During this time, he came home one evening extremely distressed. I finally got it out of him that during a discussion on sick leave, someone in senior management had told him that he needed to understand he was like any plumber RTÉ would contract to fix pipes. If he did not pitch up to do the work, he would not get paid. Despite his respect for plumbers, Gerry could not believe that after almost 30 years of working for the organisation, being absolutely passionate about promoting the public broadcaster and being a major revenue-earner for them, this comparison would be drawn. To him, it illustrated the complete disdain they felt for him.

Even though he was probably the worst-affected by the public fallout after the salary issue, he felt deeply protective of his colleagues. He not only convened meetings between them, but also got legal advice for them all, involved a PR person, and spent hours advising them on e-mails and memos to management. He wondered if management knew this, and if that was why they were treating him so badly.

While all these battles were going on with RTÉ, his money situation was getting worse. The perfect storm was starting to build up: even though Gerry had made dramatic cuts in his expenses, he was still running deeper into the red every month. His financial obligations were just too high, his salary had been cut back, and as a result of the recession, outside work had dried up. He desperately wanted to finalise the separation as quickly as possible, but found the process extremely stressful. Still, I had detected a change in him. Gerry had always insisted that he wanted for all the parties to exit the marriage with dignity and with the family finances intact. He now accepted that this would never happen.

'I have no money and almost no friends left and people think I am a bastard!' he said angrily one night after a long day involving accountants and lawyers. 'Things have to change soon.'

25

I had a very busy start to the year 2010. On 12 January, a magnitude 7.0 earthquake hit the tiny country of Haiti; 316 000 people died, 300 000 were injured, and a million were left homeless. Like all global agencies, UNICEF made an emergency appeal. This meant all hands on deck and very long hours.

I was still sick from the vertigo and felt awful, but I spent long days and nights managing the Irish operation. I had a special affinity with Haiti. In the late 1990s, I had spent two weeks there at the invitation of the Republican caucus. Two ANC colleagues and I helped with constitution-writing and negotiations. In Haiti, I saw poverty and desperation like nowhere else. The country received very little help, and remained the poorest state in the Western Hemisphere. On our visit in the late 1990s, we met Hillary Clinton, George Soros and Bill Gates Senior at a cocktail function in the US embassy, and it was clear that a global strategy was needed to help Haiti.

Knowing in 2010 that not much had improved, I appreciated how desperate the situation would be. Apart from all the awareness and fundraising we were doing, we also decided to have a memorial service at Christ Church Cathedral, Dublin, for the victims. I did various interviews over the week, and on the day at the cathedral the press mobbed me for sound bites. Gerry had arrived with me, and he quietly stood back and waited for me. No one paid any attention to him. The service by candlelight, with a lone piper playing, was emotional, and left us with more determination to do whatever we could to help the victims. In the end, we raised more than €1 million (R10 million) for Haiti, an extraordinary achievement given the recession, which had hit all charities so hard. It would be the start of an extremely successful year for UNICEF Ireland.

On the home front, the next two months were busy socially. We entertained Sir Roger Moore and his lovely wife, Lady Christina, who came to Dublin for a UNICEF fundraiser. Gerry and Sir Roger got along well and we had enormous fun over the few days the Moores were here. In the middle of February, we went to the baptism of Gerry's eldest brother Mano's baby. It was a great evening, even though Gerry was tired and wanted to get home early. The next day was Valentine's Day, and Gerry and I took his youngest children, along with my two, for lunch. Not very romantic, but it was a great lunch. Of course a guest in the restaurant spoke to the press about it, and one of the tabloids ran a story about the romantic family lunch.

Three days later, Gerry and I went to the cocktail function welcoming the new South African ambassador, Jeremiah Ndou. I felt so supported with Gerry by my side, and that night I wrote in my diary: 'It was so great to have Gerry with me . . . just there lovingly and quietly.' A week later, we went to the Irish Film and Television Awards (IFTAs) in the Burlington Hotel, where Gerry was presenting one of the awards. He was not keen to go, and complained throughout the evening. Still, he was delighted when he announced Pat Kenny as the winner of his category.

On 26 February, we went to a lecture that Kader Asmal gave at Trinity College. Afterwards Gerry and I went up to say hello. Kader had been one of Gerry's lecturers during his time in Trinity. Apparently, he did not always approve of the more fun-loving side of Gerry and his friends, but he did describe them as the brightest of all the students he had ever taught. 'Oh, Mr Ryan,' Kader greeted him. 'Are you still creating problems?'

Gerry smiled, 'Ah yes, professor! And proud of it!'

Kader threw his eyes heavenwards and snorted.

'And he's my partner now, Kader,' I intervened, while Gerry took my hand.

Kader looked at me sharply. 'You could have done so much better,' he sighed dramatically.

'Kader!' I exclaimed. 'That's not nice!'

But in true Kadar style, he just shrugged and said goodbye.

Gerry was indignant, but amused at the same time. Over dinner afterwards, he had his old friends Eoghan O'Neachtain and John Fitzpatrick in stitches over the story.

I enjoyed introducing Gerry to my African contacts and friends. A few weeks earlier, I had invited Archbishop Tutu, who was in Dublin, to dinner with a couple of friends in the Residence Club. Gerry had never met 'the

Arch' before and to me, it felt as if I was introducing my new partner to my dad. Tutu pretended to be very serious when they first shook hands, and Gerry was on his best behaviour. We had a lovely evening, with a lot of serious discussions on, among other things, Northern Ireland and the peace process. However, in the middle of a very intense and heated discussion, the door to the private room suddenly swung open and two scantily dressed burlesque dancers came in.

A silence fell in the room as we all stared at them. 'Hello,' the two women purred.

Luckily, before anything else could happen, a frazzled manager ran in.

'Wrong room, wrong room,' he said anxiously. 'Your function is upstairs!' There was a slightly uncomfortable pause after they left, but then the Arch winked at Gerry. 'That was not very Christian to chase them out like that. We should invite them back for something to eat. They looked hungry,' he said. Needless to say, and Gerry got on like a house on fire.

But during this time, Gerry's health deteriorated. He had never been 100 per cent healthy, but things were now getting worse. When he accompanied me to a scan as part of my vertigo treatment, the doctor, who knew Gerry, raised concerns with him because he looked so bad. My diary has numerous entries about him being ill and exhausted, and about how worried I was. On 21 February, for example, we went for a family lunch, but that afternoon and night he got severe heart palpitations and could barely sleep. My diary also recalls the many evenings he fell asleep on my couch, too tired to move or get undressed, as well as him waking up repeatedly with heart palpitations. I continued to beg him to go to the doctor, but he kept insisting it was only stress.

At the end of February, he asked if I would come to the recording of the final episode of *Operation Transformation* to support him, since he felt so tired and down. As always, once the adrenalin kicked in he was brilliant, revealing the new look of all the contestants with flair and enthusiasm, but at home he collapsed, exhausted, and had another bad night. On St Patrick's Day, we took a short walk along the seafront in Sandymount, but he was quickly out of breath, so we went home, where he fell asleep on the couch for the rest of the day.

On 19 March, we went to the opening of the Grand Canal Theatre for a performance of *Swan Lake*. Gerry was one of the directors of the theatre, and since it was the coming to fruition of his big pal Harry Crosbie's dream, Gerry was delighted. We posed for photographers outside the theatre and I stepped back while he spoke to journalists. I heard them asking him about his health (I think it was in relation to *Operation Transformation*), and he told them how I despaired of him sometimes. They took it as a joke, but in real life I was very worried.

I once asked Gerry why he would not go to the doctor when he was feeling so sick. He was very knowledgeable about medical issues and he had regular blood screenings. So why, when he was getting so tired, had chest pains and was short of breath, would he not go? Apart from saying that he was convinced it was 'just stress', he also said he worried that he would be booked off work for a while. 'I can't afford that, with RTÉ's new sick leave policy,' he insisted. He kept referring to the hard time RTÉ gave fellow presenter Joe Duffy when he needed time off to have an operation after someone ran into him with a car.

At the end of March, my children and I moved to Upper Leeson Street. Gerry and I had wanted to move in together, but as we could not afford a big enough house for all the children, we decided to have our own 'Woody Allen' arrangement. I found a house a few doors down from Gerry. It was lovely, but expensive. Gerry pushed me to take it, since he felt we would shortly live there together and he would then help with the rent. My lease in Dalkey only expired in mid-April, but Gerry was adamant that I should move in as soon as possible. He helped me as much as he could with the packing, and by the first week in April we were in our new house. We immediately settled into a routine, with Gerry coming over every afternoon after work and staying the night. My cat Tigger would sit on the back of the couch at the front window staring out at the gate around the time Gerry would arrive. As soon as Tigger saw Gerry coming through the gate, he would jump down and run to the front door to say hello.

I was so happy during this time. Things were really looking up, and Gerry and I were starting to make more definite plans. We were talking more and more about the future, getting married, and dividing our time between South Africa, Ireland and New York. I was delighted, and for the first time in my life I started to trust that life would be good and I would have a happy future.

Shortly after we moved into our new house, I sent Gerry a text: 'I am so happy!! Life is good! I have a fantastic boyfriend, great house and great kids!' And in my diary on 6 April I wrote: 'I am just so happy. It feels as if everything in my life just fits perfectly – as if everything will be fine in the future. Of course there is this thought: is it too good to be true? But I just have to relax and know that everything will be fine. And that I (finally) deserve this happiness.'

But I was still worried about Gerry. In mid-April I woke up one morning with a sore hand. It felt like a sprain, but I couldn't think of anything that could have caused it. That evening I was cooking and mentioned it to Gerry. He said he was not surprised. I asked why. 'Because every night you hold on to me, no matter how we sleep, your hands always find me and hold on to me. Sometimes you get yourself into the most tangled positions. It's a wonder you haven't been stiff before. It's as if you want to protect me or that you think I'm going somewhere. Are you worried about something?' he asked.

I was truly surprised to hear this. Gerry and I slept really closely at night, turning in unison, and I loved snuggling up to his broad back or lying on his chest listening to his heartbeat.

But I also knew that I was worried. I often lay awake for hours watching him sleep fretfully, sometimes propped up on one arm. I would stroke him gently, hoping to sooth him and willing him to sleep easier, but I did not realise that I even did it in my sleep. Thinking of all this, I suddenly became overwhelmed with fear and started crying.

'What's wrong?' Gerry asked.

'Oh God, Gerry, please don't die on me,' I wept. 'I wouldn't survive that. Anything else is okay, I'll manage, but not your death. Promise me you won't die on me.'

Gerry pulled me into his arms and calmly, in a deep, low voice, he said, 'You know I will die before you, but I am not going anywhere soon. There's too much that we're still going to do. Sure, our life is only really starting, once I finalise the separation.' He held me so tight I could barely breathe. 'But you will remember to hold me one day when I die, right? Now, enough tears. Please finish that food before I die of hunger.' We kissed, and after making him promise that he would go for a complete physical soon, I went back to cooking.

A few days later, the topic came up again. Gerry was again keeping me company while I cooked. I had just returned from the funeral of a staff member's dad and was telling Gerry about it. Suddenly Gerry said: 'You must promise me you will talk about me after my death.'

I turned around to face him. 'What?' I asked, surprised.

Gerry had an intense look in his eyes. 'I know you. You would just want to withdraw and be private. But you have to promise me that you will tell people everything. You must make sure they know I was a good man.'

'Gerry, what's this all about?' I asked. 'People love you.'

'You will see, after my death – all kinds of people will try and make out that I was an evil bastard. They will lie; the stories will become worse and worse. I need to know that you will tell the truth. That you will tell everything,' he said, his voice rising.

'Everything?' I asked surprised.

'Everything,' he said firmly. 'That's the only way.' He got up from the stool and held my shoulders. 'Promise me, please,' he insisted.

'I promise, Gerry. I tell you what, we'll write it in a book together in about twenty years, and then I'll get it published after your death, okay?'

'Okay,' he said, sitting down again, while I returned to the cooking. Then he added, 'Do you think people will come to my funeral?'

'Yeah, I think one or two would pitch up,' I said, with irony in my voice.

He burst out laughing.

26

I turned 43 on 18 April 2010. Gerry had returned a few days earlier from Austria, where he and DBK had recorded an interview for the next series of *Ryan Confidential* with Heather Mills, Paul McCartney's ex-wife. All had gone well, and after the interview he had phoned to say they were all going for a late dinner. Just before midnight he had called again, to say he was too tired and was going to bed. The next day he kept texting me on his way back, and when I opened the door at my house that afternoon, he opened his arms wide and with a big grin said: 'Hey girl! Your boyfriend's back!' We were like two lovesick teenagers and were delighted to be back in each other's arms.

Yet for some reason I was very sad and down the week before my birthday. I put it down to missing my family and South Africa. Gerry was understanding and tried to help, with hugs, jokes and supportive texts. The Sunday morning of my birthday he sent me a text at around 7am, wishing me a happy birthday, and an hour later he turned up at my door with gifts, cards and flowers.

That evening I wore a new dress and shoes and we went for dinner. We had a lovely evening and spoke at length about our plans for the future. Gerry also wanted to know about my will and how it provided for my kids after my separation. I told him I had made sure all the money would go into a trust for the children with my sisters as trustees, and with strict instructions as to how my children should be cared for.

'I'm going to do that in the next few weeks,' Gerry said. 'I need to make sure my kids are protected.' After filling me in on the details of his life insurance, he took my hand and said: 'I need to make sure you're taken care of. I want to make sure you'll be okay, either through property or some additional life insurance.'

I had had enough of the death talk, and told him that we still had many years to sort that out.

Gerry insisted: 'No, I want to do it soon.'

'Let's wait a while, Gerry. You have so much financial pressure.' Thankfully, the arrival of a plate of chocolates with a sparkler put an end to all the sad talk. Late that night, as we went to sleep, I thanked Gerry for a wonderful birthday.

'Just the beginning of many more, my darling. Many, many more,' he replied.

Two nights after my birthday, we went with Rita and Harry to a Whitney Houston concert in the big O2 concert venue. The concert had already started when we arrived, so we stood for a while at the back of the theatre, close to the VIP lounge. We then spotted two empty chairs at the end of a row and slipped into the seats quietly, or so we thought. The women around us were on their feet dancing, but suddenly one looked around and spotted Gerry. During a pause in one of Whitney's songs, she shrieked at the top of her voice: 'Oh my God! It's Gerry Ryan!' The whole block of people turned around to have a look. Of course then he had to pose for endless photos and everyone wanted to dance with him. Soon afterwards we had to escape back into the Audi Lounge.

Although we had a good evening, on our way home in the taxi Gerry became annoyed again about his, as well as the country's, money situation. He started to go on about the recession and how he hated what was happening in Ireland. I was worried about the taxi driver overhearing it, but Gerry could not care less. When we arrived at my house, Gerry paid the driver, who said: 'By the way, I totally agree with you, Gerry.'

Towards the end of April, Gerry had his youngest two children for the weekend. On Saturday evening, we all went for a meal at a nearby restaurant and Louis Walsh, the manager of – among others – Westlife and Boyzone, came over to say hello. The next day I encouraged Gerry to take a walk with me around the block, but we had barely walked for five minutes when he became dizzy and short of breath and had to lean against the fence. It was clear that all the pressure was getting to be too much. He was trying to finalise the separation (always stressful), but the banks were also constantly phoning him and his accountant. The demands from Revenue were also becoming more threatening. Gerry needed money fast. I had nothing left, having paid for most of his living expenses for months, as well as loaning him money so he could meet his obligations. Gerry did not want to ask Harry Crosbie, since he was embarrassed that he had not been able to repay the rent Harry had lent him for the previous year. So he asked many acquaintances from the past for help, as well as a few people he had given money to before. One came through with a smallish amount but the rest all said no.

He then got in touch with his old friend Michael Flatley. They had kept in contact through the years, and even though Gerry found it humiliating, he asked to borrow some money from him. Gerry was over the moon when he told me Michael had indicated it would not be a problem. He also told me they had discussed the possibility of arranging some meetings in Los Angeles for possible work in the future.

On Monday 26 April, Gerry and his accountant went to see his bank manager. The meeting did not go well, and Gerry told me and David Blake Knox separately how he had started to feel so sick during the meeting that he had to leave for a while because he felt he was going to faint.

On their way back, he and the accountant stopped for coffee. While they were in the restaurant, Gerry got a text from Michael saying there might be a problem, and that his accountant would be in touch. A few minutes later, the accountant got in touch. Gerry phoned me immediately after the conversation, on his way home. I could hear that he was extremely distressed. He said that the accountant had told him that 'it was not opportune for Mr Flatley at this time to be lending you money'. Gerry was devastated. When he arrived home, he was distraught and panicked. He did not know what to do.

Although he felt awful, he decided to go to Dave Kavanagh's child's birthday party that evening. Dave, a music promoter, and Gerry had rarely seen each other in the two years since the separation, but after bumping into him a few months earlier, Gerry had been trying to meet with Dave in the hope of discussing a possible loan. So when he got an invitation to the birthday party, he felt he had to go. He texted me during the evening to say he was having fun but missed me, and shortly after 11pm he arrived back at my house. In bed, he said he was now pinning all his hope on getting some money from Dave and hoped to meet up with him later that week.

The next evening, we went to a cocktail party in Bewley's Hotel, across from the Four Seasons Hotel, to celebrate South Africa's national day. Even though he was very tired, Gerry wanted to come with me. It was good to see so many familiar faces again, and of course many diplomats and officials from the Department of Foreign Affairs wanted to speak to Gerry. He looked exhausted but was – as always – entertaining and jovial. RTÉ colleague Marian Finucane and her husband John Clarke were there too, and came over to say hello. They invited us to join them for a late supper in the Four Seasons Hotel. Gerry and I were keen to get away, and agreed.

I started to say my goodbyes and walked towards the exit. Gerry was right behind me, or so I thought. At the door I turned to say something to him, but he was nowhere to be seen. This was nothing new: it would sometimes take an hour to get Gerry out of a venue. As a rule, I would walk behind him so that I could 'rescue' him if he got stuck with people who wanted to say hello. I scanned the room to see if I could spot him, then suddenly heard loud whoops of joy and whistles coming from the dance floor. I should have known.

Gerry was surrounded by a big group of African women: he was jiving away and quickly getting the hang of the African dance moves. He was having the time of his life. When he stopped, there were loads of hugs, photographs and kisses from the women before I finally got him away. I heard one woman say: 'Aauw, Nkosi yam!' This Xhosa expression of extreme affection is usually reserved for children.

I looked back at the group of women who were watching us leave and realised that the words were directed at Gerry. 'Hey, he's my Nkosi yam,' I joked back.

They laughed. 'You are so lucky, Melanie,' shouted one.

'What was that?' Gerry asked, taking my hand. I translated for him.

He smiled broadly. 'You see, I told you, the black birds always fancy me.' I sighed and gave him a playful poke in his side.

My high heels were hurting me, so I stopped and took them off. Gerry looked at me with an amused and slightly exasperated expression. 'You can take the girl out of Africa, but never Africa out of the girl,' he said.

'Yes, but thankfully for you, us birds from Africa fancy you.' We laughed, but I could see Gerry was exhausted and short of breath. 'Are you sure you're up for this?' I asked him.

'Yes, I'm just tired. It will be good to see Marian. We won't stay too long.'

Marian and John were waiting in the bar for us, and as soon as we sat down, Gerry and Marian started to talk about the situation at RTÉ. It was obvious how badly it was affecting both of them. Gerry opened up to Marian

about how much stress and anxiety it was causing him and how much resent-
ment and anger he felt towards the management in RTÉ. Halfway through
the meal, Gerry suddenly said: 'We have to go.' He looked pale, sweaty and
exhausted. 'Right now!' Marian and John offered to pay, and we left. We went
back to my house, and Gerry went straight to bed.

We had a terrible night. Gerry was fretting and could not sleep at all. He
had terrible stomach cramps and diarrhoea. He complained of severe palpitations and shortness of breath, and he was running a high fever and sweating profusely. I begged him to let me call a doctor or take him to the emergency room, but he would not let me. He insisted that it was just stress and
promised to see Dr Crosby the next day. At around 3am he was sweating so
much that I had to change the sheets, which were soaked. I spoke to him for
hours, assuring him that we would sort something out. He asked if I would
meet with his accountant in the morning and see if I could find a way out.
Of course I agreed.

The next morning Gerry was pale and looked awful. 'Please stay in bed,'
I pleaded while helping him to the shower. 'I'll phone Alice.'

'No, I can't,' he responded. 'No sick leave, I can't afford it.'

As soon as he left for work, I phoned the accountant, who agreed to see
me within the hour at the Burlington Hotel. We spent hours going through
various scenarios. The biggest problem was the Revenue bill, which needed
to be paid immediately. In the end we narrowed it down to three possible options. It was clear that Gerry would have to borrow some money somewhere
and arrange a grace period with the bank on some of his repayments.

Feeling a lot better, I went home just after noon and called Gerry. I asked
if he wanted to come for lunch, so that we could look at the various options.
Over lunch I showed him the three scenarios, but I could see he was so tired
that he could barely concentrate. 'Why don't you go to bed for a while?' I
suggested.

Gerry nodded. 'Will you come with me? I don't want to be alone.'

My heart ached for him. I hated seeing him like this. In bed he held me so
tight I could barely breathe, and when he eventually relaxed a bit and fell
asleep I carefully crawled from under his arms and out of bed. I quietly took
his phone, left the room and called Dr Crosby, hoping that he would pick
up if he saw Gerry's number. He did. I explained that Gerry had been very

unwell and told him how worried I was. He said Gerry had spoken to him and that he felt it was stress, for which he would prescribe Xanax (a sedative) and Stilnoct (a light sleeping pill). I asked whether he thought he should see Gerry, but Dr Crosby said to call back if he got worse, or else to tell Gerry to phone him if he was worried. A few minutes later, he texted to say he had phoned the prescription through to Boots in Donnybrook. I put Gerry's phone on silent and left it on the bedside table with a note to say where I was going.

The pharmacist at Boots gave me the medication. Seeing the name on the prescription, she warned me that Gerry should not take the sleeping pills too late in the evening, since they took at least eight hours to clear the system. After the pharmacy, I popped into the shop to buy food for dinner and a chocolate muffin for Gerry, before heading home.

When Gerry woke up he looked a bit better and happily munched away at his muffin with some tea while reading *Time* magazine. He did not mind that I had called Dr Crosby, but was not sure he wanted to take the medication. But he knew he desperately needed some sleep. I prepared an early dinner while he stayed in bed. He got up around six to have dinner with Wilmé and me. He had some chicken pie and roast potatoes, but when I poured him a glass of wine he pushed it away, saying he did not feel like any. At the end of the meal he helped to clear the table and, standing at the dishwasher, I heard Wilmé asking him if he was okay.

'No, Wilmé, I am really totally banjaxed – just exhausted and broken,' he answered truthfully.

Wilmé said she was worried about him, but he told her not to worry and just to look after her mum.

We had promised my son that we would make an appearance at his school that night since they were celebrating international night. Gerry had fallen asleep in front of the television and I suggested that we either not go, or I go on my own, but Gerry insisted he wanted to go too. He had told Wian he would and did not want to let him down. On the way to St Andrews, we stopped at Gerry's house so he could put on some lights and feed the fish. When we left, I pointed out the beautiful cherry blossom tree in full bloom close to his house. 'Look Gerry, it's so beautiful.'

Gerry looked at it and sighed.

'You know, things will get better. In a year from now, we'll look back and laugh at this time,' I said positively.

Gerry looked at me and said: 'Let's make a promise. Next year on this date, when this tree flowers again, we'll stand under it and drink champagne. We'll laugh and have fun.'

International night was a huge success. Wian was delighted to see us and took Gerry around to taste the different foods and introduce him to his teachers. I felt very emotional watching my son and Gerry, especially at the South African stand, where Wian proudly explained the food to Gerry – who in turn made a huge fuss and ate loads of food. Shortly afterwards, though, Gerry looked pale again and I saw him struggling for breath. Wian went to get him a drink from a vending machine and we left a few minutes later. In the car, Gerry again promised to see a doctor 'soon', although he insisted that he just needed some sleep and to sort the money out. 'All will calm down as soon as the separation is complete, in the next two to three weeks,' he said.

After we returned from Wian's school (and rescued the cat, who had got himself stuck on the roof), I made Gerry some tea and suggested that he take the Xanax and Stilnoct so he could get some sleep. He agreed, but when I returned with his tea he was busy reading up about Xanax on the internet. Having never taken it before, he wanted to be sure what he was taking. 'This is very strong stuff,' he said, showing me the information. 'It can become addictive. I'll only take it for a few nights until I've had some rest.' After he took the pills, I offered to run him a bath. He laughed and said: 'My great feminist! This could seriously ruin your street cred.'

'Well, kind gestures aren't against feminist principles, you know. But just in case, don't tell anyone!' We laughed.

I was passing the bathroom door when he came out after a long bath. He had a big white towel around his waist and his hair was wet. He pulled me into his arms. I nestled against his wet chest, listening to his heart beating. 'Thank you for looking after me,' Gerry said into my ear. 'I know it's not always easy, but I would never have survived without you.'

I looked up at him. 'Gerry, I love you so much. We will get through this. You just have to hold on, okay?'

He gave me a tight hug and said 'I love you.' Then he went to bed.

A few minutes later, he complained that the Xanax and Stilnoct had had no effect.

'Just give it a few minutes,' I replied, 'and stop reading about the war in Iraq in that *Time* magazine. It will excite you too much. Try this.' I handed him a book I knew would fascinate him: *The Brain that Changes Itself* by Norman Doidge.

He started reading as I quickly dipped into the bath he had left for me. When I returned five minutes later, he was fast asleep across the bed with the book lying open next to him. I breathed a sigh of relief and carefully, so as not to disturb him, climbed in under his arm.

At 4am I woke as he got up to go to the bathroom. I could hear from his groans that he was feeling awful. I asked if he was okay. He asked for some Imodium, which I gave to him, and a few minutes later he came back to bed. Awake, he again complained of heart palpitations and started to fret about everything like so many nights before. How was he going to meet all of his obligations? What would the press do if he went bankrupt? What if Dave Kavanagh could not help?

We spoke for a while about this before I changed the subject, talking about things we would do and trips we would take once the crisis was over. Gradually I felt his body starting to relax against mine and his breathing becoming a bit easier. I stroked his hair and back and eventually I sensed that he was nodding off again.

'I love you, I love you, I love you,' he whispered.

As always I struggled to fall asleep after the conversation. I was lying in the semi-dark, feeling panic rising in me. The stress was taking such a toll on Gerry's body and spirit. It had to stop soon. I also needed some sleep. The sleepless and interrupted nights were starting to exhaust me. I stretched out to find an eye mask in my bedside table and thankfully soon fell asleep.

About two hours later, I gradually surfaced with a sense that someone was watching me. I lifted the eye mask from my face and looked into Gerry's eyes. He was sitting on his knees next to my side of the bed looking at me intensely. He was calm and I realised he was already dressed.

'Hi,' I smiled sleepily. I stretched out to touch his face. 'Are you okay?'

'Yes,' he answered. 'I'm just watching you sleep. You're so beautiful.'

I smiled. 'With an eye mask and mad hair? I don't think so!'

Gerry looked at me with an intense expression. 'I love you so, so much,' he said quietly. 'I hope you know this.'

I nodded. 'I love you too – more than I thought humanly possible, Gerry.'

He bent forward and gave me a long, deep kiss. Then he pulled the eye mask back over my eyes. 'Now go back to sleep. You're exhausted. I'll see you later today.'

He gave me a little kiss on my neck and got up. I listened to his footsteps going down the passage and up the two small steps to the lobby. I heard him unlock the front door, and then it slammed shut behind him . . . for the last time.

27

Gerry was scheduled to meet Dave Kavanagh at around 3pm. We had planned to go to the Gate Theatre afterwards with David Blake Knox, but I was so tired after the previous night that I asked Gerry if he would be able to go on his own with David. He was fine with that. During the afternoon he phoned a few times to say how nervous he was about the meeting with Dave Kavanagh. He felt it was his last chance, since the Revenue bill had to be paid the next day.

At 5.24pm, I texted to ask how things were going and whether he wanted some dinner before he went to the Gate. Gerry texted back that all was going well, the money was forthcoming and he was giving the Gate a miss. I was relieved about the money and also about giving the Gate a miss, thinking he might come home earlier so he could rest. But a while later I got a call from Gerry's accountant saying she had just given him some bad news: the bank had declined the request of giving him a holiday period on some of his loan repayments. She said Gerry was extremely upset and she asked me to call him to check if he was all right. I asked if he had indicated where he was and she replied that he was just outside his house.

I called Gerry a few minutes later, hoping that he was on his way to me. He said he had just arrived at Dave Kavanagh's house (which was a few doors from Gerry's house) after dropping his car at his own house, and that they were going to dinner. He asked me to wait a few minutes so he could step into another room and we could talk privately. In the background I heard Dave asking Gerry what he wanted to drink, and a few minutes later our conversation was interrupted again as a drink was handed to Gerry. We spoke for almost fifteen minutes. Gerry was upset. At first I thought it was only about the news from the bank, but then I realised that the conversation with Dave had not gone well either. I asked Gerry directly if Dave had agreed to lend him the money.

'No,' Gerry said. 'But his accountant will speak to mine in the morning.'

'Gerry, that sounds like Michael Flatley all over again. Did he promise to lend you the money?'

'No,' Gerry said tiredly, 'but the accountant has some plan.'

Now I was really worried. 'Gerry, that's nonsense. Your accountant and I worked through all the scenarios. I showed it to you. There are no other plans. Either he lends you the money, or not. If not, it's no good to you.'

'I know,' Gerry replied, sounding exhausted. 'That's why I'm going to dinner with him. I have to keep him onside.'

I could hear that Gerry was beyond tired and said he did not sound up to it. 'Come home to me. I'll make you some dinner and we can crawl into bed.' I pleaded.

'I'd love that, but I have to see if I can tie this down. I'll try not to be too late.'

Our conversation ended at 8pm. During the evening I sent him a couple of texts and at 11pm we spoke over the phone. He had just arrived home and again he was frustrated. Clearly, nothing more was resolved and Gerry was panicking. I tried to calm him down and suggested that I come over to his house. I was already in bed, but was happy to throw on a coat and run over.

'No, you need a good night's rest and I've locked up already,' Gerry said. 'I'll be okay. I'm going to take a Xanax and a Stilnoct now. I'll see you tomorrow.'

I reminded him of the pharmacist's warning that it takes eight hours for the medication to clear the system. Checking the time, I made a mental note to make sure he was up the next morning.

We had another brief conversation at 11.22pm, in which I asked again if I could come over to see him, since he sounded so anxious. He said he was already in bed and just needed to sleep. At 11.39pm he phoned to say good-night and we had a lovely few minutes on the phone. From his phone records, I know that he then phoned and left messages for his producer Alice and Joe Hoban from the RTÉ press office and that Alice called him back just before midnight.

Just before 4am the next morning, I woke up covered in sweat. I was shivering and my heart was racing. I thought I had heard Gerry's voice. I knew he was not with me, so I looked at my phone to see if he had phoned or texted me. There was nothing, but I felt extremely restless, anxious and scared. I started to dial Gerry's number, but then stopped, thinking that I had to let him sleep, given his exhaustion of the previous days. I felt sick and scared for a long time before I finally fell asleep again.

The next morning I did not get my usual call from Gerry at around 7am. I was on the treadmill and after a few minutes I phoned him. The phone rang out, so I assumed he had put the phone on silent and forgotten to turn it back on. But when I did not get the usual call from the car on the way to RTÉ, I got worried.

Given that he had taken the sleeping pill so late, I thought he might have overslept. I got off the treadmill, threw a coat over my exercise clothes and ran down to his house. When I saw the car in the driveway, I assumed he was not up yet.

I tried to get into the house through the basement door we always used, but as usual he had put the various locks and chains on the previous night, and I could not open the door with my keys. I rang his cell phone a few more times from outside, but it still rang out. Eventually I called Alice, his producer, and asked if Gerry was there. I thought he might have taken a cab – something he did on a few occasions if he was not feeling well or the car would not start.

To my relief, Alice said he had called her the previous evening just before midnight, saying he was very tired and needed a rest the next day. I was thankful that he had decided to take a day off, knowing how bad he had been feeling that week.

So I went off to work feeling confident that he would call me shortly after the sleeping pill wore off. We were supposed to go to Athlone after lunch for work he had to do for RTÉ, so I phoned him a while a later to check if he was up. There was still no response. During meetings I kept texting and phoning him, with a growing sense of unease. When it got to 11.30am, I suddenly felt very anxious and a feeling of dread came over me. *Even if he has slept in, he would have woken up at some point and phoned me,* I thought. 'Something is wrong with Gerry,' I told my assistant, and suddenly felt close to tears. 'I have to go to him.'

I grabbed a cab and on the way I phoned my son and asked him to meet me at Gerry's with a hammer or screwdriver or something to break in. I kept phoning and texting Gerry.

As soon as I arrived, Wian came down the road. I realised that I could perhaps open the front door slightly, even with the security chain on. So I unlocked the door and Wian and I tried to get the security chain off from the outside, but we could not. I stuck my head partly through the door and shouted Gerry's name, knowing he would be able to hear me if he was in the bedroom.

There was no response, so I ran to a house two doors down where they were doing some building work. I asked one of the builders if he could help me to saw the chain off, saying I had locked myself out. He used a hacksaw, and as soon as the door was open he left.

I will never forget the next few seconds as long as I live. I ran up the stairs calling Gerry's name. I knew something was wrong, but I hoped against hope that he was okay. When I got to the bedroom door, there was no sight of him, and for a moment I thought with relief that he had gone out or was in the bathroom. But then I saw his feet on the floor on the opposite side of the bed. And I knew the worst had happened. In an instant my world fell apart.

I ran to Gerry and touched him, but he was so cold. I screamed for my son, who ran into the room. My son turned ashen, but in those next few minutes he would turn into a man. He immediately took charge and pulled me away from Gerry. 'Call an ambulance,' he said. Panicked, I could not remember the number. He gave it to me and started CPR .

The emergency operator took all the details. 'Please, please, hurry,' I pleaded. 'I think he is dead!' The man stayed on the line and insisted that we keep doing CPR. Wian followed the instructions I relayed, but at some point he looked up at me in despair. That said it all.

'Please, Wian, please keep going!' I begged.

'It's no use, Mum,' he said, almost in tears.

Just then I heard the sirens outside. I ran downstairs and members of the fire brigade and ambulance service ran in. They asked me to wait outside the room. The police followed a few seconds later.

Wian came downstairs with Gerry's phone. It was ringing. 'Answer it,' Wian said. 'It's Harry.'

I answered it and asked Harry to come over. I told him that something awful had happened.

Harry passed the phone to Rita. They were in the car close by and minutes later they arrived. I was in the sitting room hoping the paramedics would come down and say they were taking Gerry to the nearest hospital.

Instead, one of them touched my shoulder and said those awful six words: 'I am sorry for your loss.'

My brain would not register what I had been told, and I felt panic rising. *Oh God, I am going to lose it*, I thought. But then, out of the blue, a strange calmness came over me. To this day, I think Gerry guided me. I suddenly knew clearly that I had to get to his family. They could not hear this from the Gardaí or, worse, from the press. I decided to call their GP. I could hear his shock, but he agreed to go down to the house. However, a few minutes later there was a call from Gerry's elder son, Rex. He said that Dr Crosby was too shocked to talk. He wanted me to tell him what was going on. It was the worst news I have ever had to give anyone.

I then called Gerry's two brothers, Mano (Vincent) and Mick, and Noel Kelly, Gerry's agent, in the hope that the latter would be able to manage the press – who I knew would arrive in due course. In fact, the press was outside in less than 30 minutes. Immediately texts started to come in on Gerry's phone from friends and colleagues. They all wanted to know if he was okay, and some were making jokes about the ridiculous story that they had just heard about him having died.

I was increasingly panicked that all the children had not been told yet, so I called the house in Clontarf. I was told that everyone except Gerry's younger son Elliot had been told. Elliot was at school, around the corner from Gerry's house, and they did not know how to get to him. I was asked to go and get him.

Noel Kelly and I went over to the school, and I had to break the most awful news you can ever give a child. As I helped Elliot into the car, I realised that the radio was on. The presenter from Newstalk said: 'Folks, we have shocking unconfirmed reports . . . '

'Noel!' I said sharply.

He quickly switched off the radio. Noel suggested that he take Elliot home. I hated leaving Elliot, but I felt I would not be welcome at the house in Clontarf. I also needed to get back to the house. Gerry was still there . . .

Back at the house, the police sealed the scene to take samples for forensic evidence. Mano and Mick had arrived, and then the undertakers came to take Gerry away. I was not ready to let him go, but they strongly suggested that I not go back into the room. Gerry had been dead for hours – probably more than twelve hours at that stage. Rigor mortis had already set in when I found him, and it was an awful sight. They told me that it had got worse since then. I wanted to say goodbye, but I did not want to remember him like that. To this day I cannot remember what his face looked like when I found him. I constantly have flashbacks of his body, the room, even the smells, but not his face. Psychologists tell me that this is a defence mechanism – for which I am thankful. At least I remember his face with a smile and big happy eyes.

But I was panicking that I would not see Gerry again. Mano and Mick promised me repeatedly that they would ensure that I would see his body before the funeral to say goodbye. So I didn't go back into the room. Yet I wanted to be with him when they took him out of the house. I didn't want him to make that journey alone. But people took me into a room and closed the door. They insisted that I could not do that, since the press were outside and it would be insensitive to the rest of the family. I was bitterly upset, but before I could convince them otherwise it was all over and Gerry was gone. I now know that this was the moment he was gone from me forever.

When I arrived home there were a few people waiting. I can remember certain parts of the next few days in great detail, but the rest is a haze. I know I was in shock, and my body started to react. I felt numb, sick and shaky. I wanted to be alone yet I could not bear the idea of being alone with my thoughts and the images of Gerry. It all felt completely unreal – so much so that I put the TV news on at 5.30pm telling myself it would not be on the news; it was all just a bad dream. But of course it was everywhere. TV3 news led with it. At 6pm I switched to RTÉ news and, to my horror, unlike TV3, they did not lead with it. I watched a report on life insurance as sadness grew in me. They could not even honour him at his own workplace with the lead story. When the story came up, I listened as they merely reported that his body had been found before lunchtime, without any mention that it was his partner and her son who found him. They then sympathised only with his family. Brid, who was sitting next to me, gently took my hand as the reality sank in.

A little while later, David Blake Knox arrived. He looked shaken. After we hugged, he said that there would be a special *Late Late Show* dedication a few hours later, and he had been asked to go on. He was not sure whether he could do it, or if it was the right thing to do. I asked who else was going on. It was Pat Kenny, Dave Fanning, Gay Byrne, Brenda O'Donoghue, Joe Duffy and possibly David. I immediately begged him to go on. I knew that he was the only one of those people who was truly close to Gerry and who had been around him in the last two years as his friend. I also knew that anyone else who was really close to Gerry during this time would be too upset and shocked to go on TV that night.

Shortly after 9pm our sitting room filled up. My children's friends had arrived to give them support, and Brid and Niamh were there. Everyone watched in shock and in tears as the images of Gerry flashed across the screen. Halfway through, one of my daughter's friends said: 'Why aren't they mentioning Melanie as his partner? It's as if their relationship didn't exist.' Brid responded that they might still, but tension was building up in the room. As the segment on Gerry ended, without a word being said about our relationship, the room fell quiet and all eyes turned towards me.

I felt confused. How could Ryan and David not even mention us being together or how much Gerry meant to me? It was truly as if our relationship of the last two years had never existed. I could not understand why people would completely ignore our relationship. This confusion would grow over the next few days and weeks, as I desperately tried to make sense of what was happening around me.

I had an awful night. Wilmé slept beside me and held my hand, but I could not sleep at all. The next morning I needed to get out of the house and took a walk around the block at around 6am. As I walked past the taxi rank outside the Burlington Hotel, I overheard the taxi drivers talking about Gerry. They saw me but, clearly not recognising me, they started to talk to me. 'Awful, isn't it?'

'Yes,' I said, fighting back the tears.

One talked about how he had heard that people shouted out the news of Gerry's death in shops and how everyone was talking about it in town. I was so moved that tears started to flow. One of the guys looked at me closely and suddenly recognised me. They both pulled me into a tight hug.

Someone brought me the papers later. They were filled with stories of Gerry – as they would be every day for the next two weeks. People came and went, and in the late afternoon Gerry's children dropped in. They were with a PR agent and a driver Gerry had used years ago who was still close to the family. I took the children into the sitting room with me, and Brid took the

PR agent and driver into the kitchen. It was so good to see the children, and over the next few days I saw them a few times and we texted all the time.

After they all left, Brid came over to me. 'Do you know that the PR agent and driver were told to clean out bits of Gerry's house?' she asked carefully. 'They were also instructed to take the car.'

I was shocked. Were people going in and clearing out things, without even talking to me? This was our house that we had made together, and they had no business doing that. There were still some of my things in Gerry's car, and it was now gone. Why? Did they think I would steal the car? Very upset, I phoned Mano. He knew nothing about it. He promised to have the car returned.

Over the next few days, I tried again and again to see Gerry's body, so I could say my final goodbye. This was complicated by the fact that it was a bank holiday weekend. When I phoned the Gardaí to ask if they could help, the Garda in charge said in an irritated tone that Mr Ryan's body had been identified and claimed late on the Friday night by his wife and that I had no legal rights or standing. Unless the coroner agreed to it, I would not be able to see him. I reeled with shock.

Eventually someone I knew got in touch with the coroner's office on my behalf. Late on Monday afternoon, I received a message that I would be able to see Gerry under two conditions: 1. It had to happen in the next hour; and 2. I had to get written permission from his next of kin, which was still his wife. I was desperate. I knew I had to say goodbye properly in order to stand any chance of ever being all right in the future. So I phoned intermediaries to ask if they could arrange the permission for me. Almost immediately, the message came back. The answer was no. I am not sure if the intermediaries did indeed ask permission, but in any event I would not be able to see him. I was distraught.

Over the next two days, I kept speaking to Mano and Mick, who promised to do what they could. Eventually, on the Tuesday afternoon, they called. They said they had organised a few minutes for me. So as not to let anyone know that I was going to see Gerry, they had had his body taken to another funeral home. Even though all the secrecy made me feel like a criminal, I was extremely thankful for all their efforts.

Mick came to pick up Brid and me. In the car he was constantly on the phone, while I was trying to keep my growing panic under control. What would Gerry look like? What if I could not cope with seeing him?

At the funeral home, the undertakers took me to a room. As they opened the door, I panicked. I had only once before seen someone in a coffin, at an ANC funeral, since we normally do not have wakes or open coffins in South Africa. Now I had to go into this room to see my love. I was not sure I could cope.

'Are you okay?' the undertaker asked gently.

'I need Brid,' I said anxiously. He fetched her and we went in together.

Gerry was so cold, so quiet. *How can Gerry, of all people, be that quiet? It doesn't look like him at all.* I kept looking at him, willing him to take a breath, to sit up, but he just lay there, lifeless. *This isn't right!* I looked over at Brid. 'He's not here,' I said, confused.

'No, he's not,' she said softly.

How did this happen? It must be a nightmare. We had so many plans. If only I could do something, maybe everything would go back to normal.

Mick had come in, but left again, and I could sense that my few minutes were running out. I had wanted to put something in the coffin from me, but I knew that anything obvious would be removed. So I had cut a piece of my hair and when no one was looking I put it under Gerry's jacket, close to his heart. And then I left behind the body of the man I had loved so much.

In the car I sat in the back while Mick was on the phone again. I felt numb and sick but at the same time relieved. I had been very worried that when I saw Gerry, I would not be able to let go, that I would want to hold his body tight and protect it. But he looked so strange, so quiet, that it did not feel like him at all. And I knew he was not there. Gerry was elsewhere. At least it helped to know that. I vaguely registered that Mick was speaking to Mano on the phone. 'The coast is clear,' he said, while catching my eye in the rear view mirror.

I knew I would not be invited to take part in the wake. So my friends had insisted that I give him some sort of farewell. I was too shocked to think of anything, but they knew how important it would be, and they organised it for the Sunday after his death. It was a difficult day, but friends finally got an opportunity to talk to each other, to cry and even to laugh. They stayed for hours, drank whiskey in memory of Gerry, and just talked and talked. Many

274

of my African friends came too. They did not stay in the sitting room with us but, according to African custom, sat in the kitchen and prayed and sang for hours. At the end of the evening, they came in and sang a prayer for us all. 'Hamba kahle umkonto' (Go well, spear), the lament rang out. It was incredibly moving. Gerry's children and Mano and his wife Nessa also came, and I was deeply thankful for that.

The emotional outpouring from the public was amazing. Books of condolence were opened in numerous places and people queued for hours to sign them. A Facebook page dedicated to Gerry had more than 100 000 followers within two days. Thinking of Gerry's concern two weeks earlier as to whether anyone would come to his funeral, I hoped he was seeing it all.

The press ran for weeks with page after page on Gerry and his death. Of course there was no shortage of 'friends' who were now talking about Gerry as if they had been his closest and dearest friends. They were often the same people who had hurt Gerry so much in the two years before, while his real friends (with the exception of Fiona Looney and David Blake Knox, who bravely spoke about him) were too shocked and traumatised to talk to the press.

Radio stations also dedicated programmes to him, and I heard stories from across the world of Irish people commemorating Gerry. RTÉ in particular had various shows to commemorate him. On the day after his death, there had been a special *Ryan Show* on RTÉ Radio 2, which his colleague Evelyn O'Rourke bravely presented. Alice phoned to warn me, and I asked if she would mind if I came in to be with them. I needed to be with people who loved Gerry. She said, 'Of course.' Everyone in the studio was clearly in bits, but Alice was amazing. She kept everyone together despite being visibly heartbroken. I sat quietly on a couch in the control room and tried not to catch Evelyn's eye in case it became too much for both of us. But when the last song played she looked at me and we both disintegrated.

Halfway through the show, one of the members of senior management came in to convey her condolences. She also said that Marian Finucane was about to start her show on Radio 1 and offered to take me to her studio. I went in quietly. It was completely different from the noisy *Ryan Show* studio, where phones were ringing and people were coming and going. Marian was alone in the studio and her production people barely noticed as I took a seat in the quiet control room. I do not think Marian saw me either.

At the beginning of her show, Marian referred to Gerry's death and gave her condolences to everyone close to Gerry. She then talked about the dinner we had had together on the Tuesday night and remarked on how stressed Gerry was about various things, including the situation at RTÉ. Those truthful words from Marian would cause her a lot of difficulty in the weeks to come. Members of RTÉ management, among others, expressed 'surprise' at her comments and denied that Gerry had been under any stress or pressure at work.

I did not stay long, wanting to be back at Gerry's studio. At the end of *The Gerry Ryan Show* special, one of his researchers came up to me. 'I want to give you this,' she said shyly, handing me a mangled paperclip. I knew that Gerry always played with a paperclip while he was on air as a way of coping with stress. I often found the deformed paperclips in his jacket or pants pockets when I did the washing. 'It's the one he played with on the last show,' the researcher said. 'I thought you would like it.'

Of all the kind gestures that people would make in the months to come, this was one of the kindest. I have kept that paperclip close to me, and at the funeral and inquest I had it in my hand all the time. It became a tiny little metal bond to Gerry, and gave me strength when I needed it most.

28

On the morning of the wake, I received a call to tell me there might be a possibility of me paying my respects at Clontarf later that day. I was relieved. Since the day of Gerry's death, I had repeatedly asked intermediaries to try to arrange this. Apart from wanting to pay my respects, I did not think it would be good for first meetings to take place at the funeral in the (very) public eye and in front of all the press. I also knew it was a source of great stress to the Ryan children and I wanted to try and reduce that. But the message that had come back was that I was not welcome. So when the call came that morning, I was surprised, relieved and yet very stressed at the same time.

'When?' I asked.

'Well, I'm not sure,' was the answer. 'Just be on standby, be ready, so you can come when everyone is ready.'

A sense of unease was growing in me.

'I'll try and give you thirty minutes' warning before we send a car,' the caller said.

'Can I bring someone, a friend?' I asked, suddenly feeling panic rising.

'No, we have to do this on our terms,' the intermediary said firmly.

I stood with the phone in my hand for a long time after the call ended. She had warned that there might still be a change of mind, but to get ready just in case. I felt anger rising in me, which I suppressed quickly. I was so exhausted, so distressed. But Gerry would have wanted it to be easier for the kids, which I wanted too, so I had to do it. And perhaps the visit could lay some foundation for a relationship that would make things easier in the future.

I suddenly thought about arriving with nothing to give, so I phoned my assistant, who brought over a beautiful bunch of flowers. Then I waited and waited. Just before 1pm, a call came. 'A car will be there shortly,' she said. 'And I've been told it's okay if you want to bring your children, since it would be good to spend time together with all the children.'

Again this surprised me. I was also worried about the timing. I had repeatedly asked that I come when there were no photographers outside the house in Clontarf. I assumed that everyone in Clontarf was also not sleeping, so I had suggested that I go over late at night when we could meet away from the public eye. But now, it was just over an hour away from the public wake. Desperate not to be caught arriving at the house as people started coming for the wake, I rushed to find my children. Wilmé said she would come, for my sake, and to see the children, but when I asked Wian I saw the panic in his eyes. I knew he was still in deep shock after finding Gerry with me and would find it impossible to see Gerry's body again. So we agreed that only Wilmé would come with me. A few minutes later, former producer on the Gerry Ryan show, Willie O'Reilly, arrived in a BMW with a chauffeur. Willie wanted to make small talk, but I could not cope with that. Thankfully Wilmé took over for a while, after which Willie started making business calls on his phone.

As we got closer to Clontarf, I felt more and more tense. I kept thinking of the various occasions when Gerry had stopped around the corner to drop things off, and of waiting in the Starbucks with the children while he went to the house so I would not be seen. And now here I was, about to go into the house, with Gerry's coffin inside. I was not sure I could go through with it. 'Please help me, Gerry,' I pleaded in my head, and suddenly calmness came over me. 'I can do this, I have to do this.'

It registered vaguely that Willie was giving instructions on how to get out of the car and who would go first. 'Why is he choreographing this?' I wondered. Ignoring him, I opened the door and got out. I just wanted to get inside and see the children. I knew that once I saw them it would be easier for Wilmé and me. As I got out, I heard the endless shutter action of the cameras. I had not registered until that point that there was a sea of photographers. I waited at the door with the flowers in my arms and someone opened it. 'You can go in there to the left,' the person said.

As I walked into the room I saw Gerry's body in the open coffin. The room was dark, with incense and candles burning. *This is wrong, all wrong,* I thought. *He would not want to be here. I should have done something. I should have insisted that the wake was in his house. I've failed him. He would have hated this.* The sudden stream of distressed thoughts was interrupted by a sharp intake of breath by Wilmé behind me. She had never seen a body be-

278

fore and I realised she was battling with the shock and pain of seeing Gerry, whom she loved so much, in the coffin.

I put my arm around her. 'You okay?'

My brave and immensely strong daughter pulled herself up straight. 'Yes, are you?'

I looked at Gerry closely. It still did not look like him, although now that he had his glasses on, maybe a bit more like himself. I went to sit next to his head and whispered into his ear: 'Hey, can you believe this? Me and you together in the house? By the way, it's not fair that you left me to do this on my own!' I looked at his face and thought again how much his mouth had this expression of 'Oh God, this wasn't meant to happen'. The next moment, I heard footsteps coming down the stairs.

According to the press, I was inside the house for less than seven minutes. To me it felt shorter and also longer at the same time. The meeting was cool and distant, and not what I had expected at all. I tried to say some words of comfort, but I do not think it made any difference. I asked to see the children but was told that this was not possible, and then I was asked to leave. Willie O'Reilly had stepped back into the room, ready to escort us out. I was shocked at how the meeting had turned out and asked him just to let us go on our own. Willie nodded. I looked over at Wilmé, who was pale, shaken and clearly furious.

As the front door opened, the cameras again clicked non-stop, and as I got into the car I felt awful. I could not help wondering why we had put ourselves through this when it was very clear that no one really wanted to see me or let me see the children.

As we got close to my house, my phone beeped. It was a text from a newspaper editor. 'Sorry to disturb you. Just wanted to check, did you ask for your flowers to be put outside on the fence in Clontarf? Willie O'Reilly came out after you left and put them there. Every photographer and journalist was truly shocked, but then we thought to check if this was your wish?'

I could not believe it. Of course I did not ask for my flowers to be put outside. By now I was so wound up, so tired, that I could barely register anything. I wanted to be alone, and somewhere I could feel Gerry, where I could remember us. So I went over to the Four Seasons Hotel, where Gerry and I had celebrated my birthday less than two weeks earlier, and hid away in a corner of the empty residence lounge. The staff came over one by one, looking truly upset. They sympathised and then left me alone. I ordered coffee, and when the manager Simon brought it over, he put a Martini on the table, in front of the seat opposite me.

'It's for Gerry,' he said quietly, before leaving. He would later tell me how, on the night of Gerry's death, they kept Gerry's favourite table empty in the dining room with only a candle and a Martini on it.

I sat there quietly remembering, weeping. At some point one of the staff quietly placed a box of tissues next to me and another put a fresh coffee in front of me. Niamh and Brid arrived, worried about me. I was calmer then. Brid held my gaze and said: 'We have to talk about tomorrow. It's going to be hell and I only just realised that you don't fully understand Catholic funerals and the role of the family.'

29

I was not sure I would be able to cope with the funeral. I still could not accept that my love was gone. And now I had to go into the public eye and say goodbye during a ceremony I had no say in, no part in, and where I would be the stranger.

In the days before, Gerry's older children had tried to give me an idea of the running order, but they were not sure of all the arrangements. I repeatedly asked intermediaries what was happening, but got stonewalled. Eventually I was told I could bring my family and that I should be thankful I was allowed to attend. I was also told to be in the church early so I did not draw attention when the coffin arrived. I was asked to sit against the wall, away from the aisle, and to leave via a side entrance afterwards. I was given no details about the proceedings at the graveyard.

I was in such a haze of shock and grief that I could not even bring myself to protest. I just wanted to get through it so I could retreat back into the privacy of my house. By the time we left for the funeral I was feeling ill from stress. I was holding on to Gerry's paperclip, as I would for the rest of the day. By the evening, my fingers were bleeding from holding it so tightly.

Kathy Gilfillan (Paul McGuinness's wife) had kindly arranged two cars for my family and me. My parents had arrived from South Africa, and because they had never fully understood how famous Gerry was, they were bewildered by all the media attention. My children were with me, and I took my friends Brid and Elaine as well.

As we got close to the church, I started to see people lining the streets. There were thousands of people. 'See, I told you a few people would turn up,' I whispered quietly to Gerry.

At the church I got out quickly – so quickly that I think only one photographer saw me, and only when I was almost past him. My poor dad was stopped by security and had to explain who he was before he was allowed in. Again I was told to sit against the wall – because President McAleese wanted to greet me but did not want to make a fuss. Months later, someone close to the president related how it caused a problem that I had 'chosen' to sit against the wall, since protocol dictates that the president always walks down the centre aisle. 'But I was told that was what the president wanted,' I said. No, it was confirmed, quite the opposite.

I sat in the third row, on the opposite side from the family. Westlife, who would later sing 'You Raise Me Up', sat behind me. The president arrived and made her way to where I sat and spoke very kindly to me, then gave me a warm hug. 'Courage, my dear, courage,' she whispered in my ear. As soon as she sat down, I realised I could not see anything from where I was so I moved closer to the aisle.

Outside, the coffin had arrived, followed by the family and 'close friends'. It occurred to me afterwards that Harry Crosbie must have been deeply hurt that he was not asked to walk behind the cortege. As he was Gerry's closest friend, it seemed to me like a huge snub.

The ceremony, which was broadcast live, had beautiful moments. Yet I felt like a stranger. At least three people told me there had been instructions that I was not to be acknowledged during the service. I had asked if a few words could be read on my behalf, but was told this would not be acceptable. I accepted it at the time, since throughout those horrible days and in the months to come, my wish and motivation was always to make things easier for everyone involved. Still, I was an important part of the last years of Gerry's life. He chose to share them with me and we were deeply in love. The only reason we were not married was because of the Irish law that requires a four-year separation before a divorce is granted. Surely I had a right to mourn the death of my partner at his funeral. I had spoken to the priest the previous day; he had seemed more open-minded and had reassured me that he would take care of things. Yet when he welcomed everyone, he referred to me in passing as 'Gerry's good friend'.

During the funeral, Gerry's children kept looking at me. The girls were all wearing the jewellery I had bought them a few days earlier at Tiffany's. Gerry had always said that nothing lifted anyone's heart more than a little blue box from Tiffany's, and I knew he often gave the girls a little blue box on special occasions. So I felt it would be something to give them on his behalf. I bought cufflinks for the boys and different heart necklaces for the girls. It just broke my heart, but all I could do was try and give them reassuring looks.

Each of the children spoke, bravely and beautifully. Every one of them looked over at me before they spoke. These small actions meant more to me than I can ever describe in words. I love those children so much.

Father Darcy gave the eulogy. Gerry had once mentioned Father Darcy as a friend of his mum, but said that they were not very close personally. The eulogy was very long, and increasingly I was struggling. Father Darcy was followed by various other speakers. I started to feel panicked and wanted to get out. I felt I could not stay any more, a string of thoughts tormenting me. I knew Gerry would not have liked this – the selected group of invited celebs, some of whom had hurt him so bitterly, and the incongruous speeches.

Gerry would have wanted a big funeral, with the people of Ireland, his listeners, there. He would have wanted lots of music. He would have wanted his Presbyterian background acknowledged, as had been done at his father's funeral. It was so Catholic, and he was so proud of his Presbyterian roots. *Oh God, I failed him, I should have intervened,* I kept thinking.

At the end of the service, the coffin was carried down the aisle past me. I was at breaking point. I was told that it would take at least half an hour before everyone would leave for the graveyard, since the family wanted to greet everyone outside. I left through the side gate, but photographers had clearly realised what was going on and they pushed cameras into my face as I tried to get into the car. The driver wanted to know where we should wait, but I asked him to go past the front of the church before we decided. I was anxious that I would miss the graveside ceremony. As we drove past the front of the church, it became clear that the cortege was already moving. If I had waited half an hour, as I had been told, I would have missed it.

We followed the cars, which sped to the graveyard. It was clear this was going to go fast, so fast that people like Rita and Harry would not have time to get into their cars and make it through the traffic on time. On the way, women came out into the street with their aprons on and applauded as we drove past. This was one of the most poignant moments of the day for me – Gerry's fans, the women who listened to him every day, saying their own goodbyes. At the graveyard there was a huge security presence and the Gardaí removed a few photographers who were hiding behind gravestones.

Gerry was buried in the grave of his mum and dad, where four months earlier, on Christmas Day, we had visited and lit candles. On that day the world was bright, as sun reflected on the snow, and we were looking forward to a year of new beginnings. But on this day everything was dark, cold and grey, and I felt the deepest despair. I stood at the back. I knew I was not part of the ceremony. I could not see the lowering of the coffin and afterwards I went to sit in the car. I waited until everyone had left before I went to the open grave to say my goodbyes. I was thankful for a few minutes on my own. As I knelt looking down at the coffin holding the body of my love, Thomas Hardy's poem 'She, at His Funeral' went through my mind.

> They bear him to his resting-place –
> In slow procession sweeping by;
> I follow at a stranger's space;
> His kindred they, his sweetheart I.
> Unchanged my gown of garish dye,
> Though sable-sad is their attire;
> But they stand round with griefless eye,
> Whilst my regret consumes like fire.

30

Music promoter Denis Desmond and his wife Caroline had organised a meal in the Shelbourne Hotel after the burial. Caroline had sent a message to say she had reserved a table for me. I was thankful, but once I got there I just wanted to leave. I did not want to be with people socialising and drinking. The only reason I was there was to see the children. As soon as they arrived, Babs came over and climbed onto my lap. Finally I could hold her and say some words of comfort. My children and I spent a few hours with Gerry's children and agreed that they would come for lunch or breakfast a couple of days later.

A few days after the funeral, Gerry's brother Mano told me that the house in Leeson Street was to be cleared. Others had already warned me that I was a 'stranger' in the eyes of the law and had no right to anything in the house, even though I had bought much of it, so that Gerry and I could start our life together. I did not really care, but wanted time to clear my personal things out. I also asked Mano's permission to take a few of the kitchen things I had bought. I wanted to remember the happy times spent around the big kitchen table. He had no problem with that and said to take whatever I had bought. He also gave me an undertaking that no one else would do anything in the house until I had been. Going back to clear things so soon was gruelling. In particular, the idea of going back into the bedroom, where I had found him just over a week earlier, filled me with anxiety. I arranged for three of my friends to help me, knowing I might not be able to cope on my own.

I entered the house apprehensively. I was shocked at the sight that greeted me. At first I thought someone had broken in. TVs had been ripped off the walls, the books were on the floor in piles, and all the kitchen cupboards had been emptied. Paper had been shredded in the office and, worst of all, a hard disk was busy backing up everything on the computer. I phoned Mano to ask what was going on in the house. He knew nothing about it and could only suggest that it must have been Robbie Wootton, a former night club owner and friend of the family, trying to get a headstart. I had been told he would be helping and he had asked me to meet later that afternoon to show him which furniture belonged to the house and which to Gerry, so I let it be.

I took five small boxes of kitchen stuff: the plates, cutlery and pots I had bought. I also took my clothes, documents and photographs. After I got over the initial shock of going back into the bedroom, I took a shirt and a tie to remember Gerry by. Then I said goodbye to our house and left, heartbroken. As soon as I got home, the editor of a newspaper phoned. He said that two photographers (one from the *Evening Herald*, the other a freelancer), using a telephoto lens, had taken photos of me carrying things out of the house. He could do nothing about the *Evening Herald*'s photographs, but offered to buy the freelance photographs so as to take them off the market. He undertook not to publish them – a decent and kind act.

I felt awful. My GP said my blood pressure was extremely low and put me to bed with strict instructions to rest and nothing else. I sent Robbie a text explaining that I was ill and asking to postpone our meeting to the next day. I also confirmed with Mano what I had taken and that I was finished at the house.

Early the next morning Robbie phoned. He said he was at Gerry's house and needed to see me. Within a few minutes he was at my door. He was clearly furious. I could not understand why. He lashed out at me for removing things from the house, warning me that I had no rights and insisting I had removed things illegally. My children, who heard his raised voice from their bedrooms upstairs, were so concerned that they came down to protect me. He clearly thought my postponement of our meeting was an excuse to win more time, so I could take things. It was clear that Robbie did not know me at all. I tried to explain that I had been instructed to go and take my things, and cleared everything I had taken with Mano. I explained what I took and why, and that I had paid for everything I took. Robbie was having none of it.

'Well, do you want it back?' I asked, upset.

'You bet! Where is it?' he barked, looking around. Since I had felt so ill, I had not removed any of the boxes from the front hall.

'There,' I said, pointing at them. 'Take it! I don't care about a few pots and pans.'

Robbie grabbed two of the boxes.

'Are you going to walk down the road with the boxes?' I asked. 'What if the press sees you? They already took photos yesterday: it will be a big story.' But Robbie did not seem to care. He marched down the road with the boxes in his arms, then came back to get the rest.

In the end, it took months for the house to be handed back to the owner. There had been no need for the rush. Clearing someone's belongings is such a painful and deeply intimate thing to do. It can take months, and is a central part of the mourning process. But like so much of Gerry's life, this too was never going to be without drama. Although it was another traumatic experience, it was over, and I just wanted to have some space and privacy to mourn Gerry and come to grips with his death.

31

C S Lewis wrote after the death of his great love, Joy Davidman: 'I never knew grief felt so much like fear.' Like Lewis, I never knew before Gerry's death how gruelling and debilitating grief and mourning could be.

For the first few weeks after his death, I was in a haze of shock. My brain would not function, I could not drive, and even making a cup of tea seemed an alien and impossible task. A few days after the funeral, I poured boiling water into a teacup. My thoughts were somewhere else, and only after one of my children shouted my name did I realise that I had been pouring the boiling water all over my hand. It left an angry red mark and the skin later peeled off. It was a bad burn, but at the time I had felt nothing.

The haze of shock and disconnect of the brain was a blessing. Psychologists told me later that it is a defence mechanism to allow you to survive. But of course this passes, and then you start to feel the unbelievable pain and despair. I also never understood what a toll grief and shock take on the body, and what a physical thing mourning can be. Sleep became nearly impossible: for more than a year, I rarely slept more than two hours a night. My appetite disappeared and I would forget to eat for days. This resulted in rapid weight loss: fifteen months later, I was twelve kilos lighter. It was not that I did not want to sleep or eat; with the best will in the world, I just could not. Between not sleeping and not eating enough, other side effects began to show. My hair started to fall out in bunches, and my hormones went into overdrive. Today, I am in awe of how much the body can cope with and still keep functioning, yet I know I aged a lot in the time following Gerry's death.

I was also desperately concerned about my children. Like me, they were mourning someone they had come to love and who was an integral part of their lives. Gerry had become a father figure to them. They had spent almost every dinner with him, and looked forward to seeing his two youngest children over the weekends, when they would often babysit.

Gerry had been there for all their important milestones: birthdays, debs, final school days, and sports events. When Wilmé went to hospital with a severe abscess on her tonsils, Gerry carried her to the car and sat outside her hospital room for the whole day. Nurses brought him endless cups of tea, and when I asked whether he wanted to go home he said: 'No, this is what men do. She needs to know I'm here.' Now he was gone. I could see and feel their shock and grief. I was particularly worried about Wian, who had given CPR to Gerry's lifeless body until the ambulance came, even though he knew Gerry was dead. He was in deep shock and, like me, would have post-traumatic symptoms for months.

Despite their own shock, my children minded me. In the beginning they would take turns, letting me stay in their beds at night since I could not bear to be in my and Gerry's bed. Later they would take turns on the weekend to go out, so that one of them was always with me. What made everything so much more difficult was the media interest, which continued for months. I had assumed we would get some breathing space after the funeral, but the opposite happened. Before the funeral, the press were constantly outside my house, but the majority of their attention was focused on Clontarf, where there was a much bigger media presence. After the funeral, this changed. I had not said anything publicly and they wanted my story. There were journalists outside our house almost every day for months. Frequently, when I went to work or my children went to college or school, we had to run the gauntlet of cameras and journalists. Without fail, there would be two or three journalists knocking on our door every night as we sat down for dinner.

One of the most painful experiences was when one of the tabloids published birthday cards I had written to Gerry, as well as some notes from the children. They claimed someone had given these personal items to them after finding them dumped in a rubbish bin. I do not know whether they were truly found in a bin, since everything was in perfect condition when the paper finally returned them to me, but it was upsetting to see my cards, handwritten with so much love, photographed and printed in the newspaper. I received an apology a few weeks later from them, which helped somewhat, but the violation of privacy at such a difficult time was awful to deal with.

A few journalists also got hold of my children's cell phone numbers and would ring constantly to try and get to me. I have never had any PR people, and was not interested in getting any. For me there was no PR to be made out of

Gerry's death: nothing to spin, no image to create. I just wanted to be left alone, but because there was no buffer we were constantly approached directly. So at a time when I needed to withdraw and shut down, I felt under siege, and constantly in a state of fear and vigilance, especially when I left my house.

A month after Gerry's death, I spoke to Marian Finucane's producer, Anne Farrell, about doing an interview. I felt that if I did one radio interview with someone I trusted, the press might leave my children and me alone. The producer agreed, and I set some strict preconditions: 1. It had to be pre-recorded, so I could stop if it all became too much; 2. I wanted to be able to withdraw it afterwards if I was not comfortable with it; and 3. There was to be no promotion or advertisement of the interview. Anne agreed. All the Ryans had left with Robbie Wootton for a holiday in Disneyland and Hollywood, so I asked for the interview to be done while they were away. I felt it would be easier for them if they were not here. I would warn them before the broadcast, but at least they would not have to deal with the press reports afterwards.

On the day of the pre-recording, I got an apologetic call from Marian's producer. I do not know Anne well, but from my professional engagements with her, I know she is a woman of integrity and a brilliant producer. It turned out that senior management had stopped the interview. They apparently felt it was too early and that people would not like me to speak about Gerry. I was upset. Yes, it was early, but it was not for someone else to decide when I was ready. I needed to get a break from the media camping outside my house, and even though I knew it would be a gruelling interview to do, I would do it if my children and I could get peace afterwards.

What annoyed me most was the insinuation that I could not speak about Gerry. It seemed as if everybody in Ireland had a right to speak about Gerry – and had done so – but I, who had been his partner, his companion, could not. It was as if I had committed some sin, some evil deed, by being with him, and now I should go away and hide.

Under pressure, it was suggested that we revisit the interview two months later. By then, the press were as demanding as ever, and still ringing our doorbell. Something had to give. But now the Ryan children were back in the country. I agonised about it, but in the end I knew that I had to protect my children as well, and it was clear that the media would not stop until I had said something. I agreed to do the interview, under the same conditions as before. A week before the recording, I spoke to Gerry's younger brother Mick, since Mano was in Australia. Mick had no problem with the interview and agreed to smooth things over with Gerry's children. He also agreed, at my request, to sit in during the pre-recording so he could tell me if he was uncomfortable with anything. On the day of the pre-recording, he phoned to say he had to work and could not be there, but wished me all the best.

After the interview I was exhausted, but felt it had gone well. I had talked about what a great man, partner and father Gerry was. I talked about finding each other, and about my love for his children. When asked, I said that even though I had never met their mother, I wished I had and regretted that we had never had the opportunity to meet. I said that the only way I knew her was through the children and that, knowing what extraordinary young people they are, she must be a very special woman. I also corrected some of the impressions that had been created of Gerry in the media. The next morning I phoned his family to let them know about the interview, which was to be broadcast two days later.

The day before the broadcast, RTÉ called a few times to say that they were under great pressure not to air the interview. I asked if there was anything they felt was hurtful or problematic in it. They confirmed there was not, and that the lawyers had listened to it closely.

The next day RTÉ broadcast the interview. There was massive press coverage of it, but it had the desired effect. The journalists disappeared from my doorstep and there were no more knocks on the door. The public reacted warmly and I got hundreds of cards and e-mails thanking me for the interview. To my great despair, however, all contact with Gerry's younger children was immediately severed.

Contact with the children had become increasingly difficult. Shortly after the family's return from Disneyland, I had got a text at 3am telling me not to get in touch with the children any more.

Losing contact with the children was like a second death to me. If the desired effect was to hurt me, it succeeded. I had loved those children like they were my own. Together with Gerry, I had looked after them on weekends and driven them to activities. I knew their friends, comforted them when they were sad, and tried to create a loving space for them.

Suddenly all this was gone. I was greatly distressed and so were my children, who had accepted them as siblings. I attempted to get in touch, and tried various ways to get Christmas gifts and birthday cards to them, but increasingly all doors were shut. People told me to move on, but I found (and continue to find) this very hard. I still hope that when they are older we might have a relationship again.

I also struggled with the isolation I felt in general after Gerry's death. I was excluded from all the public ceremonies honouring Gerry. Time and again I would hear about events afterwards or read about them in the press. It was not that I would have insisted on being there, but it would have been a kind gesture to inform me. One example was the Rehab Person of the Year awards. I had bumped into Gerry's agent Noel Kelly a few days before the awards ceremony. He was complaining about having to go and I asked why he was going. He said it was because some of his other clients were presenting, but never mentioned anything about a special award for Gerry.

Two nights later, I tuned in to the awards on TV just as they announced a special award for Gerry. I was happy for Gerry, but could not understand why Noel had not mentioned it when he saw me. Rightly, Gerry's older children were there to receive it, and they were sitting with Noel, who had clearly arranged it. The same was true for numerous music, TV and radio awards. And a few weeks earlier, when I asked the mayor of Dublin if I could have a look at some of the condolence books before they were sent to his family, the request was declined. These insensitive and unnecessary actions made life even more painful at an already very difficult time.

I went back to work three weeks after Gerry's death. Doctors and psychologists felt it was too soon, but I was concerned about my team and the work. I also hoped that some sense of routine or normality would help. I could see my staff were shocked by my weight loss and gaunt look, but I insisted that it was business as usual. They had left me a plant with a beautiful card on my desk. The card read: 'We are so proud to work with you.' There was a huge pile of condolence cards and e-mails, which I would take home and respond to at night.

Over the next few months my work became my escape. I worked long hours in the hope that I would get a few hours of relief from the sadness that was tearing me apart. I convinced a big donor to give a substantial amount of money to build hospitals and schools in Sri Lanka. It was the biggest personal donation ever made to UNICEF globally, and I was delighted that the careful and respectful courting, over almost eighteen months, had paid off.

I then turned my attention to an ambitious campaign I had started to work on before Gerry died. 'Euro for Zero' had started with an idea that one of my brilliant fundraisers, Edel Cribbin, had a year earlier – to ask everyone in Ireland to donate just one euro (ten rand). We made heavy use of celebrities: Liam Neeson, Roger Moore, Donncha O'Callaghan (the Irish international rugby player) and many others helped with the campaign. We got massive above- and below-the-line coverage, and a viral video designed by an advertising company spread like wildfire to more than 100 countries. David Blake Knox helped with the filming. The head of public fundraising was on maternity leave, so I managed the campaign. With the help of Aer Lingus and other corporates, we raised almost €600 000 (R6 million). The campaign was an enormous success. Apart from the money, research showed massive positive awareness of UNICEF. To our delight, we also won prizes for the best digital campaign in Ireland, the best direct mail campaign, and a prize recognising our growth in income from UNICEF globally.

Even though I was exhausted and still in deep mourning, I was delighted with the results, and my team and I were looking forward to a break over Christmas. We had survived one of the worst years of the recession, when so many charities had gone bust; not only survived but achieved huge growth, which was a big accomplishment.

32

On 10 December 2010 a public inquest was held into the cause of Gerry's death. I had dreaded the day for months. I knew there would be huge media interest, and the thought of having to listen to the details of his autopsy was almost unbearable. In the weeks before the inquest, it also became clear that things were going to be complicated for me. One of the newspapers reported that a letter had been sent to the coroner's office asking them not to disclose any information to me. Since I was not legally the next of kin, they had no choice but to agree. This was later confirmed to me by the coroner's office. I have often wondered: if they had been allowed to share information freely with me, and if I had been asked earlier about Gerry's physical condition before his death, might the inquest have turned out differently?

Still, as with the funeral, I just wanted to make things as easy as possible for everyone, so I agreed to Mano's request to arrive last. He said that he or someone else would call to say when I could go in. Brid agreed to accompany me, and Elaine, wanting to avoid the press, met us at the coroner's court. When we got close to the court, I asked the taxi to pull in at a side street and wait. I called Mano repeatedly, but he did not pick up. As it was getting late, I eventually called Elaine, who was already in the court. She confirmed that everyone else had been there for a while.

At the court we were shown into a side room before being called to the courtroom. I was sick with anxiety. When I went in I saw the family at the far end of the room. My heart broke when I saw Rex. He looked so much like his dad, and had had to mature so fast in the previous few months. What an awful day for him to go through.

I put my bag down and went to say hello and wish them strength. It was going to be a tough day. But nothing could have prepared me for how awful it would turn out. The day's proceedings have been well documented in the press. It would rank as the third most horrible day of my life – after the day I found Gerry's body, and his funeral. Since I was the one who had found Gerry,

I was the main witness. I had been offered the option to retain legal representation, but I decided I had no reason to have legal representation and that it would be an awful scenario to have the partner's and wife's legal teams fighting things out. I was just going to go and tell them what had happened the few days before Gerry had died, and what had happened on the day I found his body.

As I was called to the witness stand, I held Gerry's paperclip tightly in my hand and quietly asked him to help. I was not sure that I would cope. After my testimony, the coroner asked me a few questions. First, did Gerry ever use drugs while we were together? I answered truthfully: 'Absolutely not.' I then told him of Gerry's promise to me. The coroner also asked me a very specific question that related to the extent that rigor mortis had set in, in order to try and establish a time of death. I was struggling with this question. I had to try and remember in detail what Gerry's body looked like on the day I found him. I had worked with a trauma counsellor on this for months, but I still had severe post-traumatic symptoms every time I recalled the images. I wanted to help but I had to stay in control. I was also intensely conscious of Rex looking at me and listening carefully. I described as much as I could, but in the end I could not answer the one question that would have helped to establish the time of death, since I truly could not remember. Neither could the ambulance personnel or my son, whom I asked afterwards.

As I left the witness box, I felt sick. I made a hasty retreat to the bathroom, followed by Elaine. Shortly afterwards, a kind woman from the coroner's office came to check on me and asked if they should wait for me. Back in the courtroom, there were a few more witnesses before the results of the autopsy were to be made known.

The pathology report found that Gerry had been drinking the previous night. It also indicated the presence of Xanax and the sleeping pill in his blood, as well as trace amounts of cocaine. The moment cocaine was mentioned there was a sharp intake of breath from the numerous journalists who had packed the room. Many did not even wait for the rest of the verdict. They ran out to start filing stories. When this happened, I knew that Gerry's worst fears would come true. He would be destroyed in the press. I just crumbled. I could not keep the fear and distress under control and I started crying.

I had been tipped off the day before that many papers would send more than one journalist: one to follow the proceedings, one to watch me, and one to watch the family. Conscious of that, I was determined to stay composed, but it all became too much. The coroner kept looking at me, and through my tears I begged him with my eyes. *Please don't say what I think you are going to say!*

He ruled that Gerry died of cardiac arrhythmia (irregular heartbeat) and he stated repeatedly that he could not for certain say what caused it. Then he said what I feared most. Because there was cocaine present, even though it was only the smallest of amounts, he had no choice but to give a verdict of death by misadventure. For the second time in eight months, my world came crashing down.

After the proceedings closed, Mano came over looking shocked and shaken, and gave me a tight hug. 'It will be okay, it will be okay,' he tried to reassure me. I went back to the side room, followed by my media lawyer, Paul Tweed, who was there to observe. He insisted that I had to give the press a statement. I had drafted something the previous evening but had not brought it with me, and so I had to redraft it by hand. Outside the window I could hear the journalists phoning in their reports. They were tearing Gerry apart.

Someone from the coroner's office knocked. 'Melanie, I'm so sorry but I've been asked to relay a message to you,' she said, looking extremely uncomfortable. 'There's a request from the other parties that you leave soon and that you leave through the back door.'

'What? Why?'

'I think it's in terms of photographs for the press,' the woman said.

It took a few seconds for her answer to register. 'Please tell them that I'm still finalising a statement. As soon as I'm finished, I'll leave. If anyone is in a hurry, they can leave. I won't exit until they have left, if that will help.'

The woman apologised again and left. A few minutes later I received another message that it was not acceptable and that I should go immediately. The people from the coroner's office looked desperate. 'It's got something to do with posing for photographs for the media,' they repeated.

I was shocked, and suddenly everything became too much. I had kept it together the whole day, and the months before, and suddenly I could not take any more. Images of Gerry's dead body kept flashing in front of my eyes: the wake, the funeral, everything I had gone through over the past few months.

I felt like I was disassociating from everything and looking at the scene from outside my body. As if in a bubble, I could hear people trying to talk to me, but it felt like I could not – and did not want to – go back into my body. I wanted to die. I wanted to be with Gerry, wherever he was. I wanted just to laugh and joke with him. I needed him to tell me everything was going to be okay, that he would fix it.

Gradually I became aware of Paul Tweed and Brid looking at me, concerned. 'Are you okay?' I came back into my body, into that awful, clinical little white room, which must hold so many tears of all those who go there. I knew I could not take much more. I wanted nothing more than to get away, to get home and climb into bed. I knew I was close to collapsing, but I still had to run the gauntlet of the press outside – something I dreaded. I was terrified.

I also knew that if someone did not leave soon, it would become a big story, and I did not want that. From experience, I knew it was going to have to be me, but I felt the fury and revolt rising in me. Yet again I would be told what to do, where and when to go. And yet I had no choice if I wanted to retain some sense of dignity on this awful day.

Paul asked if I was okay to face the media, and warned me that they might scrum in on me and shout questions. 'Don't be provoked,' he warned. I knew I would not respond, but asked Paul to stay close behind me in case it became too much physically. 'I have you,' he said reassuringly. We gathered our stuff. I took a deep breath to fight the overwhelming nausea and dizziness. We opened the door and turned left into the passage leading to the lobby. As I came closer to the lobby at the front door, I could hear and then see the huge press contingent waiting with their notebooks and tape recorders. They all looked up and fell silent as I walked towards them. I steeled myself for the barrage of questions, but none of them said a word. They all just looked at me quietly, almost sympathetically. At the door there was a large group of photographers and cameramen. The camera flashes lit up as I went out the door, but there was none of the usual shouting. I looked back at the journalists scrumming around Paul to get copies of my statement, which he had photocopied at his office across the road.

The Sunday after the inquest I went to Gerry's grave. I was hoping things would be clearer once I had visited his resting place. When I got there, all the tension, fear, confusion and pain suddenly became too much and I broke down and wept. I went down on my knees in the ice next to the headstone. 'Help me, help me,' I begged Gerry.

'Sorry love, are you okay?' a man's voice asked next to me. I turned my head sideways and, through my hair, which was covering my face, I saw a middle-aged man hunched down looking at me.

'Yes, thank you, I just want to be alone,' I sobbed.

'I understand,' he answered. 'I understand what you are going through. My son also died a year ago from an overdose of cocaine.'

What? I wanted to scream at the man: *He did not die of an overdose, you idiot!*

But before I could say anything, the man said: 'Look, always remember that your dad was a lovely man who raised you well.'

Dad?

The man continued: 'I really hope that the media will leave you kids and your mum alone now so you can get some peace.'

And then it struck me. The man thought I was one of Gerry's children, probably Lottie. He was a foot away from me and thought Gerry was my dad. 'Thank you, and I hope you are okay too,' I said to the man, before he stood up and left.

I looked up at the sky. 'Okay, that was funny.' I directed the words heavenwards. I imagined how indignant Gerry would have been and felt a giggle building up. 'You sent him, right?' I whispered to Gerry.

At that moment the sun broke through the clouds. 'Thank you,' I whispered.

33

For me, Gerry had two deaths. The first, of course, was his physical death. The second happened in the days after the inquest. In the TV series *The West Wing*, Martin Sheen's character, President Bartlett, says: 'Every once in a while, there's a day with an absolute right and an absolute wrong, but those days almost always include body counts. Other than that, there aren't very many unnuanced moments.'

I have huge respect for many journalists, but as a rule the problem with the vast majority of the press around the world these days is that it only deals in black and white. It seems that they almost always take positions of absolutes. As in a game of chess, they play either with the black or the white pieces. A person is portrayed as either a hero and a saint, or a villain and a bastard. There is rarely space for nuance or complexity, and sometimes the facts and truth become secondary.

Nowhere was this more apparent than in Gerry's case. A newspaper editor told me shortly after Gerry's death that any paper with Gerry on the front page would sell on average 30 per cent more copies than the norm. So for weeks after his death, he was sanctified and glorified. Of course Gerry never claimed to be a saint – quite the opposite. If anything, he would be over-conscious of what he perceived as his deeply flawed being.

But as anyone dealing with the media knows, the press always self-corrects. The pendulum will always swing back if it has gone to one side. And so once it became clear that something had gone wrong, in an instant every piece on the chessboard seemed to move to black. This happened the moment the word 'cocaine' was mentioned at the inquest. With that collective sharp intake of breath, it was as though almost every journalist flipped over. In the days to come, there was no space for the nuances of truth. Within 24 hours, what the coroner actually said at the inquest – that Gerry had died of cardiac arrhythmia, *possibly* triggered by *traces* of cocaine in his blood (my emphasis) – seemed to have been forgotten.

Within a day almost all the papers portrayed Gerry as an addict and a junkie. Outrageous stories were printed as fact. For example, it was printed that Gerry spent €2 000 (R20 000) a week on cocaine, that he used cocaine, Valium and champagne before going on air, that he had multiple dealers, that he would sniff cocaine off the floor in front of his children, that he was supposed to go into rehab the previous summer (when we were on holiday in South Africa), and that he died of an overdose. Headline after headline shouted these ridiculous stories as if they were the truth. The stories were so ludicrous that they would have been laughable if they were not so devastating.

The press were helped, or possibly driven, by two or three people all too eager to tell – or possibly sell – their stories to the press. None of these people was ever close to Gerry and had not seen or socialised with him for years, if ever, but verification of the facts seemed irrelevant in the hysteria to crucify him. Whoever was willing to say anything would hit the headlines, and it was almost always printed as fact.

Of course, under normal circumstances papers would never be so sloppy or risk writing such unsubstantiated claims, because they would be sued. But the law determines that you cannot libel or defame a dead person, so it was open season.

Unsurprisingly, many 'friends' who had been only too happy after his death to be all over the papers, radio and TV, now ran for the hills. Thankfully there were notable exceptions, true friends like Fiona Looney and David Blake Knox. People like the Crosbies were still too upset to speak about Gerry publicly, but others who could have said 'No, not true' suddenly lost their voice. Many phoned or came to see me to say that what was said in the press was absolute nonsense, that so-and-so was not at the parties they claimed to have been at or that they did not know Gerry at all, and so on.

'So why aren't you saying it?' I asked over and over again. I got two answers: either they were scared that their own past indiscretions would be exposed or, in the case of RTÉ colleagues, they had been told or asked by management not to make any comments.

I am not exactly sure of the reason behind this request. But at a time when Gerry needed help more than ever, those who could have helped were silenced, or chose to stay silent. Of course, I also know for sure that if any of his colleagues or friends (even those who had hurt Gerry so much) had been in similar circumstances, Gerry would not have cared less about a directive from RTÉ. He would have been out there, blasting the reports as well as those who were telling the lies, with no concern for the implications for himself – but few people have this backbone or loyalty. As Martin Luther King Junior said: 'In the end, we will remember not the words of our enemies, but the silence of our friends.' Truer words were never spoken.

In the weeks after the inquest, so many incorrect statements were made to the press that it would take a whole other book to deal with it all. I will try and deal with the most important ones. But before I do, it is important for me to acknowledge that I am aware of my deep need to protect Gerry. Throughout our relationship, I was extremely protective of him. In public I constantly kept an eye on him and intervened when I could see that he felt under pressure. At home and in private, I minded him physically and mentally. I tried to get him to be healthier by exercising, taking vitamins and eating healthy food. I tried to help him with his finances and always supported him emotionally. Even though I was not blind to his shortcomings, as I know he was not to mine, I always felt that my love might buffer him against the relentless onslaughts he faced on all fronts. Now as I write this section, years after his death, I am still very aware and cautious of my deep need to protect Gerry. I am conscious that I could be seen as the 'overprotective' partner 'blinded by love', so I am careful not to defend him blindly.

Despite my deep love for and protectiveness towards Gerry, I remain a fairly rational person. Even though I know and have never doubted that Gerry kept his promise to me (not to use drugs) until the night of his death, I have also made sure that, as far as possible, I can back this up. I have spoken to his closest friends and asked them to be brutally honest with me. They were. I cooperated with the Gardaí in their investigation and spent more than six hours in interviews with them. I also spoke to pathologists and cocaine experts. Gerry's accountant and I separately checked all his accounts for the outgoings and withdrawals. We also went through all his telephone records in detail.

Although I loved and continue to love Gerry very deeply, I did not go around with rose-tinted glasses. I knew from the beginning of our relationship that Gerry had used cocaine recreationally earlier in his life. That was no secret to me or to many of his acquaintances, who, from what he and some of them told me, also used it themselves. This was the reason for the promise he made to me at the beginning of our relationship. The issue came up a few times between us during our time together, and every time Gerry was adamant that he was never addicted to cocaine, he had not used it for a good while, and he would never use it again. 'My body would never manage. It would kill me,' he said repeatedly. We also spoke frequently about his drinking habits. Even though Gerry was not an alcoholic, he was the first one to admit that he drank more than was good for him. I did not like his drinking habits, and he knew it. Even though we never fought or argued about it, we spoke openly about it.

Some people might suggest that I just missed Gerry's cocaine use and that he hid it from me. It would be impossible for me to have missed cocaine use. As I explained earlier, I had a dad who was an alcoholic and used various prescription drugs. As a child of an addict, you do not miss the signs. You know the mood swings, the erratic behaviour, the broken promises, the lies, the highs; you can spot it a mile away. There is no chance I would have missed a cocaine addiction, and none of the signs were ever present with Gerry. I spent more than two years with him, and we often spent 24 hours a day together for weeks on end. We were extremely close – so close, for example, that he never closed the door when he went to the bathroom. There is no way he could have hidden drug use from me.

Of the various inaccuracies that were printed after the inquest, a few stand out. Shortly after the inquest, many papers started to write that Gerry had died of an overdose or that he had 'a cocaine-fuelled death'. It is important to note what was actually found and said by the coroner at the inquest. There were *minute* traces of cocaine found in Gerry's blood. The toxicology report stated that there was less than 0.05ug/ml of cocaine in his blood. The coroner made it clear that Gerry died of a cardiac arrhythmia, but emphasised that he could not say if, or to what extent, the tiny amounts of cocaine played any role.

There was severe damage to his heart, which the coroner said could have been due to cocaine use years before, but could also be attributed to other factors, such as a viral infection or the diet pills he had used. The toxicology report specifically stated that no test was done for Sibutramine or Reductil.

Yet Gerry had used the diet pill Reductil for a long time. This pill was taken off the market because its use had been associated with an increase in cardio-vascular events and strokes. The damage that was evident in Gerry's heart could have been caused by many things and the coroner made it clear he was not sure what had caused the fatal arrhythmia. However, because he could not say for sure, and because small traces of cocaine were present in his blood, he had no option but to give a verdict of misadventure. But Gerry did *not* die from an overdose, nor was there a huge amount of cocaine in his system.

The fact remains that Gerry had severe heart palpitations, chest pains and frequent panic attacks for weeks before he died. He also became short of breath with the slightest bit of exercise, like walking up the stairs. With hind-sight, and with the knowledge of the autopsy, it is clear that he had a pre-existing heart condition that was going to cause a medical problem at some stage in his life. With the stress he was under, it was only a matter of time before a physical crisis developed.

Allegations were also made that Gerry was addicted to prescription drugs because of the presence of Xanax and the sleeping pill in his blood. This is untrue. I got the prescription for him on the Wednesday two days before his death. He had never taken either of these drugs before and was reluctant to take them even then. The only medication Gerry took regularly was Lipitor for high cholesterol and Losec, which was replaced with Nexium a few months before his death. Losec and Nexium control the amount of acid in your stomach; Gerry took them on the advice of his GP to deal with his ir-ritable bowel symptoms. He took daily supplements, which consisted of a multivitamin (Pharmaton), Udo's Oil capsules and acidophilus.

The other issue that came up frequently was his financial difficulties. That he was in financial trouble was taken as a sign that he must have spent thou-sands of euros a week on cocaine. This is absurd. I had helped Gerry with his accounts so I knew his exact outgoings and expenses. It was one of the issues he specifically raised with me when he asked me to talk about him after his death. So I know that, above all, Gerry would have wanted me to correct the stories about his finances that spread after the inquest, even if it meant publishing the details of the outgoings.

Some of the figures are public knowledge, for instance that Gerry's company, Balcom Management, received €517 500 (R5.1 million) from RTÉ in the 2009/2010 financial year. In addition, he got a bonus of €51 750 (R510 000). This amounts to just over €47 000 (R470 000) per month. The company had expenses and paid corporate tax of 12.5 per cent. The moment Gerry took any money for himself or the family, that was taxed at the highest tax rate. So in the end his net income was below €30 000 (R300 000) per month. This is, of course, a huge amount – more than most people earn in a year. I used to point out to him that he earned in one and a half months what I earned in a year.

I am legally prohibited from giving any details of his outgoings. I can say with absolute certainty – and various auditors and his accountant can verify this – that once he had fulfilled his obligations to his family and paid the mortgages, he had nothing left; in fact, he was running into debt. For this reason, Harry Crosbie kindly paid his rent and I increasingly carried his own domestic costs. I know this is shocking given his large salary, but it is a fact. To suggest, as so many did after the inquest, that Gerry's financial difficulties related to cocaine use is untrue.

During the Gardaí investigation following the inquest, Gerry's accountant and I were asked to go through Gerry's accounts in detail, which we did independently. Both of us came to the same conclusion: there were no unexplained cash withdrawals at any stage, nor were there unexplained expenses on his credit card or by cheque (although I assume drug dealers do not take cheques or credit cards).

Apart from the money, the press latched on to something I said at the inquest and used it as confirmation that Gerry was in contact with drug dealers. During my testimony to the coroner, I mentioned that Gerry got texts late at night that upset him very much. Afterwards the assumption was made that they were from drug dealers who threatened him about money. This is not true. Since these text messages usually went on through the night, Gerry got increasingly exhausted and because he needed to rest before the broadcast the next day, he would ask me to keep an eye on the phone and wake him if it was from any of the children. So I (and a few other people Gerry spoke to) know exactly who the person was that sent those text messages and what the content of the messages was. For legal reasons I am not allowed to say who the messages were from, but they were *not* from drug dealers and the messages did not relate to anything to do with drugs or any illegal activities. I deeply regret not saying at the inquest who they were from, but I did not want to hurt anyone unnecessarily and never anticipated that it would be interpreted in the manner it was afterwards. After the inquest, again at the request of the Gardaí, both the accountant and I went through Gerry's phone bills in great detail. There were no unexplained calls or messages to or from anyone.

It is important to remember that most of the stories relating to his alleged drug addiction came from a few people who spoke to the press. As I stated earlier, I can say with absolute certainty that these people were never friends of Gerry's. Everyone I have spoken to confirmed this. Neither did they meet up with him or have any contact with him in the last two and a half years of his life. I think that they are lowlifes who defamed a man who could not protect himself. I have no idea why they did it. Perhaps for money; perhaps they had an old score to settle with Gerry; perhaps they wanted a moment in the limelight; or perhaps they had some Messiah complex. Who knows? I cannot help wondering if their stories stayed the same when they were questioned by the Gardaí. I hope that they can all live with their consciences, knowing what they did, not only to Gerry but also to his children. I know the effect these stories had on my children and me, so I cannot even begin to imagine what they must have done to Gerry's children.

Their stories were so outrageous that I am tempted not to respond to them at all. There are, however, two stories that really annoyed me. One of these anonymous 'close pals' said in the press that Gerry needed cocaine to get him up and into the shower in the morning. This is absolute nonsense. Was this 'friend' there in the morning? Of course not. I was, and the only thing that Gerry ever took in the morning was a cup of tea with milk and two sugars. When things got tough, I physically supported him into the shower and, morning after morning, sat with him while he showered, shaved, brushed his teeth, got dressed and fed the fish before leaving for work at around 8.20am. He would *always* call me from the car and we would talk until I heard him arriving in the building and greeting his team. His team would confirm that he had a set routine of having toast or cereal and ample cups of coffee while reading the newspapers and going through the various briefs in the 30 minutes before he had to go into the studio.

Another story run in a national newspaper quoted an anonymous source, who claimed that Gerry was taking cocaine, champagne and Valium before his show every morning. Every person who worked with him in RTÉ assured me (and I knew) that this was utter nonsense. Apart from the fact that Gerry did not like champagne and would simply not have been able to do a three-hour show after taking all those things, the simple question is where at RTÉ would he have taken it? RTÉ Radio has an open-plan arrangement and Gerry's desk was in full sight of his production team, the head of 2FM, people going down to the studios and those going to the canteen. The toilets in the radio centre are low cubicles made from thin partitions. And anyone who has ever worked in RTÉ will tell you that nothing ever stays quiet in there. To suggest that Gerry could have used drugs in the building for sixteen years without anyone – except for this anonymous source – knowing and leaking it to the press or Gardaí is ridiculous. There were just too many people who had grudges against him to think it would not have got out if it had been true.

What annoys me most is that the most basic questions have never been asked or answered. For example, if Gerry was a cocaine addict, as has been alleged, why did he not lose weight? Cocaine can bring about a loss of appetite and, when taken frequently, can result in rapid and severe weight loss. Gerry had a ferocious appetite and loved his food. He ate like a horse. Yes, he had severe problems with an irritable bowel, which was diagnosed by various specialists through colonoscopies. But this never deterred him from eating to his heart's content. He was gaining weight for months – in fact, from the time I met him, as is evident in photographs. This worried him to the extent that he started taking diet pills again during the last few months and bought a cross-trainer to get in shape. Those I consulted who counselled cocaine users raised this issue with me as one of the many reasons why they felt Gerry did not fit the profile of a cocaine addict.

Of course that still leaves the question of what exactly happened on the last night. We will never know for sure until the person, or persons, who know have the courage to tell the full story. The pathologists all agreed that with the extremely low level of cocaine in his blood, only two scenarios are possible. Either he had taken a huge amount 24 hours before his death, or he got a minute amount into his system during the afternoon or early evening of his death. Since he was with me for the 24 to 36 hours before his death, the first scenario is not possible, so it has to be the second.

I am very clear in my mind what must have happened, but I will never be able to prove it. What I do know for sure is that Gerry would not have knowingly or willingly taken any cocaine unless he felt under pressure to do so. Did he, given the pressure he was under, make a mistake on the night? Perhaps. Was he an addict? Definitely not. Was he someone who did drugs during our relationship? Absolutely not!

34

What happened after the inquest left me traumatised. Of course I was shocked at the verdict, but it was what happened afterwards that left me reeling.

For weeks I had a recurring nightmare. In my dream I was in the bush in Africa somewhere, when I would hear Gerry screaming for help. After a frantic search I would find him under a tree. The vultures would be all over him, tearing him apart. He was still alive, begging me for help. But as soon as I chased some vultures away, more would come. Night after night I would wake up in tears, drenched in sweat. I lost my appetite again and rapidly lost more weight. I despaired because I could not help Gerry, and could not stop what was going on. I kept thinking of my promise to him that I would make sure people would know he was a good man. But I knew that if I said anything, I would be portrayed as the naive girlfriend, and it could just make matters worse. In any case, how do you prove non-use?

I had arranged a trip to Swaziland for UNICEF months before that I did not want to change, so despite being close to breaking point, I got on a flight and went to Africa. As I ran to catch the connecting flight at Johannesburg Airport, I suddenly got severe dizziness, nausea and a sense of deep panic and dread. I knew this was part of the post-traumatic experiences I had been having since Gerry died, but could not figure out what the specific trigger was this time. Then I looked around and realised I had just passed a news-agent with papers piled up outside. Even though there was nothing of Gerry in the South African press, I still broke out in a sweat. It took months before I no longer had this intense reaction. Even today I get a sense of anxiety when I see a newspaper stand.

At least these feelings would become less intense over time, but the sense of having let Gerry down, of not honouring my promise to him, kept growing.

In the days after Gerry's death, RTÉ commissioned David Blake Knox to make a documentary about Gerry. As the long-standing producer of *Ryan*

Confidential – and a close friend of Gerry's – David was the obvious and correct choice. Shortly after RTÉ spoke to him, David mentioned it to me and suggested we work closely together on it. He felt it would be a good opportunity to put my role in Gerry's life and our relationship on the record.

Months later, however, I started to hear rumours that David had started filming the documentary and had asked various people for interviews. I could not understand why he had not mentioned it to me, especially since we had been working on the UNICEF Euro for Zero campaign together and had seen quite a bit of each other. I could sense that David was uncomfortable in my company and began to suspect something was going on. This was confirmed when he agreed to film a clip for a UN campaign with Mary Robinson, the former president of Ireland and later UN Commissioner for Human Rights, which I facilitated. David said that, to save costs, he would film it in the Four Seasons Hotel before another shoot he was doing the same day. At some point in finalising arrangements with one of his staff, she mentioned that the person they were filming afterwards was Gerry's good friend Fiona Looney. I knew immediately that it must be for the documentary, but when I asked David on the day who they were interviewing afterwards, he said it was just some work for RTÉ.

Then someone told me that there was an issue within RTÉ about my participation in the documentary and how to deal with the two women, past and present, in Gerry's life. Apparently, it had been decided that if there was an objection to my appearance in the programme, I should not be interviewed. This explained the awkwardness on David's part because I knew he would find it difficult to take such a position, on both a professional and a personal level. I decided to tackle the issue head-on and insisted we meet for coffee. We met at the Xpresso Restaurant close to the Dylan Hotel. We spoke for a while before I raised the issue of the documentary. I wanted to know whether the rumours about RTÉ's position regarding my participation were correct. David confirmed that they were and that he had no choice in the matter.

I was shocked and hurt that Gerry's and my relationship was being marginalised again. For once I did not hold back and told David how I felt. Although I tried to keep the tears back, it became too much and I wept as I asked him what he thought Gerry would have made of all this. I could see that David was also distraught, and the stress of doing this documentary while mourning his friend was showing. I felt sorry for him, but still felt strongly that he had to do the right thing. A few days later, David called to say that after our discussion, he had insisted in a meeting with RTÉ that no participant should dictate who else could be in the documentary. He said this was accepted and he would be in touch shortly. Although I was unsure if I would be able to talk to the camera about Gerry, I was relieved that at least the principle was established, and that David had come through.

Weeks passed and there was still no word from David. I knew deadlines were looming. After I had been told the date of the inquest, I met with David again for coffee and entrusted him with the date. I also asked if he was still planning to interview me. He said he was, but his tone worried me. I suspected there was still a problem, but I could see the stress and pain in him so clearly that I decided to let it be. I warned David that I was going to South Africa a week after the inquest and asked him not to leave it till too close to the inquest, since I was already so nervous that I did not think I would be in a state to do an interview about Gerry and our relationship.

On 8 December, two days before the inquest, I got a call from David asking to meet. I was at my staff Christmas lunch, but agreed to slip out and meet him for coffee. David asked if he could interview me in the next few days. He said that because of deadlines, it had to happen by the next Tuesday. I was angry; this was exactly what I had wanted to avoid. I told David I was not up for doing the interview the next day and would have to see how I was after the inquest.

After the horrific day of the inquest and the weekend following, I was at breaking point and in no state to do anything – let alone a TV interview. I felt under enormous pressure and agonised about it, but I knew I could not go through with it.

In the week before the broadcast, RTÉ confirmed to the media that I was not in the documentary. Of course, the journalists wanted to know why. RTÉ implied that it was my choice. From the questions that were then put to me, it was clear that the media thought that after the inquest, I was embarrassed to be associated with Gerry. Nothing could be further from the truth, and I knew I had to correct that impression. I issued a statement from South Africa:

It was only two days before the inquest into Gerry's death that I was finally asked to give an interview for the RTÉ-commissioned documentary. I first became aware of the documentary in late May, and wanted to give an interview to honour Gerry and our relationship. This has not changed. However, due to production deadlines, I was informed that the interview had to be filmed five days after the inquest. Given this short timeframe, I did not feel emotionally or physically ready to give such a personal interview. I will therefore honour my Gerry, and our relationship, at a more appropriate time in the future.

The statement received massive coverage. I am sure it upset David and I suspect that the unfortunate run of events has damaged our friendship. This saddens me very much.

35

After a few weeks in Africa, I returned to Ireland in early January 2011. Despite the light, the summer sunshine and the heat in South Africa, my first Christmas without Gerry had been very lonely and dark. I was still devastated about the events of the previous few weeks. I was not sleeping or eating much, and felt awful.

As in the year before, I decided to throw myself into work. I would work until 2am, go to sleep and then wake up again at 4am, only to start working once more. After long days in the office, I would walk the 40 minutes home. Facing the looks and whispers on the bus was too much to bear. Often I would be so distraught that I would walk home in tears. Arriving home, I frequently stood for ten or fifteen minutes outside to try and compose myself before I could see my children.

Yet I loved my work. It was not only a distraction, but the plans I had worked on for three years were finally bearing fruit, despite the recession in Ireland. By the time the audit committee convened in April 2011, the 2010 accounts showed that UNICEF Ireland's income had more than doubled compared with the previous year. In addition, the Euro for Zero campaign showed unprecedented positive awareness ratings. I had also convinced Liam Neeson to become a Global UNICEF Ambassador. With his help, we had developed big plans for later in the year. I was delighted that, at least on one front, things were going really well.

The press attention on the personal front had died down, but I knew there would be some interest again around the one-year anniversary of Gerry's death. *Hopefully it will be a one-day story*, I thought.

As the anniversary approached, I asked Mano what was planned. He did not know for sure, but assumed that there would be a Mass at the church in Clontarf. Since I did not want to organise anything else in case it might be perceived as an opposing event or a statement, I decided to go to the Mass. I dreaded the public attention, but feared that if I did not go, it would be perceived as a snub to the family. At least afterwards I could hide away and spend the rest of the day at home with my children. Even though I did not want to organise any public occasion, for months I had wanted to do something personal to remember Gerry.

Because of what happened after his death, I felt I was never properly part of any of the rituals and that I needed to do something of my own. I also did not expect to have any say in what would be on his gravestone. Yet I would find it difficult to go back to the grave after the inscription was on it. I needed a place I could go to when I missed Gerry so terribly, a place where I could remember my time with him. I had always loved the benches with dedications in parks around the world. So it struck me that I should erect one for Gerry in Herbert Park, where we had sat for hours in the sun and where we had spent such happy times with the children. I wanted to keep it as low-key as possible, and after my request had been approved I asked everyone involved in the making and erecting of the bench not to speak to the press or anyone else about it.

About two weeks before the anniversary, the press reported that a Mass had been organised, but that it was by invitation only. I waited to hear, but there was nothing. On my birthday, 18 April, I met with Mano. 'I'm not invited, am I?' I asked.

'No. I'm so sorry, but it's out of my hands,' he replied, clearly very uncomfortable.

'But since this is a church Mass, isn't it open to anyone? Would I actually be kicked out if I just attended?'

'I think that's very likely,' Mano said and apologised again.

I felt very hurt, and frankly confused, as to how any Mass can be closed, but I decided to let it go. I would have my own private remembrance around the bench, which would be fine.

A week before the anniversary, I got a call from a journalist at the *Sunday Independent*. He wanted to know if I would confirm the stories that were in two papers on that day. I had not seen any papers, but when I looked online the papers said a spokeswoman for the family had confirmed that I had been invited to the Mass the following weekend. Surprised, I called Mano to ask if the position had changed. He made some inquiries before phoning me back. 'No, there's no change,' he confirmed. I was not welcome.

I felt that I had been set up. If I attended uninvited, I might be kicked out, and there was no way I would be part of such a public drama. If I did not go, the press would surely perceive it as a snub to the family, since they were now under the impression that I had been invited. After consulting with a few people, it was clear I had no choice. Although I had tried so hard over the previous twelve months to keep this type of story under wraps, I had to put the record straight. This was the last thing I wanted. I phoned the journalist at the *Sunday Independent* back and asked him not to make it a big story. I confirmed that I had not been invited, but emphasised that I was happy having my own quiet and private remembrance.

I am not sure how the other papers got hold of the story. The next day, the *Sunday Independent* ran a small story about it on the front page, but to my shock and horror almost all the tabloids also had the story, in some cases on the front page. I had not spoken to anyone except the *Sunday Independent* journalist, and had no idea where the tabloids had got the story. I spoke to Mano again to see if he thought we could rescue the situation, but despite his best efforts there was no movement.

The press hounded me for the rest of the week. I was followed and constantly door-stepped at home. Photographers seemed to be everywhere. I kept working, but was dreading the weekend. Towards the end of the week, the pressure had become so great that I knew I had to say something. There was no way I was going to comment on not being invited to the Mass. I wanted only to remember Gerry. After agonising for days about it, I finally drew up a statement.

> The 30th of April will always be filled with horrific memories and sadness for me – as it will be for all those who loved Gerry. However, I also want to remember the happy times, and above all the great man that Gerry was – funny, clever, generous, kind and gentle. His insistence on living life to the full meant that he gave himself completely to everything and all that he came in contact with – leaving no one untouched.
>
> On this anniversary of his death, my heart goes out to all those who loved Gerry, but in particular to the children that shared his life. He was a great father figure not only to his five children but

also to my two children. I know that they all miss him beyond description.

Just over a year ago I pointed out a cherry blossom tree in full bloom to Gerry. I reminded him that even in the darkest times there is beauty around us and I assured him that the horrible time he was going through will also pass. Then we made a promise: next spring when the cherry tree flowers again, we will have champagne under the tree, laugh about the difficult times of 2010 and celebrate a new future. He died two days later.

Over the last few weeks the tree has been flowering again, but instead of champagne and laughter there is only heartbreak and silence, left by his passing.

The cherry blossoms will forever remind me of Gerry. It is impossible to describe the void his death has left in my life. I will always love him. I will always miss him.

The bench was put up a few days earlier, but I left the plaque off in the hope of not attracting attention. I had asked the warden of the park if he could let a few friends and me into the park before it opened to the public on the anniversary of Gerry's death. He agreed, and confirmed that they would close the gates behind us so that the press could not follow us. I invited a handful of friends to join me for coffee at the Herbert Park Hotel at 8am that morning. I only confirmed the venue the evening beforehand and did not mention anything about the bench.

At 6am on the morning of the anniversary, I left my house and went to a friend's house – to avoid being followed by the press. From there we went to the park. I went in first and put up the plaque. Eight friends – including Harry and Rita Crosbie, and David Blake Knox – were let in as promised after me, and the gates shut behind us. We met around the bench, and I said a few words:

> Three years ago this amazing man came into my life. At first everything about him seemed wrong, and so different from me. And so, for a long time I resisted his advances. But in the end it took only a few hours for me to fall in love with him. Because . . . once I got a

glimpse of his extraordinary mind, his huge, gentle spirit, his kindness and generosity, and the almost unnerving way in which he could listen so intensely to you, there was no way I could resist him. And after our first night together, I could not think of one thing that did not fit perfectly.

Gerry used to say that we mirrored each other. He said that we looked like opposites and yet we were the same. A perfect fit.

I can honestly say that I loved, and still love, Gerry more than I thought humanly possible. He brought out the best in me, and for the time I was with him I not only felt safe and whole, I also completely knew who I was and who I was meant to be.

Gerry loved this park. When he first moved into Ardoyne House, he used to sit for hours on the balcony – watching people play bowls. He tried to convince me that we should join the club, claiming that he would be a hit in the white outfit. He played tennis and loved flying little model helicopters in this park. We came here nearly every Sunday – sometimes with the kids, but often alone. We would sit on a bench in the sun and Gerry would dream about a time when we would see our grandchildren running around the pond.

One of the many hard things for someone in my position is that I do not get to have a gravestone and that I have nowhere to go when I want to be close to Gerry. So I started thinking a few months ago that Gerry would not have liked to be under the ground amongst the dead. What he would have wanted was to be amongst the people of Ireland, people that he loved so much, and amongst children and in nature.

I then decided to dedicate this bench to him.

I wanted you to be here today, firstly to thank you for all your support for me over this horrible year. Secondly, I wanted you to know that this bench is here so that you can also come here when you miss your friend. Most importantly, I hope that if I leave Ireland in years to come you will come here on his anniversary and put a flower down for me . . . In memory of my love for this great man . . .

A lot of tears were shed, but it was a beautiful few minutes. The ducks and the swans were behind us and the sun broke through the rainclouds. I put a bunch of cherry blossoms on the bench and then we left before the gates opened for the public. I was exhausted but thankful. I was sure this is what Gerry would have liked. Small, intimate – and no press.

Someone from the public must have seen the bench after the park opened, because it appeared on a Facebook site that was honouring Gerry later that day. Then the press were on to it. I left my phone off for the rest of the day and we did not open the door to any of the many journalists who came knocking.

The next day there were many photographs of the bench in the press, as well as a photo of a taxi driver Gerry and I often used, who agreed to deliver some flowers for me to Clontarf. Despite feeling really hurt about the way everything had been handled, I wanted everyone in Clontarf, especially the children, to know I was thinking of them. Eight months later, on 8 January 2012, the bench was burnt down and the plaque stolen. Although those responsible were never found, I replaced the bench and plaque a few months later.

Back in April 2011 I was just relieved that the first year was over and I would be able to start healing a bit. Nothing more could really happen . . . or so I thought.

36

As I entered the second year after losing Gerry, I remained reclusive and focused on my work at UNICEF. All indications were that things were going well on the work front. Money was flowing in and my team and I had big plans for the year. The board had approved the plans, even though they were clearly not convinced that we could pull it off. To my team and to me, it was clear that we were going to have another bumper year. In my heart, I knew we could reach the R100 million target I had set at the beginning of my time with UNICEF.

My team was buzzing and we were running like a well-oiled machine. Together with Liam Neeson, I had started to work with TV3 on a massive three-hour telethon. TV3 had agreed to air it, and Liam was happy to use his black book to pull in the top A-listers from around the world.

In addition, Vanessa Redgrave had approached me to do a world première of a show she would star in and produce at the Grand Canal Theatre. I had secured the Grand Canal Theatre for free through Harry Crosbie, and Peter Aiken, who was also a good friend of Gerry's, agreed to promote the show for free. All the money would go to UNICEF. Between the telethon and Vanessa's show, I knew we could raise up to €1.2 million (R12 million).

I had flown to London for a photocall with Liam Neeson, and we had made plans to take him to Africa in August. Irish rugby international Donncha O'Callaghan was going with me to Zimbabwe in July. I knew these visits would generate massive coverage for UNICEF. One of my staff and I had also been working with the brilliant golfer Rory McIlroy's manager since we had signed Rory, with the help of a board member, as a UNICEF ambassador in a meeting in a pub in Belfast. It was agreed in principle that Rory would join us on a field visit later in the year. It was clearly going to be a very exciting year for UNICEF Ireland.

Relations with the board were fine, and after the initial drama and unpleasantness relating to Gerry at the beginning of our relationship had calmed down, neither Gerry nor our relationship was ever mentioned again. The board was clearly pleased with my and the team's performance, and congratulations were the order of the day at board meetings and the audit committee meeting. We had a few bumps along the road when, for example, the low-cost clothing retailer Penneys/Primark wanted to donate a significant sum of money to us after there were some allegations (later withdrawn) against them by the British press for using child labour. The UNICEF office in Geneva instructed me not to accept the money unless certain strict conditions were met. Although it was not my decision, it did not go down well with Penneys.

But apart from that, relations were cordial and professional. I got along well with the new chairman, Paul Connolly, who had replaced Chris Horn in early 2009. Chris, who had been chairman for many years, was now the incoming chair of Engineers Ireland and so had decided to step down, due to work commitments. At a board meeting he proposed an open process to find a new chair. However, without my (or apparently his) knowledge, some board members met privately and decided that Paul should become chair. They announced this to Chris, and I only became aware of it when Chris brought Paul over to my office and introduced him to me as the proposed new chairman. Chris seemed upset about the manner in which this had been done.

As the company secretary, I pointed out to the board that they could not decide things informally, and insisted that a formal meeting take place and correct procedures be followed. Paul called Chris, me and my PA, Niamh, to a meeting in the pub in the Berkeley Court Hotel, lined the other two directors up on the phone and asked them if they had any objections. He was then elected by the directors, and Niamh was asked to write the minutes. I hate doing business like that, but there was nothing illegal about it, so I had to accept it.

After this, Paul and I would meet on average once every month or two to discuss UNICEF matters. Paul was not very involved in the minutiae of the running of the organisation. He spent a lot of time abroad on business, so he seemed happy for me to run things. In any case, the figures were really good.

Things seemed to change at the end of 2010. Paul became much more active in the running of the organisation. This change was so dramatic that staff remarked on it. We were so busy that I did not care, and as always I was happy with any help.

But I was increasingly alarmed at the manner in which vacancies on the board were filled. During Chris's tenure as chair, he would consult with me, as well as with other board members, about possible candidates. Only when he secured agreement would he approach possible candidates. With Paul, that was not the case. When vacancies occurred, in most cases he would approach people first and then inform me of their imminent appointment. First he appointed PJ Mara, a former government political adviser and spin doctor for the late Charles Haughey, the controversial prime minister of Ireland of the seventies and eighties. Then he appointed Tom Hayes, the head of corporate banking at the Bank of Ireland. In the last few months before my tenure ended, he set up a meeting on a Sunday afternoon and arranged to meet me at the Burlington Hotel. There he introduced me to two new members of the board. One was Andrew Weld-Moore, who is married to Paul McGuinness's assistant, and the other was Sinead Kelly, an Aer Lingus air hostess.

Sinead's appointment in particular worried me greatly. I asked Paul whether this had been run past management or the unions at Aer Lingus, and he admitted it had not. Given the sensitivities at the airline, and knowing how carefully we had to manage the very lucrative Change for Good partnership, I felt it was unwise. When I carefully raised this issue, Paul made it clear that Sinead had been appointed in her personal capacity, but as I had anticipated, her appointment still caused a lot of unhappiness at Aer Lingus. Together with a staff member who managed the Aer Lingus account, I had to do a lot of damage control in the weeks to come.

Paul unexpectedly became very involved in the planned field visit for Rory McIlroy. He had never been involved in organising field visits to that extent before. He suggested that we go to Haiti and offered Rory a private jet. He also insisted that we had to travel over before the US Open, on specific dates. For many reasons it was not a good time for the visit. Firstly, it posed a huge challenge for our field office in Haiti, which already had to deal with three other visits at that time. Secondly, the timing meant I could not go on the trip since it was on the day my son's final school exam started. Being a single parent, and given the very tough year my son had gone through following Gerry's death, I would not leave him on his own. I discussed it with Paul and he said it was fine. He was happy to handle the visit with one of my staff members.

Most importantly, the trip would clash with a major report launch in Dublin. The report on the mental health of teenagers in Ireland was the second in a series of four reports we were planning to release that year. Given the nature of the report and its relevance to the stress experienced by teenagers during exams, we had arranged the launch months before, with the board's approval, to coincide with the beginning of the Leaving and Junior Cert exams. The relevant minister had been invited and so were the press, so it could not be changed. Paul also insisted on including three other board members – Tom Hayes, Una Molony and Sinead Kelly – in the Haiti trip. This meant that the delegation was bigger than the UNICEF field office was comfortable with, since it posed increased security risks to all involved. Even though our offices in Haiti and Geneva repeatedly requested us to postpone the trip – and Rory's management was happy to do so – Paul remained adamant that the trip should go ahead as planned.

During the Haiti visit, I kept in touch with my staff member and the field office. All went well. The delegation was only there for 24 hours, during which Rory saw several UNICEF projects. Paul had also arranged for Rory to be entertained by a communications company, Digicel.

In the meantime, I was back in Dublin handling the report launch. In the two days before the launch, we briefed journalists on both the report and Rory's visit, and started to get good coverage. We had the report launch at the Base Youth Centre in Ballyfermot, and to our joy and surprise the press followed us there. The day of the launch, I did endless interviews with radio, TV and print journalists about the report. The minister arrived and we had a very moving event, in which the young people participated.

Afterwards, the minister agreed to be shown around the centre. The director of the centre and I accompanied her, and photographers took photos of us throughout the building, including in a sound studio they have there. After the minister left, I did some more press work, and then one of my staff told me that Ken Sweeney from the *Irish Independent* newspaper had been waiting for a while to speak to me. I was surprised to see Ken, since the *Irish Independent* had already published a story on the report on page two that morning. I asked Ken why he was there and he assured me that his interest was in the report. So I answered his questions about the report at length. At the end he asked: 'How are you anyway?' I told him that I did not want to answer the question since I did not want him to write about me. Ken responded something to the effect that I looked very well.

From his response, I knew that he was probably going to write something about me in any case. I was worried about the line he would take, so I responded: 'You know that the last year has been hell, but I choose to focus on my work at UNICEF.' I went on to elaborate about how important it was to try and save the lives of children, and that this was what I chose to put my energy into.

The next day there was widespread coverage about Rory McIlroy's visit, as well as the report launch. Ken had kept to his word and covered the report extensively on page three. On the front page, however, there was a cropped photo of me at the launch, under the headline: 'My life has been hell without Gerry.' On page two there was another photo in the sound studio, and again the photo had been cropped so that the minister and the director of the Base Centre were cut out of the picture. I knew this was not Ken's doing, but I was not happy with the personal angle to the story. Nonetheless, the coverage of the report, and Rory, was huge, and I got numerous calls congratulating us on all the attention UNICEF was receiving.

The next day Paul phoned. He was on his way back from Haiti and wanted to meet the next evening in the Burlington Hotel. I asked if everything was okay and he said it was. So I assumed it was one of our normal catch-up meetings. At the meeting, we talked about various things, but at the end he told me the board had a problem with my public profile and the press coverage around Gerry. He said it was felt that this was damaging to UNICEF and suggested that I should not represent UNICEF at public events or talk on behalf of UNICEF for an undefined period.

I was shocked. I questioned his assertion that it was damaging to UNICEF. In the charity world, people complain almost instantly if something worries them, and they vote with their wallets. The year following Gerry's death had been the most successful year ever for UNICEF Ireland. We had more than doubled our income, while keeping costs stable. There had been no complaints to the office relating to Gerry, our relationship, or me. I emphasised that the press coverage relating to Gerry had died down dramatically and reminded Paul that, as agreed, I was about to go on two months' leave, so would not even be in the country. Why was this being raised now? Paul kept saying I was on the front page and Rory was not. I replied that I could not do anything about that, but that there was still enormous coverage about Rory and the report launch. In fact, we would later calculate the ORTs (a way to measure how many people read an article) of all the coverage and how it compared to the coverage of Gerry and me in the *Irish Independent*. The coverage relating to Gerry and me amounted to less than 6 per cent of UNICEF coverage during that time. Rory's coverage was about 75 per cent and the report launch roughly 19 per cent.

I told Paul how much I hated the coverage about my private life and how I tried to avoid it, but that it was not within my control. I emphasised that I would continue to avoid it and, as always, prioritise my work with UNICEF. I was concerned by his suggestion that I should not represent UNICEF publicly, since this would fundamentally change my job description and, I felt, would raise serious questions from the press. I asked to be given some time to think about it.

On Monday morning when I arrived at work, my PA told me Paul had called her to add the issue as an agenda point for the board meeting three days later. That meeting was gruelling: I was put on the block about my private life. I prepared well and repeated the points I had made to Paul a few days earlier. I asked what they wanted me to do. At first there was no consensus about this, and two board members supported me. After a long debate, it was agreed that I would train other members of staff to do some press work, and I undertook, as always, to try to keep the press coverage relating to my private life to a minimum – as much as was within my control. It was also minuted that the board fully supported me. As we left the meeting, however, I could see that Paul was not happy. I thought I had not seen the end of this yet. I felt extremely stressed, worried and bruised by it all.

Two days later, I woke up to find photographers in front of my house. I had no idea why they were there. I slipped out through a back gate and went to the local shop to see what was in the papers. It was clear from the front pages that the probate on Gerry's will had been filed at the Probate Office, which is open to the public and press. The papers reported that I had got nothing – as if this had come as a shock to me. The implication was clear: Gerry did not love me enough to leave me anything. A few reports mentioned that his will was an old one that had not been updated, but some did not bother. They also reported that 'close friends' said that I was deeply shocked and traumatised by this 'snub'. What utter nonsense! Even though no one had ever discussed the will with me after Gerry's death, I knew I would not get anything. I also knew the exact amounts of the insurance policies, the properties, and the debt. Gerry and I had discussed this on my birthday just twelve days before his death, and I was the one who had told him to wait a while before changing his will. In any case, I could not care less about his money. All I wanted was to have him back.

I was so adamant that I would not take any money that I had declined to make a claim against the estate when asked by the executors a few weeks earlier. Gerry's accountant knew I had lent Gerry a substantial amount of money so he could meet his financial obligations towards the family before his death. Legally, the accountant was obliged to inform the executors of all outstanding debt, including what was owed to me. But even though I was in real financial difficulties earlier that year because of the loan, I did not intend to make a claim against the estate. I never wanted any of Gerry's money and I knew that I could work myself out of the debt. So despite my children being very angry about it – they knew how short money was for a while – and being advised otherwise by lawyers, I told the trust I would not make any claim. Yet no one had the decency to warn me that the probate was being filed the previous day.

In the newsagents I waited as a middle-aged man stood in front of the papers. He was looking at the headlines, which described where Gerry's assets, including approximately €1.3 million (R13 million) from life insurance policies, would go. He said something to me. At first I could not hear what it was, but he repeated it. 'I said good! Finally, justice against this woman,' he said loudly, pointing at my photograph.

I tried to stay calm. 'I'm sorry?' I said, making sure that he saw my face. 'You know you're talking about me?'

The man looked at me and said: 'Yes I do. And you're a self-contained feminist from Africa who has no right to be here. Go back to where you belong!' By now he was shouting and the whole shop was looking at us.

'And you are a very cruel, ignorant man,' I said quietly and turned away, shaking.

Despite this incident, I was thankful it was finally known that Gerry did provide amply for his family. At least some of the awful stories could now be exposed as untrue, even though none of those commentators who wrote after his inquest about how his 'selfish drug-inflicted lifestyle now left nothing for his poor family and that they were even going to lose the house' ever apologised.

I was upset about the coverage relating to me, not only because it was factually incorrect, but also because it could not have come at a worse time. Yet it clearly showed I had no control over the coverage. I had no idea that the probate was being filed and had had no engagement with the press about it. Yet it was all over the papers. The one good thing was that there was nothing more that could be said about Gerry. So it should all have been over. If I did not talk publicly – and I did not intend to – I should have been able to get on with my life and job, as well as mourning Gerry privately.

Late on Monday evening, as I was preparing to leave for Zimbabwe with Donncha O'Callaghan, I got an e-mail from Paul. In an attached letter he stated that the board had met again and 'that it had considered the negative impact on UNICEF of ongoing press reports concerning your private life'. The letter went on: 'Regardless of whether or to what extent you can control or avoid such reportage, the fact remains that your profile has become inextricably linked to your relationship with the late Gerry Ryan, the circumstances of his death, and subsequent disputes with his family, however accurate or not reports may be. These associations are extremely damaging to the reputation of the UNICEF brand.' It asked me to attend a meeting to discuss the matter on my return with Paul, and either Tom Hayes or PJ Mara.

I went to Zimbabwe where we looked, as always, at very disturbing situations of children suffering. Donncha and I did interviews with the Irish media from there, and on the Sunday after Donncha left I did a long interview with Marian Finucane to highlight the challenges facing children in Zimbabwe.

Yet I was deeply concerned about the upcoming meeting. Having thought everything had been resolved at the previous board meeting, I could not understand why I could not be given the time to implement the plan as agreed. I loved the job and, after seeing the horrendous conditions of, among others, premature babies at Harare General Hospital, I was more determined than ever to resolve matters so that I could focus on the work of the organisation.

Back in Ireland, I asked if I should bring a lawyer to the meeting. When the answer was yes, I knew things were going to be tough. The meeting took place between Paul Connolly, PJ Mara, my legal representatives and me. It was an awful meeting, where my life with Gerry was again at the centre of everything. Both my lawyer and I repeatedly asked what the board wanted me to do. I emphasised that as long as it was legal and did not damage UNICEF, I would do whatever they wanted. The response was that it was not for the board to tell me what to do.

After the weekend, I got a call from my lawyer. 'They want to discuss termination of your contract,' he said. Eight small words and, just like fifteen months before, my life again disintegrated.

My lawyer said there would normally be a process of negotiation in situations such as these, and that I had to think about what I wanted. Of all the things that were done to me after Gerry died, this was the cruellest. I loved the job, I loved my team, and we were doing really good work. I had done nothing wrong; I had thrown my heart and soul, and all my energy, into the work. How could I be asked to think about what I wanted in exchange for leaving? I was very upset and only wanted to be allowed to do my job.

Before any negotiations could take place, I received an e-mail from Paul on 15 July. A letter was attached, which was password-protected. He wrote that the password had been conveyed to my solicitor but, given that the e-mail was sent after 5pm, his offices were already closed for the weekend. Thankfully my lawyer saved me the anxious wait by calling me. I could hear that he was shocked. 'I never thought they would, but they fired you,' he said.

The letter stated again that it was the opinion of the board that my 'engagement with the media' was causing damage to UNICEF's name and reputation. It said that the board had lost confidence in me and was therefore terminating my contract with immediate effect. It instructed me to 'deliver up all correspondence, documents and property belonging to UNICEF' and then stated that they were giving me an 'ex gratia payment' which they 'trust that I would welcome'. I can honestly say I did not think about the money for a second. I have never been in my line of work for money. To me, my work was always a calling. All I wanted was to keep my job and to be able to do it effectively. I was devastated.

We wrote back to the board saying we did not accept the dismissal and that we would issue proceedings against them. Again we stated my willingness to do whatever was legal and would not damage UNICEF. We asked them to get back to us with suggestions and to withdraw the dismissal. The board responded that they would not, and that they stood by their decision.

In the meantime, members of my staff called me on Sunday to ask why Paul wanted to meet with them first thing on Monday morning. I could not believe he was going to tell the staff before giving me a chance to talk to them. I asked the staff to meet me that day. With the exception of two who were away, everyone arrived at short notice at the Morrison Hotel. There were many tears; even the men cried. We had been such a close team and had done such good work. I truly cared and continue to care about every one of them. We had weathered the storms in 2009 and were celebrating great results. And now suddenly it was all over.

I knew that once people knew, the story would quickly become public. Five days later, the *Sunday Independent* asked for confirmation, and I gave them a short statement confirming that I had been dismissed. As soon as the paper appeared, my doorbell and phone started ringing. For the next week the press ran with the story. The board's response was extraordinary. They had hired a PR firm, despite having a PR department in the organisation, presumably because they wanted to put their own spin on the story. The PR firm was left to do the talking. Not once did any board member, or the chairman, go on record to explain or defend their decision. After my confirmation of the dismissal, the response from the PR firm was: 'UNICEF does not comment on speculation.' This was baffling to both the journalists and me.

The pressure kept mounting on UNICEF, and the press continued to run with the story. Finally, on Wednesday, three days after the *Sunday Independent* article, and a week and half after the meeting with the staff, the board issued a response. They denied that my dismissal had anything to do with my relationship with Gerry or the media coverage relating to him following his death. They claimed that we had been unable to agree on the future of UNICEF or my role. I could not believe it. There had never been any disagreement about the future direction of the organisation. In fact, they had agreed with all our plans and budgets for the year. They further claimed that I had settled with them after they had offered me two years' pay. All of this was inaccurate.

Before I could respond, Vanessa Redgrave, Liam Neeson and Roger Moore issued a joint statement condemning the board's actions. Vanessa and Liam also withdrew from all their planned activities with UNICEF. I was very moved by this. In addition, comments supporting me had exploded on Twitter, and I was told that there had been hundreds of calls and e-mails of complaint to the UNICEF office, as well as numerous cancellations of donations.

The press now wanted a response to the board's statement that my dismissal had had nothing to do with Gerry. After enormous pressure, I released another carefully drafted statement, attaching the letter of 20 June.

The letter made it clear that my dismissal was because of the media coverage relating to Gerry, and together with the public and celebrities' responses, the board was under a great deal of pressure. I anticipated that they would try and spin the story, but had not predicted how far they would go. The PR agency was left to do the talking, but some board members then spoke off the record to the press.

For example, on 31 July 2011 the *Mail on Sunday* reported in detail part of the off-the-record briefing they had been given. Apart from a string of inaccuracies about the manner of my dismissal, the source of the *Mail on Sunday* story (which could only have been a board member, since he or she used the word 'we' when speaking of the board) also said: 'We felt she was egotistical. We also got the impression that she thought she was the love of Gerry's life. We knew Gerry Ryan longer than she knew him. All he was interested in was putting stuff up his nose, and drinking, drinking good whiskey. They didn't live together; he was still married. They would go to the odd function together.'

The board member also claimed that I had 'launched into Gerry' at a press conference I had given, which of course was nonsense. The anonymous source also claimed: 'That was the problem all the time – she would drag Gerry Ryan into everything. Nobody cared about her relationship with Gerry Ryan.'

In another article, an unnamed board member was quoted as saying: 'I don't want to talk about Melanie Verwoerd or whatever her name is. I'm really bored with that woman. I'm not interested in her.'

During the next week, the press coverage continued. Photographers caught me taking my belongings from the office and saying goodbye to my staff. There were still photographers outside my house, but the initial interest had died down to some extent. However, towards the middle of that week I got a tip-off from someone in UNICEF that the *Irish Independent* was planning to 'turn on me' and that an article was to appear the following Saturday.

The PR firm had sent an e-mail to various people in UNICEF stating, in reference to the *Irish Independent*, that 'the same paper is planning to do a lead article on Saturday in the Weekend Review section "exposing" the other side of MV. They have told me they are offering us a gilt-edged "opportunity on a plate" to get back at MV and court public opinion. Why would they do this, having backed her so far? I was told that it was purely for commercial reasons and that anything to do with Gerry Ryan sells papers for them.'

On Saturday the article appeared in the Weekend Review section, as predicted in the e-mail. It was a hatchet job and completely incorrect on many fronts. The *Irish Independent* had been in touch with me throughout the crisis and my cell phone number was widely known. I had always got on well with journalists at the *Irish Independent* and could not understand why the journalist had not checked the facts with me or given me the opportunity to respond.

For three weeks I had dealt with the strain of losing my job, press interest in me, and fear of the future. But when I saw this article, I sat down on the pavement outside the Topaz service station where, three years earlier, I had launched a big fundraising drive with Roger Moore, and wept. Afterwards, I walked home through Herbert Park and went to sit on Gerry's bench. I truly did not know how to go on. I had nothing left in me. I had lost the man I loved. Since his death, I had gone through so much: the funeral, the inquest, the anniversary and the publication of the will. I had lost my job and my source of income, and now it seemed as though some people were trying to destroy me in the media. How had it all come to this? All I had done was to fall in love with a man who had asked me to love him. Why was I paying such a high price for that love? I felt defeated, and could not gather the strength to get up from the bench. I just wanted to vanish, to stop having to exist.

Out of the corner of my eye, I saw a woman approaching me with the *Irish Independent* in her hand. She walked up to me and apologised for intruding.

'I just want to say how awful it is what UNICEF is doing to you. You must not give up. You must fight them and know that all my friends feel like I do,' she said kindly. With those few kind words, this complete stranger rescued me.

After I had thanked her, she left and I felt life slowly returning to normal.

With the ducks and swans in front of me, I made a few decisions. I would go to South Africa the next day and stay there for a month to recuperate. Then I would come back to Ireland and fight against this injustice. And I would keep my promise to Gerry.

I would write a book. And I would tell it, warts and all, like he had asked me to . . .

Epilogue

Two days after Gerry's death, while going through e-mail condolences on my laptop, I suddenly went cold. There was an e-mail from Gerry, sent the day before he died. Attached was an MP3 track of the song 'When We Dance' by Sting.

'My darling,' Gerry wrote, 'in New York you told me to ask again. So now I am. I can't do it any more beautifully than Sting himself. So:

> I'm gonna love you more than life
> If you will only be my wife
> I'm gonna love you more than life
> If you will only be my wife
> I'm gonna love you night and day
> I'm gonna try in every way
> I had a dream last night
> I dreamt you were by my side
> Walking with me baby
> My heart was filled with pride
> I had a dream last night
> When we dance . . .

'I love you TMD! Xxxx G'

Notes

Melanie Verwoerd is happy to acknowledge that David Kavanagh was and remains a good and loyal friend to the late Gerry Ryan. Indeed, it was to David Kavanagh that Gerry turned for financial assistance when he was under intense pressure shortly before his untimely death. David Kavanagh had indicated that he would help in whatever way he could to alleviate the financial pressure on Gerry. Melanie Verwoerd never intended to suggest and does not suggest now that David Kavanagh behaved in any way inappropriately on 29 April 2010.

The *Irish Independent* paid damages to Melanie and published the following apology on 23 June 2012:

'In an article in the *Irish Independent* of 6 August 2011, references were made to Ms Melanie Verwoerd, former CEO of UNICEF Ireland. It has been pointed out by solicitors for Ms Verwoerd that it was not acceptable for us to have repeated third-party suggestions that Ms Verwoerd was unwilling to follow instructions given by the board of UNICEF Ireland, that she used the charity to promote her personal profile and her relationship with the late Gerry Ryan, and that her work with UNICEF was not her priority. We accept that any such suggestions were without foundation and that Ms Verwoerd's work with UNICEF has always been her priority. We are happy to clarify this matter and apologise for any suggestion to the contrary.'

The same apology was also printed in the *Sunday Argus* and the *Sunday Tribune* in South Africa, which had published similar stories.

The events on the day of Gerry's death (in Chapter 27) is an edited version of a transcript of an interview Melanie did with Marian Finucane on 26 June 2010.

'If some lives form a perfect circle, others take shape in ways we cannot predict or always understand.

Loss has been a part of my journey. But it has also shown me what is precious. So has a love for which I can only be grateful.'

Message in a Bottle